REFLECTIONS ON THE IRISH STATE

Reflections on the Irish State

Garret FitzGerald

IRISH ACADEMIC PRESS
DUBLIN • PORTLAND, OR

First published in 2003 in Ireland by
IRISH ACADEMIC PRESS
44, Northumberland Road, Dublin 4, Ireland

and in the United States of America by
IRISH ACADEMIC PRESS
c/o ISBS, 5824 N.E. Hassalo Street, Portland
Oregon 97213–3644

Website: www.iap.ie

British Library Cataloguing in Publication Data

A catalogue record of this book is available from the British Library.

ISBN 0–7165–2775–8

Library of Congress Cataloging-in-Publication Data

A catalog record of this book is available from the Library of Congress.

Typeset by Carrigboy Typesetting Services, County Cork
Printed by ColourBooks, Dublin

Contents

Foreword

It takes considerable skill, tenacity, ambition and luck to climb to the top of the greasy pole of politics in any democratic state. Few succeed. Since the foundation of the Irish State eighty years ago only eleven politicians (all men) have been elected to head government. In office a tradition of Cabinet confidentiality and strict adherence to a doctrine of executive secrecy has kept them silent on many aspects of their experience. In retirement almost all have maintained a virtual Trappist-like custody of the tongue. So even the kindest students of the Irish government system and its closest observers have been deprived of that particular perspective of political life shared by this privileged few.

Garret FitzGerald has already put us in his debt with his autobiography, *All in a Life*. Now, once again, he has broken the mould – and to our advantage. In *Reflections on the Irish State* he goes well beyond the stage of memoir. He combines experience, interests, capacity and formidable intellectual prowess to offer a unique, insightful and challenging account of the evolution of contemporary Ireland and an analysis of the problems and opportunities that face the state at the start of a new century.

In less than a dozen chapters he faces all the issues from the rationale and foundation of the independence project, through constitutional and electoral concerns, economic developments and the impact of EU membership and on to aspects of demography, education, integrity in public life, Church–State relations, and of course the tangled triangular web of Northern Ireland. It is difficult to imagine anyone better equipped to undertake this tour de force with such authority, resources and skill.

Fellow ministers who served under him sometimes commented (not necessarily as a compliment) that 'Garret's Cabinets were like academic tutorials'. On the showing of this volume one might suggest that Plato would have welcomed this contemporary statesman to join his symposium. *Reflections on the Irish State* is far from being a catalogue of superficial general observations, still less a litany of sound bites. But flashes of insight and information illuminate every chapter; many will incite response.

There is his comment on the paradox that 'the delay in the introduction of civil divorce may have contributed to the undermining of marriage' and the complaint that 'failure to grasp that the politicians' task of reconciling interests and ideals is both extremely complex and also more persistently morally demanding than that of almost any other profession' (p. xxvi). Among a number of acute observations about the 'Protestant minority' he notes the intriguing fact that 'throughout the whole history of the independent Irish State, the Protestant population of the Republic has fully maintained its favourable socio-economic position' and that this has not even been cause for comment (p. 150).

Just occasionally sharp judgements puncture the calm, objective style and reveal the political passion beneath: 'in the 1990s, the Revenue Commissioners spectacularly failed to maintain public confidence in their capacity to carry out their task with visible even-handedness as between rich and less well-off' (p. 101). On *Humanae Vitae*, he comments that 'attempting to make a fundamental moral distinction between "natural" and "artificial" contraception is not merely unconvincing but is the kind of thing that gives theology a bad name' (p. 124). On the question of corruption in public life he makes the point that an 'all-too-widespread admiration for what was widely seen as political "cuteness" left little room for healthy moral indignation' (p. 73). He suggests that the way recently revealed clerical paedophile scandals have been handled 'has not conveyed the impression that celibate bishops' emotions are in tune with those of parents. And this aspect of celibacy has placed a totally new kind of barrier between laity and episcopacy' (p. 144).

This is an important and extraordinary testament by an extraordinary and important participant in Irish political life. It must be required reading for all who wish to understand Ireland's past, evaluate its present, and are concerned about its future welfare.

BRIAN FARRELL
Dublin
September 2002

Preface

Why this book? After all, many excellent political histories of modern Ireland now exist, and first-class work has also been done by economic historians, in addition to which there are distinguished studies by political scientists, constitutional experts, sociologists, and so on. And in none of these areas have I a professional competence that would enable me to compete with the expertise of those engaged in them.

But, in the first place, I am not aware of any work accessible to a general reader that covers these inter-linked 'areas' in a multi-disciplinary way. In particular, our schools of political and economic history do not seem to me to have cross-fertilized in a productive manner, and this has left even the best of our political histories of modern Ireland somewhat unidimensional.

Second, many important aspects of modern Ireland have been the subject of specialist works only, and some issues seem to me to have been virtually overlooked. Let me instance some aspects of Irish life that I believe merit some further treatment in works for general readers.

In the purely political sphere there is little material accessible to the general reader on such matters as the rationale and relevance of our present political party structure and the nature of the forces that have drawn almost all these parties to the political centre, to the effective exclusion of some key policy choices for the electorate; nor has much been written on the effectiveness and adequacy of a political structure which has been shaped by a unique electoral system – one that has very specific consequences in terms of the preoccupations of the politicians that it produces.

It also seems to me that little has been written – by politicians at any rate – about some of the ethical issues that arise in politics or on the shape and adequacy of the expert back-up sought by and available to politicians; the distorting effects upon politics of the power of major pressure groups and single-interest groups; or the adequacy of our public service structure to the rapidly evolving needs of Ireland in the modern world.

Issues in the economic area that seem to merit some further discussion include the profound impact of demographic changes – some long-term and others temporary or even perhaps cyclical – upon our economic performance, and in particular upon the levels of employment, unemployment and emigration. And this economic performance needs to be placed firmly within the context of contemporary economic progress elsewhere during the past three-quarters of a century.

There is also room for more discussion about how and why our patterns of taxation and income distribution differ in significant – and perhaps socially and economically negative – ways from those of some of our neighbours. I feel that not enough attention has been given to the problem of reconciling ideological pressures for lower taxation – some of which we have imported from better-endowed societies – with the exceptional social and infra-structural deficiencies of what was until recently a very poor country by Northern European standards.

A quite new issue that emerged in the second half of the 1990s has been the social and psychological, as well as economic, impact of the pace at which our average material living standards have been catching up with those of our near European neighbours. In the last one-third of the twentieth century the speed with which a traditional society has been radicalized has led to a more rapid decline in marriage and in marital fertility here than elsewhere in Europe during this period. And associated with these developments has been the decline in the influence of religion as a moral force, and the evident inadequacy of any alternative lay or civic ethic, especially in the face of the double hazard of the siren call of individualist liberalism on the one hand and of the off-putting face of right-wing fundamentalist Catholicism on the other.

In the social area I also would instance such issues as the effectiveness and productivity of an educational system upon which our unique demography has placed enormous strains – and in particular the sharp contrast between its many successes and its simultaneous failure to make inroads into under-education and even illiteracy amongst a minority of pupils.

Insufficient attention has, moreover, been paid to the manner in which Church–State relations in Ireland have evolved under intense pressure in recent decades, or to the changes in attitudes needed on both sides in order to minimize consequent strains. There are also issues posed by the rapidity of the change in attitudes among very many Catholics towards the institutional Church and by the nature of the forces influencing the Irish Church as an institution in its response – or lack of response – to these changes.

In relation to Northern Ireland we have faced the paradox on the one hand of a quite deep-seated partitionism in the South, and on the other hand the evident inability of Northern unionists to throw off their historic sense of being a threatened minority, underlying which is their persistence in thinking in all-Ireland terms – for, of course, it is only in that context that they are a minority. At a deeper level both communities in some measure belie their publicly stated positions on the political division of the island. There is also the related issue of the nature and consequences of the partial transformation of the mainstream of Southern nationalism from an exclusivist and irredentist model to one which as well as being somewhat partitionist has also become more inclusive, pluralist and tolerant.

All this has imposed a strain, about which little enough has been said, upon the relationship of Southern with Northern nationalism. And there is also the long-term impact of the IRA's activities domestically and upon the wider Anglo-Irish relationship, as well as the likely effect of the belated emergence of Sinn Féin as a political force in the Republic at a time when the established political parties here have lost the confidence and trust of a substantial part of the electorate.

Moreover, the effects, economic, political and social, of a parallel partial shift in Irish nationalism that has taken place in the context of our relationship with the European Union need to be considered, as well as the disturbing lag between public policy stances and public opinion in relation to Europe, demonstrated by the Nice referendums. We have also seen a gradual, but still somewhat confused, re-evaluation of Irish neutrality in the post-Cold War era.

In the European context we also need to reflect upon the problem posed for a small country like Ireland by the need to match in quality, and to some degree even in numbers, the personnel dedicated by larger States to European affairs, as well as the adequacy or otherwise of adjustments hitherto made by our political system to the demands of European partnership.

Many, although not all, of these issues are addressed in this book – sometimes drawing on articles I have written or lectures I have given in Ireland or elsewhere in recent years. Some parts of this volume draw more heavily than others on such material – for example the chapter on

Irish demography, much of which appeared in *New Century, New Society: Christian Perspectives*, edited by Fr Dermot Lane and published in 1999 by the Columba Press.

I am, of course, conscious of the extent to which issues I have sought to address here reveal both some of my own biases and also huge gaps in my range of interests. Whole areas of great importance are missing, including the crucial subject of the arts and literature: in respect of such sectors of activity I have no competence and could add nothing of value.

I must acknowledge the assistance and encouragement I have received from Irish Academic Press and from some of my friends who have helped me in several different ways, and I am very grateful for the comments of my daughter Mary on the draft and of Enda McDonagh and my son John and daughter-in-law Eithne on several chapters, as well as for the editing by Joe Joyce, copy-editing by Anne Macdona, and indexing by Suzanne Buggy. I should add that the book would certainly not have seen the light of day in the year 2002 without the very hard work of my secretary, Sharon Kelly.

But no one except myself is to blame for the contents!

GARRET FITZGERALD
Dublin
September 2002

INTRODUCTION

General reflections on politics

From childhood I have always been very conscious of the morally demanding aspect of politics. My own motivation in entering politics almost forty years ago derived mainly from practical concerns about such issues as defective economic policies that were then inhibiting economic growth, failure to address social disadvantage, irredentist nationalist attitudes towards Northern Ireland, and concern to prepare Ireland for EC membership. But I was also conscious of the challenge posed by the huge widening of moral choices that I knew political life would entail: the constant dilemma between doing what is right and doing what is popular, and the resultant test of one's capacity to plough a judicious course between these two alternatives.

I say 'judicious course', because realistically, to do 'the right thing' on every occasion, however unimportant the issue and however unpopular this action may be with some segments of the voting population, would be to condemn oneself to a short, and consequently worthless and unproductive, political career. On the other hand, to fall into the trap of perpetually seeking to be popular would be equally worthless and unproductive, a complete waste of one's life.

The moral challenge in politics is to balance these choices in a constructive but also realistic way: that, indeed, is what democratic politics is really about. The true test of a politician is whether he or she succeeds in combining principle and prudence in such a way that, over time, as many as possible 'right' decisions are made, without in the process being persistently defeated at the polls or losing his or her own seat, thus undermining or even destroying the possibility of doing further good.

Looking back on it all, I think that when I first contemplated an eventual career in my teens, I was attracted by this moral choice aspect of politics.

I had always admired those who took responsibilities, especially responsibilities involving moral dilemmas, when these could have been avoided by opting for an easier life, free of such agonizing choices. Thus, as a schoolboy, I was preoccupied by the drama of Pétain and de Gaulle, by the spectacle of the old man choosing what I felt at the time he must have known would be the path of personal dishonour in order to protect his people – in retrospect I realized this was a romantic illusion – whilst the younger man chose what then seemed to me the easier path of *la gloire*.

In our own history, I had always been fascinated by the moral issue of the Easter Week Rising which, as my father recounted in the fragment of autobiography he left behind, caused mental agonies to Pearse and Plunkett during those days in the GPO. I was equally absorbed by the cruel moral choices that faced the first government of the State, as the country dissolved around these men in civil war.

Conscious that I was unlikely ever to have to face the kind of dilemmas agonized over by Pearse and Plunkett, by the leaders of our first Government, or by Pétain and de Gaulle, I nevertheless always felt that it would be hard to justify a failure to seek and play a part eventually in a field of activity that raises moral issues which so many opt to avoid and whose attempted resolution by those engaged in politics is so often the subject of moralizing criticism by those who stay safely away from involvement in public affairs.

Beside those hugely difficult moral decisions of earlier periods, the choices that I was likely to face in politics were going to be tame indeed. But they would still offer far more of a challenge than I was likely to face in any other career that I might embark upon in the later part of my working life, when politics might become an option for me.

What bothers me is that none of this moral challenge aspect of politics seems to enter the heads of most people who write or talk about the subject.

Of course, other careers also involve taking many difficult and potentially unpopular decisions. Judges face this all the time, but judges have security of tenure as do clergy, at least of the Roman Catholic and Anglican Churches. In both cases that security of tenure is designed to enable them to speak and act without fear or favour.

But it is the combination of the huge number of potentially controversial decisions to be taken in the absence of any security of tenure that makes politics such an extraordinarily difficult career: not just in terms of the workload but, above all, through its morally demanding character.

The fact is that politicians face a much larger number of moral dilemmas than people in other professions simply because they are constantly faced with choices between doing what they know or believe to be the right thing in the public interest that they are elected to serve, or, alternatively, of avoiding, watering down, or delaying such decisions because they know that taking such action will lose them votes at the next election.

When civics is taught in our schools this whole issue of the moral challenge of politics should, I feel, be given a prominent place. Only if each new generation is brought to see and to understand something of the uniquely morally demanding nature of democratic politics will democracy endure. Then, perhaps, a few young people in each new generation might in turn feel challenged to try their hand at this demanding career, instead of – as seems to be the case with so many today – dismissing it out of hand as simply a dodgy and disreputable way of earning a living.

Of course, contemplating the morally demanding nature of politics as a career is unlikely to be the commonest factor motivating people to enter the profession! Most entrants to politics will probably be motivated by some combination of wanting to be of service to others and of finding satisfaction in being prominent in the public eye – which is, of course, a form of vanity. At the very least, one can say that anybody who shrinks from the public gaze is unlikely to contemplate a career in politics!

However, the fact that some element of vanity in this sense must be present in the mind of anyone going into politics does not mean that one should ignore or dismiss other positive motivations, which for most people take the form of a desire to be of service to others, or of a wish to improve society by making it serve people's needs more effectively in terms of economic efficiency or social justice, or by eliminating or at least minimizing evils such as war, disease or famine.

Inevitably most politicians have *mixed* motivations; few are wholly inspired by either vanity or self-interest, and few, if any, are wholly free of such flaws. And many may not even be conscious of their own mixed motivations, or at any rate may not have been endowed with that relatively rare quality – intellectual honesty – which would enable them to see themselves, and their underlying motivation, in objective terms.

At the practical level, politics involves making constant choices about the allocation of scarce resources. Quite aside from the basic issue of the extent to which private resources should be taken through taxation to meet public needs, there are always choices to be made between different ways of raising taxation, as well as endless choices to be made between huge varieties of demands made upon whatever resources are raised in this way.

Taxation issues are complex but finite. By contrast, expenditure choices are virtually infinite. Very many items of public expenditure could with some advantage be given additional resources: politicians allocating scarce resources are thus forever choosing between an enormous number of different needs, having to decide how much to add each at the margin, or, more rarely, to subtract.

Although cost–benefit analysis can often be employed to rank capital projects, in the case of current expenditure there simply exists no conceivable rational quantitative basis for choosing to give to one need rather than to another. Endless value judgements have to be made and conflicts between the value judgements of ministers, each concerned with his or her own department's needs, have to be reconciled at government level.

Finally, on top of this ever-present resource allocation problem, there are, of course, many other political choices to be made, including nowadays choices in relation to the European Union and also the wider world, where, through our membership of the Union, we have both the capacity and the responsibility to influence events constructively.

Some of these many choices will be influenced by different political philosophies, for example the traditional left/right divide on the relative merits of lower taxes on the one hand and better public services and social provisions on the other. A new right/left dichotomy opened up in recent decades is that between some forms of economic development and the preservation of the local or global environment.

Again, at a practical level, where social welfare is concerned there are choices to be made in regard to social provision between standard and targeted provisions, and between universal provision and means-tested assistance, as well as choices between allocating scarce resources to prevent crime or ill health or providing resources to deal with the consequences of these evils.

Almost all these choices are seen by some people as having negative consequences for them, and, unfortunately for politicians, voters are more inclined to vote against those who make decisions they do not like than to vote in favour of those who take decisions of which they approve.

Another political issue that divides electorates is the extent to which governments should seek to intervene in what may be regarded as the private affairs of individuals. Liberal pressures have increasingly been operating against some interventions of this kind, and State actions that can be represented as 'judgemental' are increasingly liable to attack from a liberal angle – whilst 'political correctness' in respect of some other issues admits of no dissent. As values shift, many old taboos are dismissed, but some new ones have taken their place as our society has reacted against various forms of discrimination that in the past were not sensitive issues.

Politics has thus become increasingly complex and demanding and, correspondingly less attractive as a career, even to people concerned for the good of society.

Looking at politics in a more general way, there are, I believe, four principal motivations for political actions apart from the enjoyment one gets from being involved in it: ideals, interests, ideologies and, lastly, emotions, whether of hope or of fear.

By the concept of *idealism* I mean the adoption of policies or the taking of actions which are of an altruistic character, namely ones designed to benefit individuals or groups other than those actually taking these decisions. Such decisions may not correspond with, and may even run counter to, the perceived interests of these decision-takers.

By the pursuit of *interests* I mean policies or actions designed to further what politicians perceive to be their own interests or the interests of groups with which they are associated, but also, of course, more widely and less selfishly, the interests of their community or state.

By *ideology* I mean actions and decisions motivated primarily by an academic or social theory.

And by the force of *emotion* I mean feelings such as hope or fear which inspire actions that may not correspond to a cool calculation either of self-interest or of the interest of others.

It is also necessary to distinguish decisions and actions motivated by concerns for *ends* from those taken with a view to securing the necessary *means* towards the achievement of these ends. In the latter category fall the many practical decisions taken by politicians with a view to securing their retention of power or their re-election. This purpose, though clearly self-interested, may nevertheless be justified, either subjectively or objectively, or both, by a belief that the continuation of these politicians in office or their return to power after an election is desirable. Desirable, not merely for their personal benefit or that of the party or group to which they belong, but also perhaps so that they may be enabled to implement the policies which they espouse and which they believe to be in the public interest.

Clearly a large number of political decisions are taken on these latter grounds and are concerned not with the *ends* of politics but rather represent *means* towards the achievement of genuine political goals. The biggest single temptation for politicians is, however, to believe that their contribution to the public interest is of such importance as to require for their continuance in power the adoption of a whole range of actions or strategies unrelated to, and possibly even running contrary to, the goals which they see themselves pursuing.

In other words, the means of securing political changes all too often become ends in themselves – and ends that may run counter to the true end of politics, namely the public interest. This is so widely perceived as the besetting sin of politicians that it is not necessary to develop it at length, and I am concerned here specifically with the ends of politics rather than with the means. Nevertheless I want to comment briefly on two aspects of this matter related to the concern of politicians to retain power through re-election within a democratic system.

First of all, concern for re-election tends to operate as a strongly conservative force in politics for a reason that is not, perhaps, always understood by people outside politics. This is the fact that politicians feel that they know who their existing supporters are, and are particularly concerned not to lose these familiar votes. They would, of course, like to gain new support, but their image of potential new supporters is a much vaguer one. They cannot put names and faces on these potential new supporters in the same way as they can on those who they know already vote for them. And in these circumstances politicians in office – and to a lesser, although nevertheless quite surprising, degree, politicians in opposition – are often reluctant to espouse changes or reforms that might lose them some of their existing support, even though there may exist a large unrepresented constituency favouring such changes or reforms. This is a clear case of a bird in the hand being worth two of them in a very uncertain bush.

I have to say that I found this one of the more discouraging aspects of politics after my election to the Oireachtas thirty-seven years ago. My naive belief that political parties were interested in winning votes was shattered by the discovery that changes that seemed to me likely to be good in themselves as well as popular with many voters who had not hitherto supported my party were rejected by my colleagues because they might evoke hostility from quite a small number of known party supporters.

Political parties are, moreover, in varying degrees oligopolistic. Entry of competitors to the parliamentary party market is in many cases difficult to the point of virtual impossibility, especially in polarized political systems, like those of Britain and the United States, which are not proportionally representative in the way that other electoral systems are in Europe.

For these two reasons political systems have built into them powerful inertial forces, inhibiting change. As a consequence many of these systems are antiquated and unresponsive to modern needs, whether these needs be economic or social. And this inertia and lack of responsiveness to changing needs can produce tensions, resentments and frustrations within the community, which in certain cases can become explosive but more often may simply lead to disillusionment with politics.

These tensions and resentments are sometimes intensified by another feature of the democratic political system that is strongest in, but by no means exclusive to, cases where the political party system is a polarized duopoly rather than a broad spectrum with a number of components. This is the disproportionate influence of small but strongly motivated single-interest pressure groups.

Whilst politicians are relatively insensitive to quite substantial generalized pressures for change, especially where acceptance of the ideas in question might threaten their existing support base but does not seem to offer an assurance of new votes, they are often very susceptible to pressures from quite small single-minded groups who appear to be able to 'deliver' a specific batch of votes that might make the difference between victory and defeat in a number of marginal constituencies. And in constituency-based political systems, which are the norm, there are *always* a number of marginal constituencies.

This susceptibility to single-interest pressure groups is strongest where the pressure is *against* change, even when a much larger but less committed constituency exists for the change in question. And this has the curious effect of producing a situation in which governments may be retained in, or alternatively removed from, office by very small groups of self-interested people rather than being really elected by a majority of the electorate, as will appear on the surface to be the case.

But I want to return for a moment to the motivations of political actions.

The *ideological* motivation of politics is quite common, underlying much of the structuring of the political system itself into parties and groups, and providing a strong motivating force for many political actions. But the strength of this factor varies considerably. On the one hand there are parties and groups and individuals who are primarily and very strongly motivated by ideology. On the other hand there are those for whom ideology is merely a significant background consideration in the course of the pursuit of individual issues and of little, even of no, importance, because they adopt an almost totally pragmatic approach to the political scene.

Leaving aside such ideological factors as racism, the main categories of ideological imperatives are those inspired by individualism and those inspired by considerations of society as a whole. These two sets of political attitudes have in turn led to two quite separate sets of polarized attitudes in the economic and social spheres.

In the economic sphere during the twentieth century this polarization took the form of one between liberal capitalism on the one hand and socialism on the other. Eventually, however, such extreme polarization was rejected by a huge majority in most countries. Instead, social democrats now accept the market system but are concerned to modify its operation in such a way as to ensure a more equitable distribution of the fruits of the capitalist system than would emerge if that system were left to itself. By contrast, economic liberals, whilst not in principle opposing some social provisions for the disadvantaged, prefer to let market forces prevail as far as possible, and resist pressures to ensure a more equitable spread of resources through State action.

In the social, as distinct from the economic, sphere, however, there is a different kind of polarization, namely that between the liberal concern with minimizing societal constraints on individual behaviour, and the conservative (with a small 'c') concern for the preservation of such values and standards, even at the cost of accepting many such constraints.

Originally there was, of course, a philosophical connection between the economic and social forms of liberalism, both of which place their emphasis on minimizing interference by the State. But there was never a similar relationship between their antitheses – collectivist socialism and societal conservatism. On the contrary, collectivist socialism and societal conservatism were strongly polarized in relation to each other.

This curious double polarization in politics is not always understood, and can be a cause of considerable confusion, especially in countries like the United States where politics is bipolar, and where as a result, antithetical economic and social ideological views have to be accommodated within a single party. Moreover, in the US there has often seemed to be considerable confusion in the public mind between collectivist socialism and the modified form of liberal capitalism known in Europe as social democracy.

In the terms that I have been using one might say that the Republican Party in the US is economically liberal but is in social terms conservative, while the Democrats are socially liberal and in some degree also social democratic. Collectivist socialism, for its part, has simply never featured in any serious way within the polarized party system in the US.

I am inclined to the view that this dual structuring of ideologies which emerged in Western civilization owed a good deal to the particular synthesis of societal and individualist values espoused by the Christian Church over a millennium and a half – from the time of Constantine until the eighteenth century, at least. This synthesis laid stress on the one hand on the uniqueness and individual value of man, seen as made in the image of God, but on the other hand on the need for a wide range of social constraints on human behaviour through a tightly drawn moral code, designed to preserve the fabric of society in a form seen by the Christian Church as optimal for personal human development, of a kind meriting reward in the next life.

Individualism, leading to both social and economic liberalism, and collectivism seem to me to represent two great heresies from this Christian tradition of balancing individual and societal considerations. And in the nineteenth and twentieth centuries these two 'heresies' became very powerful, and often quite lethal, forces in world politics.

Today, many of these ideological considerations are implicit in political attitudes rather than being primary motivations. Nevertheless some politicians and some parties remain strongly ideological in character, whether of the left up to the end of the 1980s, when the forces of collectivist socialism were left in total disarray as a result of events in Russia and Eastern Europe, or on the right, where in that same decade Ronald Reagan and Margaret Thatcher espoused a revival of the ideals of nineteenth-century economic liberalism in their purest form, with mixed results in social terms.

However, much of modern politics is motivated only implicitly or subliminally by ideological considerations of a theoretical character and tends to reflect rather the pursuit of idealism or of material interests, or else is motivated by emotions such as fear.

Much of the impetus of social democracy, as distinct from socialism, derives from an idealistic rather than an ideological political view, a simple concern that society be structured in such a way that the benefits of material progress are more widely spread than would happen if the liberal capitalist system were left to itself. Modern social democracy is *not* a form of socialism; it accepts and works within the liberal capitalist framework, but seeks to mitigate the highly skewed distributive effects of this system if left to itself.

The social democratic model has strong support within Western Europe, where two main variants exist under the confusing labels of 'Socialist' and 'Christian Democrat'. The Christian Democrat label spans quite a wide range including some social democrats but also supporters of a form of liberal capitalism that is less ideological and more open to ideas of worker participation than British Conservatism. This is one of the reasons why the British Conservative Party has experienced such difficulty in finding a comfortable niche within the general European political spectrum.

The social democratic position has a strong altruistic element because it involves a good deal of emphasis on the need for a readjustment of resources away from the pattern that emerges in the first instance through the operation of the market system. Many social democrats are in fact urging policies that, at the personal level, would involve a transfer of resources away from themselves towards more disadvantaged groups in the community.

I have to say that the force of altruism is a more powerful one in the political system than is generally realized. Many outside politics are so conscious of the over-preoccupation of many politicians with means rather than ends – with securing or remaining in office rather than with actual policies – that they underestimate the extent to which many politicians actually do pursue altruistic policies – policies designed to benefit others, regardless of the prospect of electoral reward or personal financial advantage.

As this proposition is likely to give rise to widespread cynical disbelief, I shall illustrate it with a concrete example from recent Irish political history.

Redistributive policies are known to evoke resistance amongst taxpayers, many of whom resent increased taxation for redistributive purposes. At the same time such policies do not evoke corresponding favourable reactions from the principal beneficiaries, such as pensioners, whose voting patterns have been fixed by age, or from the unemployed or the young, whose participation in voting tends to be low. Accordingly such redistributive policies are generally seen by politicians as electorally counterproductive, and their pursuit on a significant scale must thus reasonably be characterized as altruistic, so far as the politicians are concerned.

An example of such redistributive action was to be found here in Ireland between 1960 and 1982, the initial period of post-independence economic growth. This was a period during which there were eight different governments and four changes of government leadership – so in presenting this example I am not making any party political point.

During this period of over two decades, the pre-tax purchasing power of the industrial wage before tax doubled, although because taxes were much higher at the end of the period, the after-tax purchasing power of incomes increased by a somewhat smaller amount. But, during this period political action trebled the purchasing power of such social pensions as the old age pension and unemployment assistance.

Now, some on the right may argue against the *wisdom* of such a significant redistribution of income away from those at work to retired and unemployed people, especially as the number of people on the Live Register trebled during this period. And there are also people who, although not ideologically right wing, are critical of such a large scale of redistribution of resources as between the economically active and inactive members of society.

However that may be – and for my part I tend on the whole to disagree with these analyses – what one can *not* reasonably argue is that the political decisions taken at various times during that twenty-two-year period which led to this redistributive process were motivated by concern for electoral advantage by one or other, or both, political groupings. For the politicians of that period were certainly not naive enough to have thought that by these actions they would gain more votes from the completely unorganized and – in Ireland at least – politically inert body of unemployed and retired people than they would lose by having to impose the higher taxes needed to pay for that scale of redistribution. The motivation of these substantially improved social benefits can only have been the existence, at that period, of a widespread concern, felt on both sides of the Irish political divide, to mitigate social deprivation.

It is not the purpose of that example to extol the virtue of politicians in Ireland or elsewhere, or to highlight their altruism – especially as this process of redistribution did not resume after the recovery from the financial crisis of the early 1980s, during which the much improved relativity between earnings and social welfare was maintained, for Irish politicians of that time fell under the influence of a new right-wing liberal ideology antithetical to further redistribution. No, I merely wish to record the objective reality of the existence of this factor of idealism within the political system at a particular period of our past history.

Leaving aside the idealistic element and the ideological factor, many people presume that for the rest politics is merely a matter of the pursuit of material *interests* by sectors of the public operating through the political system, and also, of course, internationally by governments on behalf of their states. Material interests are, indeed, a very important factor in democratic politics, where many, although not all, interest groups are highly organized with a view to putting pressure on the political system so as to favour their interests and to distribute public resources in a way that will benefit them.

Obvious major interest groups of this kind are trade unions, the farming organizations, and the industrial and financial communities. Less obvious ones, which, however, have an altruistic rather than a selfish motivation, are the multitude of 'disinterested interest groups' which seek support from the State for their voluntary work on behalf of others.

It is important to note in this context, however, that some groups are not organized at all, including as I have just mentioned the retired in our society, although these have a quite powerful organization in the United States. This is also notably true of youth who, because of the constant turnover of the age group, are unorganized, not having yet become part of the established social structure.

Now, there can be a serious unbalancing of the thrust of State policies in favour of those who find it easier to lobby in a well-organized way at the expense of those who in the nature of things cannot organize equally strongly in their own defence. One of the principal duties of politicians is to seek to offset this imbalance by giving higher priority to the needs of the underrepresented – as was in fact done within the Irish State from the 1960s to the early 1980s.

But there are broader interests than sectoral ones, and these may centre upon divergent views on the interests of a state, or in the case of Northern Ireland of different elements in what might be styled a sub-state. It is in relation to a community or state of this kind that we are most likely to find a conflict between an objective assessment of where the interests of that community or state lie and *emotional* factors, often relating to issues of identity.

Just such a conflict is, in my view, evident in British politics at the present time, and has been for some decades past, on the issue of Britain's relationship with the European Union, and this seems also to have been emerging in Ireland.

In Northern Ireland, the intercommunity division has led to the emotional factor almost totally displacing other motivations in politics. Unionists in particular have been motivated almost completely by the emotion of fear – fear of losing their identity within an all-Ireland context which they have visualized as being dominated by an alien and exclusivist Catholic, post-Gaelic culture. And because emotion drives out reason, this factor of fear led Unionists to use the power devolved to them as a local majority to discriminate against nationalists, thus building up a head of resentment that eventually brought down their regime. The fact is that fear consistently inhibited, and today still inhibits, very many Unionists from making an objective assessment of how best to secure, through their relationship with successive British Governments, the interests of their community and of Northern Ireland as a whole.

The truth is that emotions of this kind have no useful role to play in politics. Nor, in my personal view, has *ideology* – a motivating force in politics that often distorts actions in an unhelpful way. I believe that politics ought to be about reconciling ideas and interests – a difficult enough task for sure, but one often capable of resolution, if both emotion and ideology are kept at bay.

Failure to grasp that the politicians' task of reconciling interests and ideals is both extremely complex and also more persistently morally demanding than that of almost any other profession lies behind a good deal of popular disillusionment with politicians. There is no point in gainsaying the fact that politics is, perhaps, the most vulnerable of all professions to low public esteem. But while the fact of the low esteem in which it is held is often adverted to, the fundamental reason for this vulnerability is rarely addressed in any depth, either by politicians or by journalists writing about the subject.

That fundamental reason is, I believe, the fact that the public interest demands that politicians in office take – or, if on the backbenches of a government party, accept – responsibility for an extraordinarily wide range of decisions involving changes that affect the lives of the whole community. But many such changes made in the general public interest are of their nature bound to have negative effects upon private interests. And those whose private interests are thus adversely affected have the opportunity (normally at intervals of five years or less, but in Ireland a period that has averaged less than three years), to drive the offending politicians from office, and indeed from their careers as members of parliament, by switching their votes.

1 Irish independence: rationale and timing

In September 1962 when I was Chairman of the Irish Council for the European Movement it was suggested to me on behalf of the then Taoiseach, Sean Lemass, that the Council invite a group of journalists from member states of the European Community and from Britain to come to Ireland to study the preparations we were making at that time for membership of the Community and to hear the views of the various parties and interest groups on this subject.

The reason for this move was that the recent Irish application for membership had not been as well received within the Community as the Government had hoped; whilst the negotiations with Britain and Denmark had made progress, our application had been put on one side pending consideration of the state of readiness of the Irish economy for accession to the Community. This was probably because as recently as 1958 the Irish Government had pressed the need for a twenty-year transitional period for Irish industry in the context of the negotiations for a European Free Trade Association designed to link other Western European countries with the six-member European Community.

In the light of that stance, the European Commission was not convinced that our economy could have been sufficiently transformed in the short period since 1958 to be able to accept the kind of five-year transitional period that they had in mind for acceding States.

Amongst the journalists whom we invited on that occasion was A.P. Ryan, a distinguished journalist then near the end of a career with *The Times* which had begun well before the outbreak of the Great War. At the end of my initial briefing session to the group he came up to me and put the following question: 'When I first came here in 1920 I met your father in the Shelbourne Hotel. As Director of Publicity of the underground Dáil Government on the run from the British forces, he sought to convince me that Ireland should be a sovereign, independent State. Now, just over forty years later, I return to find his son seeking to persuade me that Ireland should give up much of that sovereignty. Can you reconcile these two positions?'

I did my best to effect the requested reconciliation, although whether I convinced him I do not know. I should, perhaps, have said to him that my father was also passionately European and would, I believe, have welcomed enthusiastically our proposed involvement with the rest of Western Europe, but that personalized response did not occur to me at the time.

When I later reflected on the challenge that A.P. Ryan had thus posed to me I eventually became convinced that far from there being any contradiction between our demand for independence from Britain and our later accession to the European Community, Irish membership of the European Community ultimately justified that independence.

For, if we had not become independent during the first half of that century, and if as a result we had joined the Community as part of a recalcitrant and unenthusiastic United Kingdom, we would have had neither the capacity to secure our interests within the Community nor an opportunity to express our personality and to make our own distinctive, if inevitably modest, contribution to the development of this new political structure for Europe.

Given the extent to which Ireland's assessment of its own interests and the ideals it wishes to pursue within the Community diverge from – and in some respects are indeed antithetical to – those of the United Kingdom, it seems clear to me that Ireland would have suffered a permanent and enduring disadvantage if it had been unable to become a member in its own right. Europe, too, would, I suggest, have been at least marginally the poorer because of our absence as a separate member state – a verdict that I believe virtually no one in the Continental member countries of the Community would now contest, despite our reduced popularity in Europe following such developments as the controversy over our corporate tax structure and our Nice referendum vote.

It is, of course, very difficult for us today to make the imaginative leap back to the mood of the 1912–16 period in Ireland. To generations born after independence the existence of an Irish State based on a powerful tradition of separatism with regard to Britain is so much a fact of life that it has been increasingly hard for these generations to conceive of an Ireland in which, up to a century or so ago, the existence of a sovereign, independent Irish State was to the vast majority of a people a remote and uncertain objective, and one to which very few were in fact totally committed.

The following is an assessment by one participant in 1916 and in the subsequent movement that led to the emergence of an independent Irish State in 1922, in which he later recalled the fluctuating mood of separatists like himself between 1912 and 1914.

> Home rule was in the air. The overwhelming majority of the people supported Redmond. In so far as that support had waned it was due to a growing cynicism among the people. Home Rule had been promised so long and had not materialised. If it failed again there was no evidence to lead one to expect that the people would do more than shrug their shoulders and say they expected as much.
>
> On the other hand it did really look as though some Bill would become law. Those of us who thought of Home Rule as something utterly inadequate were a very small minority, without influence, impotent. In the circumstances of the time, in the cold light of reason, one could really have foreseen only the success of the Home Rule movement with a subordinate Government established, whose restricted powers would be acclaimed as fulfilling all aspirations, or the failure of Home Rule, which would have been acceptable to the majority of the people as a proof that it was too much to hope for.
>
> Then came the War.
>
> I think our first reaction was one of jubilation. England would now be beaten and resurgent Irish nationalism would assert and make effective our claim to real autonomy.

But that was not to be. He continues:

> Whatever degree of exultation possessed us soon gave way to a condition very close to despair. On the very declaration of War Mr. Redmond made a statement assuring the English people that the Irish volunteers would protect Ireland. But more disturbing than that mere statement was the fact that immediately it became apparent that it really represented the views of the majority of the Irish people. There were reports of the success of recruiting, of Volunteer bands marching to the station to see off their comrades who had volunteered for service in the British Army. The movement on which all our dreams had centred seemed merely to have canalised the martial spirit of the Irish people for the defense of England. Our dream castles toppled about us with a crash. It brought home to us that the very fever that had

> possessed us was due to a sub-conscious awareness that the final end of the Irish Nation was at hand. For centuries England had held Ireland materially. But now it seemed she held her in a new and utterly complete way. Our national identity was obliterated not only politically but also in our own minds. The Irish people had recognised themselves as part of England.

That was my father, Desmond FitzGerald, writing some quarter of a century after the events in question, but, I believe, accurately reflecting his mood, and that of his friends, at that earlier time. I should perhaps add that he was recognized amongst his contemporaries as having an exceptionally accurate memory.

It has always seemed to me a huge paradox that the success of 1916 – in conjunction, my father always held, with the impact of the conscription controversy of 1918 – in changing utterly the attitude of Irish people towards Britain and towards the continued participation of Ireland in the United Kingdom has been such as to make it virtually impossible for anyone in later decades to understand the mood of despair about Irish nationalism that actually provoked the Rising.

The subsequent attempt, sustained for two generations, to portray the Rising as part of an unbroken tradition of armed resistance to British rule effectively negated the actual rationale of that Rising, which had the unfortunate effect of totally obscuring that reality. In time, however, this false presentation of history produced its own reaction. In 1966, when the golden jubilee of the Rising was celebrated, this reaction was really only starting to become evident; it did not feature largely in the rhetoric of that celebration. But in writing about it at that time, several years before the outbreak of violence in Northern Ireland, I commented that public attitudes to 1916 were becoming more critical, a trend which I suggested had been intensified by the growing abhorrence of violence that marked the advanced cultures of the world, our own included.

Furthermore by 1966 the spurious claims made by the propagandists of extreme nationalism were, in my view, already beginning to alienate the sympathies of many younger people and contributing to a growing cynicism about the National Movement of 1916 and the years that followed.

Indeed, I wrote at that time that it seemed to me that the case for the Rising had for some time past been allowed to go by default because of an easy assumption by many speakers and writers that the

1916 tradition was shared by everyone and that it required no explanation or justification. Because of the treatment of pre-1916 Irish history in schools up to that time and the silence with which the events of the intervening half century were being passed over, younger people had in fact been largely prevented from understanding why the gesture of the Rising had been judged necessary by its leaders.

The case against 1916, which I also outlined when writing on the subject in 1966, was, of course, that violence, once unleashed, was difficult to chain again. At its birth the Irish Free State had nearly succumbed to armed anarchy; young men who had been taught to glorify violence against Britain had found it hard to eschew violence against a native regime which they were persuaded to regard as a British puppet government. The achievement of Irish freedom, which should have been a glorious event, had degenerated with frightening speed into a civil war of assassination, arson, executions and reprisals. And even after that war had petered out, the tradition of violence still lived on: a Cabinet Minister, many detectives and other policemen, jury members doing their duty, landlords, innocent bystanders, and many members of the IRA died violently in our state during the thirty-five years that followed the Civil War.

Moreover, apart from the death and destruction thus wrought on the new state, there was the demoralization that followed these political divisions, and the perpetuation of old hatreds by some, although by no means all, of the protagonists. Because of the circumstances in which the new state had come into being, the inferiority complex, the xenophobia, and the inverted snobbery that were all inevitable legacies of British rule were kept alive for decades after they should have disappeared.

To these factors has since been added the appalling violence in Northern Ireland, which I know for many people has shifted the balance powerfully against the case for 1916. That violence undoubtedly contributed to the deep-seated national reluctance to celebrate, or even to commemorate, the seventy-fifth anniversary of the Rising in 1991.

Clearly we have not yet come to terms with our history of the first quarter of the twentieth century.

Let me now pose in somewhat different and, perhaps, more fundamental terms issues that have been only implicit in these arguments about 1916.

It seems to me that two sets of fundamental questions arise in connection with the issue of Irish independence. The first of these is whether, and if so why, Irish independence was desirable. And the second question, which would follow from a positive answer to the first, is when and how Irish independence might best have been achieved. In the context of possible answers to these two questions the Rising of 1916 can better be evaluated.

As to the first matter, the question of whether a country ought to continue to be independent scarcely arises where it has been an independent state for a considerable period of time. It could be relevant only where strong evidence emerges that the state in question was a failure, and would be clearly better off as part of some other political unit, or else broken up into several parts.

The former happened in the case of Newfoundland earlier in the last century. And, it can certainly be argued today, that the components of Yugoslavia might have been better off had they not come together in a single state. How did that composite state come into existence? The union of Croats and Slovenes with the Serbs in the second half of November 1918 was precipitated by a very specific and temporary threat of the loss of their coastal areas to Italy. Because, for this reason, the union was created in a great hurry, the Croats and Slovenes failed to safeguard their interests adequately against the dominance of the more powerful Serbs. The result was that a decade later these two peoples found themselves submerged within a now centralized Serb-dominated state, which, despite the divisive effects of a four-year German/Italian occupation, and the subsequent Tito period, collapsed sixty years later.

A need for independence arises most frequently where some part of an existing state believes that it could manage its affairs better on its own and has a sufficiently strong sense of cultural and social identity, as well as a sufficiently viable economic base, and normally also a sufficiently distinct infrastructure, for this proposition to be tenable, or even, perhaps, compelling. This was for example the situation in Norway in 1904.

The case of Ireland is a particularly interesting one because from 1801 onwards Ireland was part of a United Kingdom within which four distinct national identities existed with varying degrees of contentment or unhappiness – the Welsh, Scots and Irish, in addition to the dominant English.

On the whole it has seemed that the Welsh have felt themselves reasonably comfortable within the union, so long as they have been allowed to foster their own culture and language, and, more recently, their own regional political institutions. For much of the period of the union with England the Scots also seemed reasonably content with the arrangement, but in recent times the balance has shifted. Scotland now has its own parliament and the idea of an independent Scottish State now commands some degree of support in Scotland.

In the case of Ireland, a desire for a separate Irish political entity survived with varying degrees of intensity throughout the whole of the period of the union with Britain, as indeed it had during the earlier period of subordination to Britain. It was always clear that Ireland was the most likely of the Celtic nationalities to break away at some point from that union.

It was not, however, clear throughout much of the period of the union that there existed amongst a majority of Irish people either a desire for, or an expectation of, a complete break with Britain, involving the establishment of a sovereign independent Irish State, as distinct from the achievement of a significant degree of autonomy for Ireland within some kind of structured Anglo-Irish relationship.

Even where they contain a considerable measure of diversity, there is much to be said in favour of reasonably large states. Both economically and politically many things can be better done on a larger scale. For one thing, sovereign independence carries an overhead of administration which can be relatively costly.

Against that background, in what circumstances is independence for part of an existing state 'justified'? Of its nature this is incapable of being determined with anything like scientific accuracy, but, I suggest, the following are amongst criteria that can reasonably be applied:

1. The existence of a significant disparity in economic interests between the area in question and the larger unit to which it is joined.
2. The existence of significant cultural differences between the two.

And perhaps also:

3. The existence of a strong and persistent will for separation on the part of the people of the area in question, or on the part of a significant proportion of them – a will for separation that is of

such a character that continuance of the existing relationship would be likely to be disruptive of either or both societies.

Whilst these criteria are somewhat arbitrary, and others could, no doubt, also be suggested, it seems to me that some such features as these must lie behind the separation of part of a state to form a new one. In the case of Ireland, it seems to me objectively that at least the first two of these elements were always present, the third less clearly and consistently so.

Thus with regard to the economic issue, it appears to me that the history of the last eighty years has demonstrated very clearly that the economic interests of the greater part of Ireland and those of Britain are sufficiently divergent for a strong case to have existed for a separate Irish State. Even when the relationship between the dominant and subordinate partner had developed to the point where the former had ceased either to exploit, or to protect itself against, its weaker partner, the differences between the two economies in the post-Industrial Revolution era were such that the policies that needed to be pursued for the benefit of each of them were fundamentally divergent – divergent to a degree that could not easily be reconciled within the structure of a single state.

(In this connection it is, I think, significant that within the complex history of the evolution of states no acceptable structure ever seems to have evolved enabling different parts of the same political entity to develop and to sustain thereafter divergent fiscal policies, and, where appropriate, to introduce customs barriers between them where these did not previously exist. On the contrary, where fiscal barriers exist within states the tendency has been for them to disappear, both in pre-existing states and in new states created by an amalgamation of existing ones, *vide* in Germany and Italy in the nineteenth century.)

A complicating factor in the Irish–British relationship was the parliamentary Union of Ireland and Britain in 1801. It can be argued that this Union may have eased the eventual transition to Catholic Emancipation and parliamentary representation for Catholics as well as the introduction of a wider franchise in Ireland in parallel with that process in Britain, which began in 1832.

For, in the absence of the legislative union of the two islands, the commitment of the 10–12% Anglican governing establishment in Ireland to preserve their political dominance in the island by resisting

Catholic Emancipation and/or the extension of the franchise might well have led to a violent confrontation with the vast majority of the Irish population at some point in the nineteenth century. And such a development could in turn have had a traumatic impact on Britain, comparable to, but occurring a century earlier than, that of the Algerian crisis on France in the late 1950s and early 1960s.

Nevertheless, whatever inter-community problems the Union may, perhaps, have temporarily eased during the nineteenth century, it was ultimately unsustainable because of the depth of the cultural, religious and social differences, but also because of the profound economic differences, between the two areas.

In contrast to the Scottish case, in Ireland these differences were alleviated neither by a common Protestantism nor by a period of rule in England by a dynasty from the Celtic periphery. Moreover, in contrast with the Scottish lowlands, which had the natural resources for industrial development, there was a huge contrast between the Irish and English/British economies: the development of each required the application of quite different policies. In practice such contrasting policies were incapable of being applied by the government of a union of the two states, for that government necessarily had to give priority to the needs of the larger and more dominant of the two islands.

As a result of its lack of the natural resources that had formed the basis of British economic development in the nineteenth and early twentieth centuries, the bulk of the smaller island had remained almost exclusively agricultural, and consequently suffered persistent and massive debilitating emigration. This problem could not be rectified without its people having the power to devise and implement economic policies specifically related to their island's very different economic situation.

There is another economic consideration to which it seems to me political historians have given inadequate attention. It relates to the development in the twentieth century of the Welfare State. Up to the very end of the nineteenth century Ireland, as part of a state without any significant redistributive income transfer system, was, like the peripheral regions of most states at that time, a net contributor to the central services of the state of which it formed a part, namely the United Kingdom.

This perverse flow was an inevitable consequence of the two islands having become a single fiscal area at a period when government expenditure was still largely deployed centrally, on public administration and defence. At that period there were almost no such activities as locally-provided but centrally-financed education, health services, public housing or social welfare, all of which involve flows from the richer centre to the poorer periphery of a state.

From the analysis undertaken by the Commission on Financial Relations in the mid 1890s we have some measure of the extent of this Irish net contribution to the British economy in the nineteenth century. The British Treasury's own analysis, undertaken for that Commission, of the relationship between estimated true revenue from Ireland and local expenditure there showed net contributions by Ireland to Imperial Services ranging between £2.5m. and £5.5m. at different periods during the nineteenth century. (In today's money terms almost one hundred times that figure.) Throughout a large part of that century the estimated true tax revenue from Ireland was estimated by the Treasury to have been three to four times local expenditure there, although this ratio had diminished to approximately 1.5 to 1 by 1889.

Moreover it would appear that these figures probably underestimated the extent of the transfers from Ireland to Britain during this period, because for one thing they included within the figure of 'local expenditure' the cost of the Royal Irish Constabulary. Given its political role that body had been accepted by Sir Robert Peel, and later by Goschen as Chancellor of the Exchequer, to be more appropriately considered an Imperial charge. And, as late as 1909–1910, the RIC represented over one-eighth of the total of public expenditure in Ireland.

During the 1890s and the early years of the last century a Conservative Government substantially increased local expenditure in Ireland (the policy of 'killing Home Rule by kindness') with the result that, by the time the Liberal Government came to power in 1906, public spending in Ireland had for the first time come approximately to equal true local revenue. The new old age pensions introduced by that Liberal government in 1908 seem to have added a further one-third to public spending in Ireland and, coming on top of the earlier Conservative reforming measures, this first significant social welfare provision changed Ireland from being a net contributor to the Imperial Exchequer into a country representing a burden on that Exchequer.

It was to counter these arguments that Tom Kettle wrote his small book on 'Home Rule Finance – An Experiment In Justice' in 1911. It is clear from that pamphlet that, as one of the more intelligent advocates of Home Rule, Kettle was deeply concerned at the disappearance of the traditional argument for Irish independence, namely that it would prove much less costly for the Irish people than participation in the Empire.

The significance of this shift in the flow of resources between Britain and Ireland a century ago was also immediately apparent to unionists who were quick to point out that separation would now make Ireland poorer rather than better off. Nationalists were thus for the first time put on the defensive on this economic issue.

From what happened to the finances of Northern Ireland following the establishment of its Home Rule parliament, and from its subsequent and indeed continuing financial relationship with Britain, we can see the extent to which, after 1922 with the development of the Welfare State, the cost to Ireland of becoming independent and standing on its own financial feet would have grown rapidly. At that time the change was still just manageable without significant financial disruption. Effectively it was met by reductions of 10% in Civil Service pay and later also in welfare payment – cuts which in purchasing terms were more than offset by a 30% fall in the cost of living in the course of the 1920s.

When we note the extent to which in the 1970s Irish public opinion was influenced, despite a strong emotional pull of nationalist arguments, to join the European Community on grounds that were almost purely economic, a doubt must exist as to whether in these conditions full Irish independence would continue to have been sought in later decades when the cost in terms of lost transfers of resources from Britain would have grown enormously.

Did the reversal of the net flow of resources between Britain and Ireland just short of a century ago contribute, perhaps even subconsciously, to the decision of some nationalist leaders a few years later to seek to accelerate the process of securing separation from Britain by organizing the 1916 Rising? I do not think we know enough about the thinking of those who took that decision to answer that question one way or the other.

But, with all the clarity of hindsight, it now seems clear that had Irish independence not been secured in 1922, well before the Welfare State reached its full shape, it might have been very difficult indeed for the people of Ireland to have broken away from a Britain which would by then have been transferring annually to Ireland a substantial flow of financial resources.

And if for that reason Ireland had felt constrained to remain in the UK rather than face the shock of the loss of what could have become one-fifth to one-quarter of its public revenues, its people would never have had the opportunity at the end of that century to catch up with Britain and the rest of Europe in economic terms. For, the scale of the subsidization of less prosperous Ireland by Britain that would have been necessary under modern Welfare State conditions would, I believe, have been such as to make practically impossible the emergence in Ireland of an internally-generated dynamic for growth.

In recent times this kind of problem of regional overdependence on financial flows from a central government has been seen to arise in three regions of Western Europe: the Mezzogiorno of Southern Italy, East Germany, and Northern Ireland. In each of these three regions the need for transfers from the remainder of the state of which they are part, to the tune of up to 20–25% of the regions GDP, has hugely inhibited the emergence of an internal dynamic of growth. Indeed in the case of Northern Ireland a significant pre-existing growth dynamic has in fact been seriously undermined by the scale of such regional subsidization, involving a very high level of public spending.

A measure of the extent to which, because of this factor (admittedly aggravated by thirty years of violence), Northern Ireland has lost ground during the past half century, is the fact that the proportion of the output of the island of Ireland that is produced in that region has fallen from 37–38% in 1953 to about 23–24% today. From having been the most prosperous part of the island, Northern Ireland now has a very much lower level of output per head than the Republic.

Within Northern Ireland this depressing fate has hitherto been accepted by the Unionist majority as a price that has had to be paid to preserve the identity of their community, which they see threatened by incorporation with the nationalist majority in the island. This acceptance of relative economic decline may also have been facilitated hitherto by a false belief amongst Unionists that this process has been attributable solely to the IRA campaign of 1970–93 – as well as up to the mid 1990s, but not since then, by a belief that Northern Ireland had at least remained better off than the Republic.

If, under the Welfare State conditions that evolved in Europe during the twentieth century, the whole of Ireland had had to be subsidized from and by Britain, eventually to the tune of something like €10–12bn. a year, this could also have created tensions in Britain.

There was, moreover, a further economic consideration relevant to the timing of the achievement of independence. If Ireland was to have the possibility of using tariffs and quota protections to develop an industrial sector, it needed to be independent. I know, of course, that there are many economists who argue that the policy of protection pursued within the independent Irish state was mistaken, but I do not myself think that the evidence fully supports this thesis.

I would not for a moment dispute that protection was introduced in a messy and ill-judged way in the Irish case and that it could have been much better arranged. But I find it hard to conceive that we could today in the Irish state have a significant manufacturing sector, half of it comprising high technology industries from abroad, had Ireland remained up to the time we joined the European Community an almost exclusively agricultural economy in a continuing free trade relationship with Britain.

It is, of course, true that many of the industries established in the Irish state behind protective barriers disappeared with the movement to free trade in the 1960s and 1970s, but the surviving sectors have expanded significantly and the experience of industrial activity gained during the period of protection, including the experience that so many individuals and families acquired of working in industry, was, in my view, a positive factor in terms of attracting new foreign industries to Ireland. These new industries would for the most part have been most reluctant to come to a European country in which there was no such body of industrial experience and where workers had remained accustomed to the totally different work-rhythm of an agricultural economy.

The economic arguments for Irish independence, deriving at a fundamental level from the divergence between the interests of a Britain pursuing a cheap food policy and the interests of a largely agricultural Ireland, and also from the need for a measure of industrial protection during an initial period, are, I believe, powerful ones. It is perhaps worth adding that the extent to which in the three decades after accession to the European Community the Irish and British governments pursued largely divergent positions in relation to both agriculture and industry has reflected the continuing fundamental divergence of economic interests between the two states.

There is yet another point that I would add in connection with the Irish membership of the European Community.

It is not easy for a new state to concede sovereignty. There may be some significance in the fact that the only European people who voted against a proposal for EC membership put to them by their government were the Norwegians – Norway being in fact the only other Western European country as well as Ireland to have secured independence in the twentieth century.

Had Irish independence been secured at a significantly later date than the early 1920s it is far from certain that Irish opinion would have had enough time to have become prepared for the sharing of sovereignty involved in an application for EC membership in the early 1960s and for actual membership in the early 1970s. Ireland might, of course, have become a member at a much later stage, but delayed independence could have involved losing out substantially by being inhibited, because independence had so recently been secured, from adopting the positive attitude to European integration that Ireland, in contrast to the United Kingdom and Denmark, was able with considerable advantage to take up at and after the time of accession. There would, moreover, have also been huge losses in terms of benefits that would have been secured in the intervening period.

In relation to this issue of loss of advantages because of delayed accession, it is perhaps worth pointing out that had Britain and Ireland been accepted as members before 1970 the Community's Common Fisheries Policy would certainly have been less disadvantageous to these two countries than the self-interested policy of communitizing fish stocks adopted by the Continental EC members in 1970 before we joined. Late accession carries significant penalties.

I think, therefore, that in hindsight there is a very strong argument that Irish independence was in fact secured almost at the latest date at which it could have been usefully achieved, both in terms of developing through a policy of protection of an industrial economy capable of surviving in the free trade conditions of EC membership, and also in terms of securing public support for independence in the face of what would have become increasingly strong short-term financial arguments for continued participation in the United Kingdom. These arguments could well have obscured in the minds of the Irish electorate the objectively strong case at a much more fundamental level for Irish independence that I have already outlined.

With regard to the other criterion for independence earlier mentioned – the issue of cultural identity – it is scarcely necessary to argue that the cultural differences between Ireland and Britain are very deep indeed, and that the Irish sense of a separate cultural identity is extremely strongly marked. The fact that in some ways it became even more strongly marked when both countries came to use the same language makes the cultural divergence even more striking.

It is curious that these issues do not seem to have been addressed in the debates that in recent decades have taken place from time to time on the relative merits of the revolutionary and constitutional 'Home Rule' approaches to the Irish question in the early decades of this century.

Although hypotheses about what might have happened are, of course, unhistorical, I believe it is, nevertheless, fair to speculate that without the arousal of national consciousness which the dramatic failure of 1916 evoked, Ireland would have moved towards Home Rule before or after the end of the Great War. At some stage, the Irish people would have secured from Britain the measure of autonomy that Home Rule implied, probably with some provision for separate treatment of the North, for a time at least. Defence, Foreign Affairs and much of Finance would have remained Imperial responsibilities, and Ireland probably would still have been represented at Westminster.

Beyond that point one advances, of course, into the realm of unqualified speculation. Starting, however, not from the Ireland we know today but from the viewpoint of the Ireland of 1915, it is far from clear that Home Rule for the whole of Ireland would necessarily have evolved much further towards independence, or that as a matter of course Ireland would have taken its place eventually among the independent nations of the world.

True, the granting of independence to almost all the parts of the great European Empires that sought independence during the decades after the Second World War might have had an influence on events in Ireland, but not necessarily so. For Ireland was not a colony in the same sense as these overseas territories, and, given that it would have enjoyed self-government whilst sharing with Britain its responsibilities in Defence and Foreign Affairs, it does not seem to be certain that the Irish people would in those circumstances have seen themselves as a colony.

Instead they might have been persuaded rather to continue as one of two great mother countries sharing an Empire – as many Irish people who were not Unionists, John Redmond amongst them – had done before the Great War, especially if Britain had during these years come to show some sensitivity towards Irish feelings in such matters.

Would the people whose menfolk had rushed to join the British Army in such extraordinary numbers in 1914 have wanted an Irish National Army in the 1920s and 1930s? Without the national revival brought about by 1916, would a people whose more brilliant men found ample opportunities for their talents in the Imperial Civil Service have sought to make the voice of Ireland, as distinct from that of the United Kingdom of Britain and Ireland, heard in the councils of Europe, or at the United Nations? Would a people so long oriented towards London, many of them apparently content that Dublin should be merely a provincial centre of the British Isles, have suddenly become ambitious to secure for it the status of a capital city of a sovereign state?

Without the national revival of 1916–21 would Ireland ever have become a largely self-reliant country, seeking to run its affairs in its own way? Or would it have shrunk as, regrettably, did Northern Ireland, into a dependent, economic provincialism, myopically preoccupied about its share of British subsidies and social welfare provisions?

In the seventeenth and eighteenth centuries England exploited Ireland. In the nineteenth century she neglected Ireland. But in the twentieth century she would have subsidized Ireland, as she has done Northern Ireland. And could Ireland's sense of nationhood, which by 1915 was already so weakened as to require, in the view of the separatists of that period, a rising to reawaken it, have withstood for long this most insidious of treatments?

Moreover if a single Irish Home Rule entity had eventually emerged, would it have been all that different from Northern Ireland, save for the switch between Orange and Green conservatives? Might there not have been the same stifling one-party rule, the same hopelessness with regard to social or political change, the same orientation towards London as the ultimate source of political power and the ever present source of financial subsidies?

I am not sure that conclusively negative answers can be given to all these questions, and if the speculative picture that I have implicitly drawn could have some substance, then the negative consequences of this possibility must be set against what are seen today as the negative consequences of 1916.

Let me sum up my thesis so far. The case for the existence of a sovereign, independent Irish State in the second half of the twentieth century is a strong one, reflecting the extent of the divergence of material interests between Ireland and Britain, and the extent of cultural differentiation between the two areas combine to make that case.

And on the timing of independence, even if an Irish State had emerged somewhat later in the century out of the twin Home Rule entities that in the absence of 1916 would almost certainly have been the product of the period immediately after the Great War – and such delayed independence is far from certain – would its people have been psychologically ready for the sharing of sovereignty involved in membership of the European Community in the 1970s? And would that State's industrial structure have been capable of developing without industrial protection, or with only a very truncated period of protection, to a point where it would by the 1970s have been capable of a viable existence under free trade conditions?

If Irish independence was objectively desirable, it is certainly arguable that it needed to be achieved within the third decade of the twentieth century, and it is very doubtful whether without 1916 it would have been secured within that time scale.

These arguments can, I believe, legitimately be set against the adverse impact of 1916 in terms of the persistence of violence in the island of Ireland throughout the twentieth century.

But, whilst political independence was a necessary precondition of economic growth, the early history of the Irish State also showed that it was far from being a sufficient condition. For, instead of seeking to deploy its new-found independence to grow the Irish economy faster than that of neighbouring Britain (which by 1922 was already well-embarked upon the relative economic decline by comparison with continental Europe that persisted until the 1980s), a combination of external events and the choice of self-sufficiency as a policy goal produced an opposite situation: right up until the end of the 1950s economic growth in Ireland was instead slower than in Britain.

The causes of this initial failure to benefit economically from political independence included such factors as the burden of reconstruction costs following the destructive post-independence Civil War, and the subsequent 'Economic War' with Britain between 1932 and 1938. (In 1932 a dispute over the payment to Britain of Land Annuities due in respect of the land reform of a generation earlier led to a tariff war between the two countries, which aggravated the negative impact on the Irish economy of the 'Great Slump'.)

A crucial negative policy choice in this period was the attempt not just to develop 'import industries' behind a temporary tariff wall but actually to seek to achieve economic self-sufficiency. That was, of course, an absurd ambition for a small underpopulated state, with few known mineral resources and a very limited climatic range. Such a state needed above all to develop its exports in order to be able to pay for the wide range of imports it would require in order to achieve and sustain a reasonable standard of living.

Finally, given the absence in the 1920s and 1930s of any alternative market for agricultural products, the operation of Britain's 'cheap food' policy – which had kept food prices, and thus wages, low in Britain since 1846 with a view to maintaining artificially its dominance in world trade – contributed to the lack of significant economic growth in a country one half of whose working population were engaged in farming.

By the 1950s this combination of unfavourable external conditions and unwise policy choices, when combined with deep political conservatism and a notable lack of economic expertise amongst the long-surviving post-revolutionary political elite, had led the Irish economy into a condition of actual economic stagnation. Indeed, for a brief moment in the latter part of that decade the resultant crisis even induced doubts amongst some of its citizens about the viability of an independent Irish state.

Eventually exasperation at this most unhappy outcome of the first thirty-five years of Irish independence produced a vigorous reaction, involving a massive public and political repudiation of the past futile policy of unlimited protectionism designed to secure an unattainable self-sufficiency. Interestingly this revolution in economic policy antedated by several years the departure from active politics of its author, Eamon de Valera.

Between 1958 and 1973 this belated attempt to deploy political independence in an effective manner secured a growth rate of about 4.25%, which was for the first time well above the 2.75% rate for contemporary slow-growing Britain, albeit still fractionally below the average growth rate for the remainder of Western Europe.

The two key initiatives deployed during this first period of economic growth were:

- The application of reduced, and later nil taxes to export profits (a provision which, after EC accession, was substituted by a 10% tax on all industrial profits), combined with vigorous promotion of foreign investment replacing the earlier restraints imposed upon it.
- This was supplemented, in the second half of the 1960s, by the initiation of a very rapid expansion of the second-level educational system. At the second level this involved additional finance for the confessional schools which had been providing three-quarters of Irish second-level education. This provision enabled almost all of them to eliminate the, often very small, fees previously charged.

Whilst this additional finance was generally insufficient to permit these schools to have student–staff ratios on the same scale as in most other European countries or to equip them adequately, teacher pay rates were relatively high and this ensured high teacher morale. Moreover, in this process the state also drew successfully on the high educational motivation of most Irish parents, who were no longer prepared to tolerate seeing their children emigrate without adequate educational preparation for decent jobs abroad.

Within a generation this policy, supplemented by a major state-wide expansion of third-level education, had at very low cost transformed Ireland from the most undereducated country in Northern Europe into one of the better educated.

However, during the first quarter of a century of economic recovery (1960–85), and even after entry to the EC (where after the first oil crisis of 1973 growth slowed to a lower average rate than that being achieved in Ireland), the benefits of Irish economic growth accrued not in the form of a catching-up of Irish living standards but rather in the form of an increase in population.

This was because, with economic growth, instead of almost half of each new age cohort being lost to emigration, that proportion fell rapidly to about 15%. Arithmetically this meant that the proportion of people born in Ireland who survived there to age 35 rose by something approaching three-fifths. And, at a time when early marriage and childbearing were still the norm for those who secured employment, this jump in the size of the young population produced a temporary increase of one-third in marriages, accompanied in conditions of declining fertility, by a rise of one-quarter in the number of births.

However, in this early period of economic growth the numbers actually at work rose relatively slowly, due to the need to re-absorb the decline in the still-numerous farm population, and also because of the expansion of the educational system which reduced the stock of young workers. Consequently the ratio of dependants to workers grew by no less than one-third during the 1960–85 period.

Irish economic growth in that period was, nevertheless, sufficient to secure that despite this disproportionate increase in the number of dependants, living standards were still able to rise at about the same rate as in the rest of Europe. But no faster until after the mid 1980s when the Irish dependency ratio started to decline very rapidly due to employment growth on the one hand and a sharp post-1980 fall in the birth rate on the other.

From the outset it had been clear that without an opening up of markets other than the slow-growing and, so far as agriculture was concerned, depressed British market, the new economic policies could earn only limited results. In the 1960s and 1970s some British and German industrial investment had been attracted to Ireland, but mainly on the basis of lower labour costs, or, in the case of British firms, to cater for the domestic market, from which they had been excluded since 1932. Major US investment was drawn to Ireland only when Continental European markets for Irish-made goods were opened up by Irish accession to the EC, by which time the first fruits of the educational revolution were also starting to emerge.

From 1965 onwards EC farm prices had been distorted on the high side by a system of protective levies. This situation had been brought about by German pressure to fix the new common EC farm prices at a high enough level to support their farmers, whose efficiency was relatively low. The initial positive impact on the Irish economy of EC accession was thus principally in the farm sector, which at the time of accession still employed almost 25% of the working population and accounted for no less than 18% of national output.

In joining the European Community Britain had lost its power to keep food prices artificially low through encouraging the dumping of world food surpluses on the UK market whilst protecting the incomes of its own small farming population by direct income supports. That policy had led to what, from an Irish viewpoint, represented a form of exploitation of the Irish small farm structure ever since the repeal of the Corn Laws in 1846 – an exploitation which had been carried forward into the first half of the post-independence period.

A certain part of the new rural prosperity in Ireland deriving from EC membership was thus essentially temporary because it was dependent upon an EC farm policy of artificially high prices that could not persist for more than a couple of decades. But, nevertheless, this agricultural boom proved of great importance during the transition to the establishment of an Irish high-tech industrial economy, based on free access to the markets of Europe, and, with global freeing of trade, to the world outside Europe.

Thus, freed from its enervating post-colonial dependence upon the small and slow-growing British market with its rapidly-dwindling manufacturing sector, Ireland became able for the first time to derive full benefit from its political independence. This was achieved by exploiting the hitherto limited benefits of its policy of low taxation on corporate industrial profits, as well as the benefits of what since the 1960s had become a well-educated, young labour force.

Figures from the Organization for Economic Cooperation and Development (OECD) show that by the mid 1990s the proportion of Irish 18-year-olds in the educational system had risen to a level 40% higher than that in Britain, which admittedly, together with Portugal, still has today the highest drop-out rate from second-level education in the EU.

In addition to this, a system of national pay agreements was developed by the government, in 1987, in conjunction with the trade union movement (which around that time had begun to give a new priority to expanding employment) and employers. In the following decade, the moderation of pay increases achieved by this process in return for cuts in taxation and improvements in social conditions, enabled profits to rise from a depressed level, with the result that, by the end of the 1990s, they accounted for almost 45% of non-farm output, as against the 1987 figure of 30%. This phenomenon was, however, largely confined to the new foreign-owned high-tech industrial sector which benefited most from the low corporate tax regime.

Finally, all these advantages, which were secured by belatedly using Irish independence to good purpose, were skilfully exploited through the efforts of a highly-professional and sophisticated industrial promotion agency, backed by Irish embassies abroad and able to draw readily on the services of Irish Cabinet Ministers travelling to the United States and elsewhere to support its efforts.

The result of all this was that, with only 1% of the EU's population, Ireland came to attract up to 25% of the number of new greenfield industrial investments in Western Europe. Between 1993 and 2001 this gave Ireland an annual GNP growth rate in excess of 8%.

The consequence of this exceptional growth was that Irish output per head, and living standards, which until the late 1980s were still running 40% behind those of the rest of the EU, have moved to that level, according to both the EU and the OECD, and Ireland has now become, within a few years, one of the richer EU countries in terms of the purchasing power of its disposable income.

It is by the exercise of its sovereignty in such domestic matters as taxation, incomes policy and education, whilst simultaneously benefiting from sharing other aspects of its sovereignty with its EU partners in relation to trade matters, that the Irish State has achieved this remarkable outcome. Without this combination of domestic sovereignty and participation in the EU as an independent state, Ireland could never have pulled itself out of the unhappy situation in which it had for so long remained. In combination, these conditions enabled Ireland to break out of its debilitating long-term economic dependence on Britain, to which it now sends only 23% of its exports, as against 60% before it joined the European Community.

Just as there was a very strong case for the separation of the greater part of Ireland from the United Kingdom not later than the 1920s, so also, it has to be admitted, was there a strong case, in purely economic as distinct from political terms, for the north-eastern corner of the island having remained within the United Kingdom at least for a large part of the twentieth century.

In 1920 it was not foreseeable that within not much more than half a century the shipbuilding industry, with its associated engineering activities, would virtually disappear, nor that the linen, textile and clothing industries would also effectively cease to be of significance. For a large part of the twentieth century the interests of these Northern Irish industrial sectors, upon which much of the prosperity of the north-east depended, were objectively better served by remaining in the United Kingdom, which provided a major market for both naval and merchant vessels, and which, as a relatively open economy, provided a useful base for exporting industries such as textiles and clothing.

Whilst these various economic considerations did not determine the political division of Ireland that took place in 1920, they certainly represented strong reinforcing factors supporting the continued participation in the UK of the north-eastern corner of the island at the moment when cultural, political and economic factors brought about the secession of the greater part of the island from the United Kingdom.

However, with the subsequent, effective disappearance of these industries from Northern Ireland, much of the purely economic rationale for the division of Ireland disappeared. In economic terms the case for Northern Ireland's continued participation in the United Kingdom is today largely limited to the scale of non-security-related transfers from Great Britain to Northern Ireland, which now represent a very significant part of disposable income in the region, but which have also had a most debilitating impact on the previously quite dynamic area. However, these economic considerations have clearly had no effect on the political preferences of a majority of the area's population which have all along been primarily motivated by non-economic considerations.

In the last third of the twentieth century significant changes took place in the capacity of the political majority in Northern Ireland to influence decisions affecting its domestic affairs. The replacement of majority-rule devolved government in Stormont by direct British rule in 1972 involved an almost complete loss of influence upon British policy, as well as a loss of control over legislative provisions affecting Northern Ireland. In respect of this legislation, the area's Westminster MPs had no power of amendment through the system of Orders in Council employed between 1972 and 1999, although paradoxically they retained power to vote on legislation affecting England, Wales and Scotland.

The restoration of devolved government on an agreed basis in 1999 has gone a significant distance towards remedying the absence of control over most aspects of the domestic life of the area. But the absence of any Northern Ireland role in the institutions of the European Union, apart from a disproportionately small role in the European Parliament where it is represented by three out of eighteen Irish MEPs, clearly reduces its capacity to influence its own future in a number of important respects.

For, in a number of key areas of EU policy, such as agriculture and regional policy, Northern Ireland's interests, like those of the Irish state, tend to diverge from, and may even be antithetical to, those of Great Britain, the interests of which naturally determine the United

Kingdom's policy stance in Brussels. Of course the same could be true of certain regions of other member states, but it is difficult to think of cases where the national/regional divergence of interest would be as marked as in the case of Northern Ireland.

At some point in the future this deficiency might, perhaps, be remedied by an arrangement under which, without prejudice to the sovereignty issue, Northern Ireland might be accorded an equal share in the Irish state's role in Europe in respect of those matters where the interests of the two parts of Ireland coincide and diverge from those of Great Britain. If pressed with sufficient insistence by a Northern Ireland Government, might the British and Irish Governments and the European Community not at some point be persuaded to accept an admittedly anomalous situation of this kind?

I should perhaps add that I have found a willingness amongst some administrators and individual members of both Unionist parties to see merit in such an arrangement in the longer term.

2 Economic comparisons

The Irish were not the only European people to have been colonized in the medieval period. Germans, Swedes and Russians colonized parts of Slav and Baltic Europe and later the Turks colonized the Southern Slavs, Greeks and Albanians. And, although in one part of our island settlers established a firm local foothold that survived the upheavals of the twentieth century which eliminated German enclaves in Eastern Europe, in the Irish case the colonization was incomplete. The bulk of the island did not become English, as the western parts of Slav territory became completely German. But neither, for the most part, did Ireland retain its native language, as happened throughout the remainder of Eastern Europe.

For a period of 120 years, Ireland was represented in the parliament of the colonizing country, as was also the case with the subject peoples of the Austro-Hungarian Empire. But in the Irish case this arrangement became particularly fraught when the franchise came to be gradually extended during the nineteenth century, far beyond the religious ranks of the colonizing minority. The incomplete character of the colonisation of Ireland, and the extension to an increasingly large proportion of the Irish population of representation in the United Kingdom Parliament, differentiated the Irish case from that of overseas colonies.

Up to the second half of the nineteenth century Ireland was also differentiated from both Britain and the remainder of Western Europe by the extraordinarily low level of the living standards of the great bulk of its population, which approximated to those of the peoples of the Balkans under Turkish rule and had no parallel in Western or Northern Europe. Moreover, this situation was aggravated as a result of annual transfers of revenue from Ireland to Britain through rents and taxation.

However, in the second half of the nineteenth century Irish living standards rose to the levels of France and Scandinavia, largely because the emigration of a large part of its population eased the problem of subsistence living, but also towards the end of the period through land reform.

Throughout that period Britain's economy was both the richest and most dynamic in Europe, and in the opening decade of the twentieth century transfers of resources from Ireland to its richer neighbour were reversed, through the provision of capital transfers for economic development in the west of Ireland and through the initiation of the system of old age pensions and unemployment insurance.

Thus, by the time Ireland became an independent state in the early 1920s its average level of income per head had come to exceed 60% of the British level. With independence this income level was slightly reduced, as a result of the disappearance of social and other government transfers from Britain.

Although it was not realized at the time, by the 1920s Britain was well embarked on a process of relative economic decline compared to the rest of Western Europe, which continued thereafter until about 1980. Consequently, for most of the period of over half a century after independence the continuing close economic and financial, as well as social, relationship between Ireland and Britain – virtually the only available market for Irish exports of goods and services – greatly constrained Ireland's growth rate.

It was only from 1960 onwards that the Irish economy began to break away from its dependence on the UK market and it was only after Irish accession to the EC in 1973 that this process gained real momentum – a process unhappily halted during the 1980s by the economic mismanagement of the late 1970s.

Ireland's institutional, social, and economic heritage from the past, including its institutional structure and common law legal system, has been markedly different from that of any part of Continental Europe. It is not surprising, therefore, that in many respects Ireland today remains strongly differentiated from those countries.

First of all, well into the second half of the twentieth century Ireland remained a much more agricultural country than the remainder of Northern Europe. In 1950, half of its working population was still on the land and it still derived almost 30% of its output from farming, as against barely 10% in the rest of Northern Europe. Even twenty years later, on the eve of Irish accession to the EEC, more than a quarter of the Irish working population was still on the land as against 8% in neighbouring European countries.

In addition to this, Irish agriculture suffered severely from the fact that the only market open to its farm products, Britain, had been operating a 'cheap food' policy from mid-nineteenth century onwards. After the Second World War this situation was aggravated by the introduction of income subsidies to British farmers, which facilitated the flow of world surpluses to the UK market.

Furthermore, for a number of historical reasons, including a heritage of English colonial exploitation from the eighteenth century as well as neglect of economic development in the nineteenth century, there had been little industrialization in the island of Ireland in the pre-independence period, and what there was had been concentrated in the north-east, which opted out of the new Irish state. The only open market for the products of the late-established, highly protected, and largely inefficient industrial sector of the Irish state was once again Britain, which, as has just been mentioned, had from the late nineteenth century until 1980 consistently been the slowest-growing market in Western Europe.

In 1973 accession to the European Community released Ireland from this economic dependence on Britain, enabling it to diversify hugely its trade pattern. Whereas before EC accession only a minority of Irish exports, 40%, went to countries other than the UK, by the end of the century this proportion had risen to 77%. And during these years Ireland's tourist trade, previously dominated by British visitors, was also diversified, with the result that in 2001 over half of three and a quarter million holidaymakers came from countries other than Britain. The opening up of new markets in Europe was crucial to the development of Irish exports, and to the attraction to Ireland of industrial investment from outside Europe.

The EC has also had a major influence on certain Irish policies, such as those relating to equal treatment of women and to environmental protection, albeit with a good deal of domestic dragging of feet in both instances.

Nevertheless, the *structure* of Irish public finances, of taxation and public spending (which had been set on a British model during the pre-EC period of independence when Ireland was still greatly influenced by British practice), has proved much more resistant to change. So far as social provisions are concerned Ireland has also remained strongly influenced by past British practice, offering much less generous welfare arrangements than most Continental countries.

However, the evolution of the public finances of Ireland and Britain with other EU countries in recent times must be seen in the context of the Irish financial crisis of the 1980s, which had a huge impact on the evolution of Irish society during the last quarter of the twentieth century.

In the years prior to the early 1980s slower growth in Britain than in the rest of Western Europe, combined with public pressures in both Britain and Ireland to move towards providing public services and social provisions closer to the Continental European level, brought both states' finances under heavy pressure. By then the scale of the public authorities' deficit in both countries was becoming unsustainable, with current public receipts already absorbing around 49% of GNP (Gross National Product) in the Irish case. This high level of public revenue could not easily be sustained, for it reflected an artificially high level of non-tax revenue.

At the same time even this very high level of public revenue was failing to finance current spending, which was running at 56% of GNP. Clearly a very substantial reduction in this expenditure was urgently needed in order to transform a large deficit into a current surplus large enough to leave an overall budget surplus after providing for substantial public capital investment.

There were two particular reasons why in the 1990s it proved necessary for Ireland to develop a very large current budget surplus. First of all, economic growth in that recent period greatly over-strained the infrastructure of what until that decade had been a relatively poor state by Northern European standards. Consequently a major public capital programme came to be needed and, with Irish GNP per head moving towards the EU average, this greatly expanded infrastructural investment was no longer going to receive support from the Community's Structural Funds. Second, the vulnerability of the very open Irish economy to external shocks required the maintenance of a somewhat bigger overall budget surplus than was necessary for most other EU states.

However, as Irish governments sought to secure such an outcome during the 1990s, they made this task more difficult for themselves by simultaneously reducing by almost one-fifth the proportion of GNP taken in personal income tax and indirect taxation. Despite rising returns from corporate taxes, these substantial tax cuts greatly intensified the already severe pressure on public spending as successive governments strove at the same time to create the required substantial current budget surplus.

The proportion of Irish GNP absorbed by current public spending was in fact cut during this period by the astonishing amount of over two-fifths. However, one half of this reduction was painless, being attributable to a sharp reduction in the share of GNP required to pay interest on the national debt and to finance unemployment payments – both beneficial consequences of economic growth.

Nevertheless, and even in conditions of unprecedented economic expansion, this huge reduction in the share of GNP devoted to public spending also required that between 1985 and 2000 the overall growth of current spending be held down to 2.5% a year. Given the huge increase in economic activity during these years and the consequent rise in the demand for public services, this tight constraint on spending inevitably contributed to a deterioration in some of these services, notably the health sector.

Thus, within fifteen years Ireland moved from being an economy bedevilled by excessive public spending and a very large budget deficit to being one marked by inadequate public spending and a temporary large surplus, with taxation reduced to a level one-tenth below that of the rest of the EU. The burden of indirect as well as direct taxation was significantly reduced, mainly through limiting increases in taxation of oil products.

Most striking of all, however, is the fact that in the year 2000 Ireland not only spent on social transfers a one-third lower share of its GNP than the Continental EU, but also one-sixth less than the share spent in the neighbouring UK. The total amount of Irish current public spending had in fact been reduced almost to the US level, one-seventh lower than in the UK and almost one-quarter below the Continental EU average.

These year 2000 figures will of course have been subsequently modified by the huge pre-election spending splurge in Ireland in 2001 and 2002. That will have raised the share of GNP absorbed by current spending from 29.7% of GNP to something like 32%, but even after this belated reversal of the expenditure squeeze of the 1990s, the current spending level in Ireland in 2002 remains extraordinarily low by European standards.

It is clear that during the late 1980s and 1990s not merely were the national finances put in order but there also took place a very marked swing to the right in the broad policy stance of Irish governments.

For more than two decades after 1960 governments of whatever political composition had pursued a policy of radically improving the lot of social welfare beneficiaries, not only absolutely but also in relation to the income levels of the working population. The truth is that the influence of American economic liberalism became much stronger during this later period, and pulled Ireland markedly away from the Continental European model of social provision.

The effects of this shift to the right in Irish public policy emerges clearly from a comparison of the patterns of Irish, British and Continental EU public finances in 1985 and 2000, which are set out in the table below:

Table 1: Public Finances 1985 and 2000 EU, Ireland, UK, USA (Percentages of GNP)

	EU		Ireland		UK		US	
	1985	*2000*	*1985*	*2000*	*1985*	*2000*	*1985*	*2000*
Government Consmptn	21.0	19.9	22.3	15.8	21.2	18.7	18.0	16.6
Social Transfers	15.5	16.1	18.6	10.9	12.9	13.3	11.3	10.5
Interest Payments	4.8	3.8	11.5	2.5	5.0	2.7	3.3	3.6
Other Expenditure	2.5	3.2	3.7	3.4	2.6	3.1	0.4	1.1
Total Expenditure	45.1	43.0	56.1	32.8	41.8	37.8	33.0	31.8
Personal Income Tax			13.3	10.4				
Corporation Tax			1.4	3.7				
Other Income Taxes			1.4	1.3				
Sub-Total	14.8	14.3	16.1	15.4	17.1	16.4	14.5	15.5
Social Payments	12.6	14.4	6.3	6.9	8.3	7.6	6.3	7.1
Total Taxes on Income	27.4	28.7	22.4	22.3	25.4	24.3	20.8	22.6
Indirect Taxes	12.6	13.8	19.0	15.9	12.9	14.1	8.0	6.8
Other Taxation	4.5	3.3	1.9	3.2	4.5	2.6	2.7	3.0
Total Taxation	44.6	45.8	43.3	41.4	39.9	41.1	31.5	32.4
Other Revenue			5.9	1.9				
Total Revenue	44.6	45.8	49.2	43.3	39.9	41.1	31.5	32.4
Current Surplus	–0.5	2.8	–6.9	10.5	1.9	3.3	–1.5	0.6
Capital Receipts		0.7		2.2		0.4		0.4
Capital Expenditure		2.2		5.0		–0.7		2.8
Capital Balance		–1.5		–3.2		1.1		–2.4
Overall Surplus/Deficit		1.3		5.4		4.4		2.3

On the revenue side the degree of reliance on indirect taxes in Ireland, even though much reduced since 1985, is striking. VAT rates are higher than in most EU countries and, although excise duties on oil products are relatively low, taxes on alcohol, tobacco and motor vehicles are very high indeed. This has been necessary in an effort to curtail over consumption of alcohol, but also in order to compensate for the very low level of direct taxation, which by 2000 was actually fractionally below that of the United States. The lower level of Irish – and to a lesser extent British – direct taxation in relation to Continental EU countries reflects the exceptionally low level of social contributions in these islands, which in the Irish case in turn reflects the very low proportion of GNP absorbed by social payments. In this respect Ireland closely resembles the United States.

Most people are aware that Ireland has now caught up with the rest of the EU in terms of per capita output and income. As late as 1989 the purchasing power of Irish output per head (measured in terms of GNP) was still 40% below the EC average, but by 2001, a mere twelve years later, Ireland had attained the EU average. Except, perhaps, for some countries whose economy had been destroyed during the Second World War, no industrialized country has ever achieved a catch-up of this magnitude in such a short period.

Clearly an exceptional burst of economic growth has been the major factor in this process: between 1989 and 2001 the volume of Irish GNP more than doubled, rising by 108%. During this period output within the rest of the EU rose by only 25%.

In addition to a rise of one-half in output per hour, i.e. labour productivity, this huge jump in output required an increase of almost one-third in the number of hours worked. However, as during these twelve years Irish workers chose to take almost one-quarter of their increased earning power in shorter working hours per week, the achievement of a one-third increase in hours worked required a rise of as much as one-half in the number of people at work. Output per worker rose by just under one-third.

Given that ouput per worker has increased by less than one-third, how has Irish GNP per head of population more than doubled during these twelve years? The answer to this, as to so many Irish economic and social questions, lies in the unusual demography of the Irish State.

The relevant figures are set out in Table 2 below:

Table 2: Output per worker & per hour 1989–2001

Year	*Nos. At Work (000's)*	*Average Hours Per Week*	*Hours Per Year (49 Weeks)*	*Total Hours (Bn.)*	*GNP (£ Bn. 1995)*	*GNP per Worker (£ Bn. 1995)*	*GNP Per Hour (£ Bn. 1995)*
1989	1,124	43.0	2,107	2,368	28,805	25,627	12.16
2001	1,738	37.8	1,852	3,219	58,282	33,533	18.11
Change	+54.6%	−12.1%	−12.1%	+35.9%	+102.3%	+30.8%	+48.9%
Change Per Year	+3.6%	−1.1%	−1.1%	+2.5%	+6.0%	+2.4%	+3.5%

Note: In the absence of data on the length of annual holidays this table assumes no change in this factor over the period. Of course, to the extent that the average length of annual holidays rose during this period, reducing further the annual number of hours worked, output per hour will have risen slightly more than shown here.

First of all, because the Irish birth rate peaked as late as 1980, the proportion of the population under the age of 20 who were pre-school or still in education in 1989 was 34%, nine-tenths of them outside the labour force. In the rest of the EC only 21% fell into this age group. Second, in 1989 only 37.5% of Irish women of working age were in the labour force compared with 53% in the rest of the EC. And, finally, in 1989 unemployment in Ireland was almost twice the level of the rest of the EC.

Taken together these three factors explain why in 1989 only 31% of the Irish population was at work, as compared with 41% in the rest of the EC. Turning this around the other way this meant that in 1989 each Irish worker was supporting, either domestically or externally through taxation, over 2.23 dependants, as against 1.44 in the rest of the Community.

Whereas between 1989 and 2001 there was only a fractional fall in the EU ratio of dependants to people at work, the huge increase in employment in Ireland transformed the dependency situation in this country, reducing the Irish dependency ratio from over 2.2 to 1.2. Thus, although the average worker's output has risen by only one-third, the fact that the fruits of his or her output now have to be shared with one-third fewer dependants (2.2 as against 3.2), including the worker concerned, reinforced the effects of the increase in labour productivity enough to more than double Irish output per head.

(Incidentally, this dependency factor is rarely adverted to in comparisons made between the economies of different countries, yet it is a hugely important element. Thus, although output per hour in Finland and Sweden is slightly below the EU average, GNP per head is higher in these two countries than in the rest of the EU because they have high participation rates and correspondingly low dependency ratios. The other side of this equation is illustrated by the fact that in Italy the ratio of dependants to workers is over four-fifths higher than in Denmark – which explains why with a lower level of output per worker than Italy, Denmark nevertheless has a much higher output per head than its southern EU partner – the highest in the Community, indeed, apart from Luxembourg.)

The consequence of all this is that, with a labour productivity rate in 2001 within 6% of the EU average – a shortfall partially offset by 3% more hours being worked each week – Ireland's lower dependency ratio in relation to the average of the rest of the EU enabled it to achieve a level of GNP per head that was about 2% *above* the average EU level. GNP per head in 2001 was about 5% above the EU average and, in these terms, Ireland must now be in the middle of the EU league table – on a par with Germany, Italy and Britain, and well above France.

Table 3: Output per worker & per hour Ireland and EU 2001

	GNP (E Bn.)	*At Work (Mn.)*	*Hrs. Per Year*	*Total Hours (Bn.)*	*GNP Per Hour E*	*GNP Per Worker E*	*Dep. Ratio*	*Pop. (000's)*	*GNP Per Head E*
Ireland	94*	1.738	1,887	3.28	28,658	54,085	1.18	3.839	24,485
EU	8,820	160.0	1,840	294.4	29,996	55,125	1.37	379.5	23.241

*£97 Bn. adjusted for Purchasing Power Parity

The achievement of the EU level of GNP per head does *not* mean however, that average Irish living standards in the broadest sense have now attained the average EU level. Because Ireland's infrastructure – roads, public transport, hospitals, schools etc. – still largely reflect inadequacies inherited from the pre-1990 period, when Ireland was 40% poorer than all its neighbours, a huge programme of public investment is required in order to expand and modernize these inadequate facilities – and will continue to be required for perhaps 10–15 years ahead.

Similarly, in order to expand its productive capacity and to cater for the market needs of what is now a much more prosperous, and somewhat larger, population, the volume of private investment currently needed is also very substantial. Since 1995 the proportion of Irish GNP invested has risen rapidly from 19% to 28% of GNP, largely at the expense of the resources available for current consumption.

Forty years ago Ireland was investing a much lower proportion of its GNP than its neighbours, no more than about 14%, as against about 23% in EC countries at that time. By the late 1960s our investment ratio had risen to the EC level, which in the meantime had fallen slightly. And, save for a brief period at the end of the 1970s when Irish investment was raised to a higher level at the cost of an unsustainable external payments deficit, thereafter until the mid 1990s it remained broadly in line with that of the rest of the EU.

However, since 1995 the investment ratio has risen from 19% to over 28% – the highest level in the Community. The only EU countries with an investment ratio coming anywhere near the Irish figure are Austria, at 24%, and Greece and Spain, at 26%. But, in marked contrast to the late 1970s, this exceptional Irish level of investment is now being achieved without external borrowing.

This high investment level is being facilitated by the low level of Irish public consumption, which in 2000 absorbed a much smaller proportion of GNP than in the rest of the EU, but very high investment has also had the effect of reducing the excessive proportion of national output available for private consumption.

Up to the 1980s Irish private consumption tended to absorb about 70% of our national output, as compared with about 60% in the case of the EC, but from the mid 1980s onwards the private consumption ratio gradually fell to the average EC level. The effect of this has been to reduce the growth of private consumption well below the rate of growth of GNP during this period, and the impact of this upon average consumption per head – the usual measure of living standards – has been intensified by the fact that the Irish population grew twice as rapidly as that of the EU during that decade, by 8% as against 4%.

Thus, whilst GNP more than doubled between 1989 and 2000, private consumption increased by barely three-quarters, and public consumption by less than two-fifths. By contrast the volume of investment rose by almost 120%. Allowing for the population increase, average living standards improved by almost two-thirds.

It is possible to measure the economic performance of Northern Ireland over a period of more than half a century and to compare this progress with that of both Great Britain and the Republic of Ireland. Official estimates of Northern Ireland's output do not go back as far as the early 1950s, but in December 1954 Professor Charles Carter of Queen's University made estimates of the Gross National Output of Northern Ireland for the year 1953. And, two years later, I used Professor Carter's data to make a comparison between the economies of North and South in that year.[1]

That comparison was not very flattering to the Republic. It showed that at that time both output per head of population and average living standards in the Republic were about 25% lower than in Northern Ireland. It also showed that, in turn, output per head in Northern Ireland was then about 30% lower than in Great Britain; thus half a century ago output per head in the Republic was no more than about 50–55% that of Great Britain, probably a less favourable ratio than at the time independence had been secured thirty years earlier.

Why was there such a marked difference between the two parts of the island in 1953? My analysis at the time suggested that the proportion of the population at work was much the same in both parts of the island, with Northern Ireland suffering from the fact that the proportion of women – then much lower-paid than men – at work there was about one-sixth higher than in the South. But this disadvantage was more than offset by the fact that incomes in services, including the public service, and incomes of self-employed persons, particularly farmers, were higher in Northern Ireland. Indeed farmers' incomes were then twice as high as in the Republic, reflecting a combination of higher farm productivity; a smaller proportion of relatives assisting on farms; higher prices for products such as pigs, milk and eggs; and UK farm subsidies.

In some sectors of industry workers' pay in 1953 was slightly higher in the Republic than in Northern Ireland, but because earnings were almost one-quarter higher in metals and engineering in Northern Ireland, and because at that time this relatively high-paid sector of industry loomed much larger in the North than in the Republic, average pay for the manufacturing sector as a whole was slightly higher in the North. Moreover the total number employed in manufacturing in Northern Ireland at that time was 15% higher than in the Republic.

Writing sixteen years later[2] I found that net output per head in manufacturing was still fractionally higher in Northern Ireland than in the Republic, but that the number employed in manufacturing in the South in that year was by that time over 10% higher than in Northern Ireland. This reflected the fact that employment in textiles, clothing, shipbuilding and engineering in Northern Ireland had halved during the preceding two decades. In addition, British takeovers of Northern Ireland manufacturing and distribution firms had started to undermine the traditional self-reliant dynamic of Northern Ireland business.

By the early 1970s the gap between living standards in Northern Ireland and the Republic seemed to have narrowed slightly, reflecting a 5% improvement in the ratio of the Republic's per capita output to that of the United Kingdom. But by that time something like half of the continuing difference between living standards in the two parts of the island was attributable to agricultural and social welfare transfers from the UK. Furthermore, Northern Ireland was exempt from contributing to defence and to the remuneration of the national debt, as well as benefiting from the particular method of calculation of the Northern Ireland tax revenue handed over to the UK Exchequer. Thus, even before violence began to create a need for UK security transfers, there were signs of increasing dependence of Northern Ireland upon direct and indirect transfers from Britain.

However, since 1969 there has been a huge change in the economic balance between the Republic and the UK in terms of both per capita output and living standards.

In the first dozen years of this period, between 1969 and 1981, the output of the Republic rose by over three-fifths, whereas output in Britain in that period grew by barely one-fifth. Some of this lost ground was made up by Britain between 1981 and 1987, when growth in the Republic was minimal because of the steps the government I led had to take to tackle the financial crisis that had been precipitated by our predecessors' huge spending increases and unwise tax cuts.

But since 1987 the Republic's GNP has risen in volume terms by a further four-fifths in contrast to an increase of just one-third in this period in the UK. The consequence of this has been that by 2002 the Republic's GNP per head, which in 1987 was still only 65% that of the UK, has since risen to about the same level as that of its larger neighbour.

Of course, all comparisons of this kind are necessarily approximate because of adjustments that have to be made to allow for currency and price level differences. Nonetheless these comparisons can give a reasonably good impression of where these three parts of our archipelago now stand in relation to each other in income terms.

Because output per head in Northern Ireland has risen slightly faster than in the rest of the UK, the 30% gap that existed between British and Northern Ireland output per head half a century ago has been slightly reduced, to just under 25%. Consequently the change in the relationship between output per head between the two parts of the island has been slightly less than that between the Republic and Britain.

Nevertheless, output per head in Northern Ireland has now fallen well behind that of the Republic. Whereas in 1953 output per head in Northern Ireland was almost 30% higher than in the Republic, today the reverse is true: per capita output in Northern Ireland now falls short of that of the Republic by about 22%. However, because the Republic invests a much higher proportion of its GNP than Northern Ireland, only 58.5% of its GNP is absorbed by private consumption, as compared with over 80% in Northern Ireland. As a result of this long-term strategy on the part of the Republic, and also because living standards in Northern Ireland are now sustained by very large transfers from the UK, private consumption per head in the Republic is still some 5–10% lower than in Northern Ireland.

Of course, in broader terms the closeness of current consumption levels in the Republic to those in Northern Ireland reflects only part of the picture, because many years will elapse before the Republic's massive investment programme will enable it to catch up with Northern Ireland in terms of the quality of its infrastructure.

Against the background of the appalling violence of the IRA and its loyalist rivals, the Northern Ireland economy must be judged to have performed relatively well in recent decades. It also should be said that during the past two decades the UK economy has itself broken away from the depressing pattern of slow economic growth that had unhappily distinguished it from the rest of Western Europe for the whole of the ninety years between 1890 and 1980. And in the recent global recession, the UK economy seems to have performed somewhat better than that of the rest of the EU and notably better than the economy of Germany.

Thus, the remarkable reversal of the historic relationship between a more prosperous – and, for much of the earlier period, also more dynamic – Northern Ireland and what was then a poorer and worse-performing Republic has clearly been attributable to the exceptional economic performance of the latter in recent times, rather than to any abnormal slowness in growth in Northern Ireland, or indeed in the UK itself.

3 The Irish Constitution

Constitutions are, in greater or lesser measure, historically conditioned. They derive from the historical experience of the particular state for which they are drafted, and specifically from the particular circumstances of the time when the draft is prepared.

The extent to which these factors, expecially the latter, influence the appropriateness of constitutional provisions for future generations depends in some measure upon the degree to which the Constitution is rigid, or flexible. By 'rigid' in this context I mean that the provisions are so framed as to be binding on the Executive and Legislature, and are liable to very precise, potentially legalistic, future interpretations. The Irish Constitution is, relative to many others, both historically conditioned to an unusual degree, and quite rigid.

These are not criticisms, and should not be read as such. However inconvenient it may seem to be from time to time, the rigidity of a Constitution is also a measure of its capacity to protect human rights, individual or collective, against threat or erosion, intended or unintended, by an Executive or Legislature. And, however irksome some of the consequences of a historically-conditioned Constitution may be for later generations, far removed in time and in context from the circumstances that gave rise to the particular shape of the Constitution in question, it may be a serious mistake to dismiss too lightly the value that such a Constitution had for the State at the period when it was enacted.

Several factors have contributed to a sense of discontinuity in relation to Irish constitutional development. These include:

- The fact that the first Constitution, the Dáil Constitution of 1919, was adopted by a revolutionary parliament, soon to be forced underground.
- The fact that the publication of the second Constitution, that of 1922, was followed within a week by (and some would say helped to precipitate), a civil war.

- The manner in which the 1937 Constitution was presented – and for reasons that seemed good at the time had to be presented – as something new and home-grown, allegedly quite distinct from its immediate predecessor.

I believe that the sense of discontinuity thus generated is in significant measure misleading.

In 1919, Dáil Éireann (soon to be proclaimed by the British Government and driven underground) promulgated a brief Constitution establishing its sovereignty on the model of the Westminster Parliament. Of course, given the situation in the country at the time, that revolutionary assembly had no effective means of providing for the protection of human rights against possible abuses either by itself, by the Executive that it proceeded to elect, or by its army, the Irish Volunteers. So, for obvious reasons, at that point the British concept of parliamentary sovereignty was retained.

After the signature on 6 December 1921 of the Articles of Agreement between the British Cabinet and plenipotentiaries of the Executive elected by Dáil Éireann, both that Executive and the Dáil divided on the acceptability of what came to be known familiarly, but inaccurately, as the 'Treaty'.

The head of that Executive, Eamon de Valera, rejected the Articles of Agreement signed by his colleagues and resigned, being replaced a month after the signing of the Agreement by Arthur Griffith as President of that Government. Michael Collins shortly afterwards became Chairman of the parallel Provisional Government, which under the terms of the Treaty was set up to carry through the transition to the Irish Free State.

Michael Collins quickly established a Constitution Committee to draft a Constitution for the new State that was to be formally established on 6 December 1922.

The committee appointed to draft this Constitution succeeded in less than three short months (oh, for the days when such things could be done so speedily!) in bringing forward no fewer than three versions, based on a study of the Constitutions of almost a score of other countries.

Whilst the particular draft adopted by the Provisional Government sought at least notionally to operate within the framework of the Agreement of 6 December 1921, in fact it substantially retained the republican ethos of the 1919 Dáil Constitution. Some of these republican features were rejected by the British Government, which nevertheless accepted a number of radical changes in the nominal role of the monarch in the new Irish State. These changes had no parallel in the constitutional practice of other dominions of the Commonwealth.

Interestingly the draft adopted by the Provisional Government was one that devoted its first two Articles to a series of declarations about the sovereignty of the nation over all its material possessions, its soil, its resources and all the wealth and wealth-producing processes within the nation. It declared the subordination of all right to private property to the public rights and welfare of the nation, and it also declared the reciprocal duties of citizens and the State to each other in the service of the commonwealth (with a small 'c'), and of the people.

These provisions, some of which had a notably social democratic, even socialist, ring about them, were subsequently modified, being substituted by the single phrase: 'The sovereignty of the nation extends to all the possessions and resources of the country.'

I am not clear on how this change came about. It may have been made by thc Provisional Government at the suggestion of Dr George O'Brien, barrister, historian, and later Professor of Political Economy in University College Dublin, who advised the Provisional Government on the draft, proposing some forty amendments. Alternatively this watering down of the original draft may have been effected by the British Government, which could have feared that this radical wording portended an attempt to overturn the land settlement of the early 1660s, which had left most of thc land of Ireland in the hands of English or Scottish settlers.

The revised property Article was also moved down to a later section of the Constitution, and in its place was inserted a new Article 1, to the effect that 'Ireland is a free and sovereign nation'. This wording was later quite closely followed by Article 5 of the 1937 Constitution which reads: 'Ireland is a sovereign, independent, democratic State'. This is a reflection of the fact that a very large part of our present Constitution is in fact the Constitution of 1922, with the language in many cases quite unchanged – some of it as drafted by the Constitutional Committee of 1922, and some of it exactly as redrafted by the Provisional Government.

The extent to which the contents and even wording of the 1922 Constitution were retained in 1937 was partially – and perhaps deliberately – obscured by the manner in which the order of Articles was re-arranged by the authors of our present Constitution.

It is, I believe, right to stress this element of constitutional continuity in the historical development of the Irish State. However in making this point I have no wish to diminish in any way the significance of the 1937 Constitution, nor the ingenuity with which it was drafted, nor the extent to which most of it, including some of the new material in it, has stood the test of time.

It is true that some of this new material introduced in 1937 reads strangely to our eyes two-thirds of a century later. But, however anachronistic or inappropriate we may find the wording of certain Articles of the 1937 Constitution, which incorporated a good deal of matter reflecting the social teaching of the Roman Catholic Church as it was understood at that time, we ought to have sufficient historical insight to understand just why de Valera felt it necessary to include some of those provisions.

First of all, he believed that it was of great importance to 'repatriate' the Constitution with a view to bringing back fully into the constitutional fold many of those who had been alienated by some of the language imposed on the draft Constitution of 25 May 1922 by the British Government of that time.

A major concern of de Valera's in 1937 was to bring as many as possible of those who had taken the republican side in 1922 to accept the new state, the government of which he now headed. He thus sought to eliminate phrases or forms that could be alienating for those who had opposed the Anglo-Irish Agreement of 1921.

Next, he believed that he could not accomplish this task if he had to fight simultaneously both the Catholic Church and the Opposition in the Dáil. And, in the light of experience in the closing decades of the twentieth century, who are we to say that he was wrong in that calculation.

By de Valera's own subsequent admission, Northern Ireland came only third in his list of priorities – after the revival of the Irish language and the establishment of the full sovereignty of the Irish State – in this as in other matters he showed marked insensitivity to the Unionists of Northern Ireland. In our generation we have sought to put this right by radically changing in 1998 the phraseology of Articles 2 and 3 so as to take account of the extent to which their wording alienated almost one million Irish people in Northern Ireland.

In a broadcast interview as Taoiseach in 1981, I proposed a review of the provisions of the 1937 Constitution to remove these insensitivities. At the time I chose to take this step in a broadcast interview because I felt that the best chance to secure support for this concept was to put it to the people directly, viva voce so to speak, rather than in a speech or statement to be reported, perhaps incompletely, in cold print in the newspapers.

Historians will, no doubt, make their own judgement on the wisdom of that approach, but I think there is some evidence that it had a catalytic effect upon an important segment of our population and that this effect continued thereafter to operate within our body politic. Something was started then which did not go away and which came to fruition seventeen years later in the form of the referendum connected with the Belfast Agreement.

I recognize, of course, that in approaching the matter in this way, rather than by raising it in the first instance with the political Opposition of the day, I was likely to evoke a negative reaction that could in the short run prove to be divisive. However, the reality was that even if I had sought to propitiate the Opposition by adopting that approach, Fianna Fáil, under its then leadership, would certainly have reacted negatively.

But to return to the 1922 Constitution: that document introduced for the first time inside the British Commonwealth constitutional protection for human rights, thus making a principled rejection of the British concept of the sovereignty of Parliament. Amongst these human rights measures were provisions guaranteeing trial in due course of law, including trial by jury in serious cases, as well as others setting out a series of citizens' fundamental rights:

- No citizen to be deprived of liberty save in accordance with law
- Habeas corpus
- Inviolability of the dwelling, to be entered forcibly only in accordance with law
- Freedom of conscience and religious belief and practice
- Freedom of expression
- Freedom of assembly peaceably and without arms
- The right to form associations and unions for purposes not opposed to public morality – any legal regulation of these rights to contain no political, class or religious distinction
- A right to free primary education

Nevertheless, despite this extensive enumeration of fundamental rights of citizens with regard to Parliament and the Executive, no challenge was in fact made by the courts to parliamentary sovereignty during the fifteen-year lifetime of that Constitution. There were, it seems, three reasons for this.

First, because at the time of the enactment of the Constitution a civil war was under way, the Article of that Constitution providing for the right to personal liberty and habeas corpus was qualified by a clause that it could not be invoked to prohibit, control, or interfere with any act of the military forces during the existence of a state of war or armed rebellion. And as, even after the ending of the Civil War in 1923, the IRA remained a significant threat to public order, this limited the applicability of the principle enunciated in this Article.

Second, the Constitution entitled Parliament during a period of eight years after its enactment, to amend it without recourse to a referendum, a power which in the disturbed conditions of that time was itself later used to extend this period for a further eight years. In those circumstances, the entrenchment of these rights being potentially impermanent, there was little disposition on the part of the judiciary to try to enforce them.

And finally, the members of the judiciary of that period, having been formed as barristers in the positivist British legal tradition, were notably disinclined to engage in judicial activism vis-à-vis with the new Irish Parliament.

Indeed in 1935 (The State [Ryan] v. Lennon), a majority of the court went so far as to hold that because the provision that no person shall be deprived of his liberty was subject to the qualification 'save in accordance with law' then 'if a law is passed that a citizen may be imprisoned indefinitely upon a *lettre de cachet* signed by a Minister, as the deprivation will have been "in accordance with law" he will be as devoid of redress as he would have been under the regime of French or Neapolitan Bourbon'.

In other words, most paradoxically, the attempt to entrench habeas corpus in the Irish written Constitution had rebounded to the point of effectively destroying this crucial protection of the British unwritten one!

In 1937, however, Eamon de Valera, put his new Constitution through the Dáil and then secured acceptance of it by the people in a referendum. And, in contrast to the 1922 Constitution, the transitional period during which this new Constitution could be amended by

Parliament was limited to three years, and that limit was not extended.

Thus, by 1940 the Constitution was firmly entrenched, and a new generation of barristers was in the process of being formed who were not dominated by British legal positivism. Moreover there was a growing interest in, and awareness of, the Constitution's potential capacity to protect human rights from erosion, however unintentional, by either Parliament or Executive.

It is far from clear that Eamon de Valera himself intended, or foresaw, the kind of extensive, indeed radical, judicial review that ultimately emerged. The late Professor John Kelly remarked that de Valera 'did not see himself as calling into existence a sort of legal "shredding-machine" which a later generation of lawyers and judges would use with devastating effect on the acts of the sovereign Irish people's own Parliament'. In Professor Kelly's view, he intended it rather to be 'primarily a set of headlines for the legislature rather than a hurdle on which that legislature would frequently stumble and fall'.[1]

De Valera may, indeed, have allowed himself to be misled on this crucial issue by the notable absence of judicial activism during the lifetime of the 1922 Constitution, and by the failure of several challenges to the laws of the Irish Free State that had fruitlessly called in aid human rights provisions of that Constitution.

Nevertheless, whilst de Valera may not have realized that judges would eventually become very willing to accept such challenges by aggrieved parties basing claims upon the human rights clauses of his Constitution, he himself made specific provision to the effect that the holder of the newly-created office of non-executive President might refer a bill, or part of a bill, to the Supreme Court for constitutional adjudication if the President were to have doubts about its constitutionality.

Before doing so the Council of State – a body comprising the Taoiseach; Tánaiste; Speakers of the two Houses; Attorney General; Chief Justice; President of the High Court; former Taoisigh and seven members appointed by the President at his or her discretion – has to be consulted. But the decision on reference is at the sole discretion of the President. The Supreme Court, after then hearing the case for and against the constitutionality of the bill, put to them by counsel appointed for this purpose, gives a single decision, and, if it finds the bill or a part of it unconstitutional, it is struck down and has no legal force. On the other hand, if its constitutionality is upheld, the

Constitution also provides that none of its provisions may ever again be impugned. This latter provision has been questioned as introducing an excessive, and potentially dangerous, rigidity into the process of constitutional interpretation. An All-Party Committee of the Oireachtas recommended, some years ago, the deletion of the provisions in respect of both the single decision and the irreformability of Supreme Court decisions on bills that have been referred to it by the President.

There has been a certain reluctance by Presidents to refer to the Supreme Court bills with multiple provisions, because of the danger that some provision impinging on a human right might inadvertently be overlooked in the court hearing, and then become irreformable by either the courts or Parliament without a constitutional referendum. Because of this, and also because a President is naturally reluctant to appear to be challenging Parliament too frequently, the reference procedure has been used relatively infrequently, no more than a dozen times in sixty years.

To what extent was the eventual development of judicial protection of human rights under the 1937 Constitution a function of changes in the constitutional formulation of these rights in the 1937 Constitution?

On the whole this does not seem to have been a significant factor. First of all, in the 1937 Constitution no change was made in the wording of the provisions in respect of liberty of the person and inviolability of the dwelling. And in respect of freedom of expression and freedom of assembly the 1937 Constitution actually spelt out in some detail qualifications to these rights, thus in principle limiting the scope for intervention by the courts. However, in relation to freedom of association, the qualification in respect of public morality in the 1922 Constitution was dropped.

The articles on freedom of religion and the right to education, however, were substantially changed, apparently in response to concerns on the part of the Roman Catholic Church. And, for similar reasons, new Articles were introduced in relation to the family, marriage (including a ban on divorce, removed in 1995 by a referendum), and private property.

Overall, these changes do not of themselves explain the growth of judicial activism, although in various ways they have, of course, been the subject of frequent consideration and decisions by the courts. It seems rather to have been the appointment in the early 1960s to the High and Supreme Courts of barristers whose careers largely post-dated the enactment of the 1937 Constitution that led to the radical shift in constitutional interpretation which developed in the early 1960s.

The most striking – one could indeed say revolutionary – example of new judicial activism in that decade came in 1965. In a case (Ryan v. Attorney General) in which the fluoridation of water was challenged constitutionally – a challenge that was, in fact, rejected – the Supreme Court asserted its power to identify unenumerated personal rights that it held to be implicit in the Constitution.

This decision was based on the combined effect of two sub-clauses of Article 40.3 of the Constitution:

40.3.1. The State guarantees in its laws to respect, and, in so far as practicable, by laws to defend and vindicate the personal rights of the citizens.

40.3.2. The State shall, in particular, by its laws protect as best it may from unjust attack, and, in the case of injustice done, vindicate the life, person, good name, and property rights of every citizen.

It was the inclusion of the words 'in particular' in 40.3.2 that encouraged the Supreme Court to assert its capacity to determine personal rights not specifically identified in the Constitution, but which it regarded as being implicit in it. The list of unenumerated personal rights identified by the Courts is now quite a long one. Casey lists them as follows:[2]

- The right to strike
- The right of dissociation
- The right to privacy
- The right to earn one's living
- The right to communicate
- The right of access to the courts
- The right to legal representation on criminal charges
- The right to protection of one's health
- The right to travel
- The right to marry and found a family
- The right to fair procedure in decision-making

John Kelly notes that the right to travel includes the right to a passport, and he also adds certain rights of mothers of non-marital children and of non-marital children themselves.[3]

From what sources have the courts derived these implied rights? In the Ryan decision, which first established the role of the courts in identifying and declaring unenumerated rights, the 'Christian and democratic nature of the State' was invoked as one guide, a principle also later called in aid in respect of the right to travel abroad, and therefore to obtain a passport. In a case where the right of a married woman to access contraceptives for health reasons was declared at a time when artificial contraceptives were still illegal in Ireland, the notion of 'justice' was drawn upon. 'Tradition' and 'consensus' have also been mentioned. Other judges have referred to the 'natural law' which has had 'a powerful influence in the evolution of human rights'.

It has also been suggested that international Conventions on Human Rights to which Ireland is a party are 'a perhaps more enlightening source of inspiration', although as against that it has been said that these can be used 'only to confirm an unenumerated right, such as one recognized at common law'.

In his 1997 address to a London Conference on Human Rights Lord Chancellor Irvine warned against the dangers of 'plunging judges into conflict with the legislature' because of possible 'mutual conflict and recrimination'. I am, of course, aware that the scale, frequency, and mandatory nature of the Irish courts' interventions in relation to human rights, and in particular their declarations with respect to many unenumerated rights, may be considered by some to raise a question as to whether they are not, perhaps, acting as a third House of Parliament. Nevertheless at that Conference I strongly challenged this assertion by the Lord Chancellor, pointing out that in a well-ordered democracy the only sources from which threats to human rights can come are the Executive and Legislature. Protection against such threats can be effective only if the courts have power to review legislation and to strike it down if it infringes such rights.

Such decisions of the courts are, of course, open to review by Parliament and the electorate, through a referendum process, which has in fact been used several times in Ireland to qualify or effectively to reverse decisions of the courts, e.g. in relation to an adoption issue and to limitations on bail.

On one occasion a minister was sufficiently incensed about a presidential reference of legislation to the Supreme Court to attack the President in unparliamentary terms, and the reluctance of the Taoiseach of the day to permit the minister to resign on this account provoked a presidential resignation and election. But that was a quite exceptional event.

In some instances governments have indeed welcomed such a reference as being likely to provide certainty about the constitutionality of key legislation. This was true, for example, of legislation with respect to rent restriction in 1983, and again several years later in relation to legislation to extend voting rights in Dáil elections on a reciprocal basis to countries that gave this right to Irish citizens. In the latter case reference to the Supreme Court was clearly very desirable so that the validity of a subsequent general election in which British citizens would vote could not be open to a constitutional challenge.

Of course the availability of a process of constitutional challenge to Acts of the Oireachtas adds to the complexity of government in Ireland, but in my view that is a small price to pay for the protection of human rights against legislative abuse.

In thus supporting the role of the courts in applying the Constitution in defence of human rights in Ireland I recognize, of course, that this process can be taken too far, and I have at times found myself in deep disagreement with some of the courts' decisions.

For example, I agree with David Gwynn Morgan in his criticism of the majority decision in Crotty v. An Taoiseach that the provisions of the Single European Act with respect to the coordination of foreign policy was unconstitutional because it imposed a significant obligation on Ireland limiting the Government's capacity to conduct foreign affairs.[4] This Treaty actually provided that the Government retained a right of veto over decisions by the member states of the EU in the process of political coordination, which fully protected the Government's role. But I think that David Gwynn Morgan pushes his argument too far in seeming to suggest that the judiciary should simply steer clear of foreign affairs.

I now regret that in Opposition in 1972 I, with others, successfully pressed for a strengthening of the wording of the proposed constitutional amendment on EC accessions so as to exempt from subsequent constitutional challenge only such decisions as might be 'necessitated' by the treaties. This was not proposed in order to open future treaties to challenge; perhaps foolishly, we simply did not contemplate such a possibility at the time. It was instead intended to deal with a rather hypothetical possibility, namely that a future government might seek to introduce, through a kind of EU 'back door', legislation that might have been unacceptable if presented to the Oireachtas. But given that this is the wording of this constitutional provision, I cannot see how the courts could refuse to consider whether a measure is or is not so necessitated by the treaties, if and when this issue is put to them.

I also accept many of the specific points made by David Gwynn Morgan in his subsequent book on the subject of judicial activism[5] and I recognize the dangers inherent in the courts purporting to require the Executive and Legislature to spend money on specific social projects, such as the provision of accommodation for juvenile offenders.

Judicial activism can, of course, go too far, but I believe it would be a pity if the courts were to resile from the active role they have until recently taken in declaring and protecting many human rights. Our society is the better for the vigilance with which the courts have for many decades past ensured that Government and Oireachtas do not, however unintentionally, prejudice the rights of citizens.

I should, perhaps, add that the constitutional vigilance of our courts has had a significant impact upon the role of the Attorney General in the Irish system of government. Because the Attorney General has to vet all legislation for possible unintended breaches of the Constitution, he has to be present when the Cabinet is considering draft legislation in respect of which it might make amendments. This has been common practice in the Irish Cabinet system which makes little use of Cabinet Committees for legislative purposes. The Attorney General at Cabinet will, where appropriate, express a view on the constitutionality or otherwise of such amendments, and indeed also of other possible government decisions, and few governments will take the risk of ignoring such advice. Thus, the Attorney General is much more intimately involved with every aspect of the work of government than I believe to be the case in the United Kingdom, for example. Moreover, as his task is to ensure that the government is not embarrassed by unintended breaches of the Constitution, in effect much of the Attorney General's work is de facto directed towards protecting citizens' rights vis-à-vis the Executive.

It should perhaps be added that because of their role as a check on the Executive and Legislature in relation to human rights, the ethos of the Irish courts has on the whole been libertarian, to the point almost of being anti-establishment, although some would hold that they have tended to be unduly reluctant to consider allegations against the police.

The role of the courts in protecting human rights is an important element in the Irish system of government, ultimately affecting the quality of the whole system in a significant way. To put it simply I can say that as a citizen I have always – even when I was Taoiseach – derived comfort from the knowledge that my rights are being protected against the Executive which, in Ireland as in many other parliamentary democracies, effectively controls the Legislature through the party whip system.

However, there remain some features of the 1937 Constitution which I believe require radical amendment.

One of these is Article 41.2, with its extraordinary paternalistic – one might even say patriarchal! – references to women. Section 1 of that Article deals with the family in terms which have also been used – perversely it would seem to me – to argue against the rights of children.

This is an evident anachronism in our Constitution, despite skilful defence of this provision by Mr Justice Brian Walsh in 1987. Whilst he was, of course, technically correct in his statement that the *legal* issue in this case was solely related to the powers of the Adoption Board, the issue as seen by the public was that of the relative rights of parents and children. And I frankly do not understand why in that address Mr Justice Walsh sought to insist that this case had 'nothing' to do with the family provisions of the Constitution, for the Supreme Court in two cases decided that on the grounds of this family Article (Art. 41) the natural parents in one case and married parents in another had a right to take custody of a three-year-old and two-year-old child respectively.[6]

In this connection it is, perhaps, worth recalling that there was a sense of almost universal public outrage some years ago when the courts held that this Article required the return to the natural parent of a child who had been integrated into an adopting family for a number of years previously. In a subsequent referendum 99% of the electorate – admittedly in a very low poll – voted to rectify that injustice. In relation to respect for children's rights, that referendum vote bore witness to a huge shift in public opinion during the half century after the enactment of this Constitution.

I believe that much greater effect needs to be given to this significant shift in public opinion through further appropriate changes in emphasis throughout this part of the Constitution.

Another matter that should, I believe, be reviewed is Article 45, which incorporates what are described as the 'Directive Principles of Social Policy'. This Article was deliberately made non-justiciable – that is, not capable of being enforced through the courts. Although it has been consulted by the courts in searching for an indication of general State policy, and as an aid in interpreting other Articles, it has no binding effect.

It should, I believe, either be scrapped, or, in so far as it contains provisions that might have a genuine impact of a positive kind in the social area, should be made justiciable to whatever extent might be thought appropriate. The present halfway house of an Article that is not binding but can be used for interpretative purposes carries dangers of increasing the uncertainty as to how the courts will interpret legislation.

In Article 43 on private property, the contrast between its terms and Article 1 of the draft Constitution of 1922, dealing with property, is quite extraordinary. I am personally inclined to the radical view that we might do worse than re-enact that section of the draft republican Constitution of 25 May 1922 – but given the huge drift to conservatism in our state since then, above all in relation to property matters, this is, I am afraid, too ambitious a suggestion!

More seriously, *obiter dicta* in cases in the 1980s and 1990s suggest that earlier Supreme Court decisions overly protective of property rights, which have had the practical effect of effecting huge transfers of financial resources to private landowners of development land, could usefully be reviewed by re-opening this issue.

In that connection I have to say that I always had severe doubts about Mr Justice Walsh's suggestion that the Constitution does not create a problem with respect to property rights because 'a claim to compensation would be only a claim to just compensation' and that consequently 'all the complaints concerning the question of compensation for land taken or for the limitation of the use of land are properly to be directed at Acts of the Oireachtas . . . and not at the Constitution'. This statement makes the assumption – with which many would disagree – that a claim for compensation for limitation of use in the public interest is, in fact, a just claim.

Over time, courts change their views on social issues. Moreover, judges are of course fallible, and some past decisions were known at the time they were enunciated to have been influenced by a strong view held by particular judges, which their successors might be happy to have an opportunity to reverse.

Another matter that might be worth revisiting in the courts is that of the role of the Executive and Legislature in relation to foreign policy, as mentioned on p. 49. To many people at the time (1987) it seemed that Irish sovereignty could not conceivably have been prejudiced by a provision in respect of which our Government retained a veto, and it is quite widely believed in legal circles that such a decision would not be upheld by the courts today. Yet, ever since that judgment, Attorneys General have felt it necessary to refer all new EU treaties to the electorate, even those which by any reasonable standard could not be held to prejudice Irish sovereignty.

This seems to me to reflect a too-cautious approach to such matters by Attorneys General, who seem to be concerned at any cost to avoid any risk of legislation, including treaty ratifications, being overturned through challenges in the courts. I believe that there is a strong case for Attorneys General and governments taking a more robust view by offering the courts an opportunity to re-visit the rationale of the 1987 decision. Had this been done in the case of any or all of the Luxembourg, the Maastricht, or Amsterdam or Nice Treaties, the Government might well have found that they were being over-punctilious in having referred all these ratifications by way of referendum to the voters who, understandably, have difficulty in addressing the complexities of such documents.

I believe that attention also needs to be given to the method of selection of the Taoiseach under the Constitution. Our constitutional practice here is out of line with that of most other democracies, in almost all of which the head of state plays a role in relation to the selection of the person whose name is to be submitted to parliament. That this practice was omitted from our Constitution was, I believe, very evidently a consequence of the ambiguous constitutional situation created by the 1937 Constitution. At that time, and for twelve years thereafter, the Irish Head of State recognized by the international community, was the King, as head of the Commonwealth. Understandably, de Valera did not wish the King, or a representative of the King, to have even a nominal role in the process of the selection of the Taoiseach or Prime Minister. And, had he conferred such a function on the newly-created President (who, of course, until the declaration of a republic in 1949 had no external recognition), there might have been a danger that the validity of the Taoiseach's appointment would have been internationally questioned. Accordingly de Valera adopted the unusual expedient of eliminating the head of state completely from the process of appointment of the Prime Minister, leaving the election of the Taoiseach entirely to Dáil Éireann.

Although this matter was adverted to in the 1967 Report on the Constitution, and although I have personally been aware throughout my political career of the problems that could be created by what appears to me a lacuna in the political system, it was only at the time of the election of Charles Haughey as Taoiseach in 1987 that the possible difficulties presented by this constitutional provision emerged in practical form.

On 10 March of that year I was faced with a situation in which there could well have been a deadlock in Dáil Éireann on the election of a Taoiseach as a consequence of no candidate securing the necessary majority in the House. Indeed on that occasion I had two different speeches ready to make, one of them to be delivered in the event of a deadlock arising, instead of an actual election of a Head of Government. In that alternative speech I would have said that following my own defeat, when my name had been before the House some minutes earlier, I was resigning from office under the provisions of Article 28.10 of the Constitution, but that under Article 28.11.1. of the Constitution I would be continuing to carry on the duties of a caretaker Taoiseach until a successor was appointed. I would then have gone to Aras an Uachtaráin to present my resignation to the President, who, I believe, would have asked me to reconvene the Dáil in an effort to break this deadlock.

Now, the Constitution is notably unclear as to whether these caretaker duties of the Taoiseach extend to the power set out in Article 13.2.1 to advise the President to dissolve the Dáil again. On that occasion constitutional uncertainty on this issue might have been at least avoided through the exercise by the President of his power under Article 13.2.2. in his absolute discretion to refuse to dissolve Dáil Éireann on the advice of a Taoiseach who had ceased to retain the support of a majority in Dáil Éireann; but that would not necessarily have been the end of the matter. For the deadlock might have persisted, and the constitutional dilemma would then have re-presented itself.

Several years later when such a deadlock did in fact arise, the confusion that surrounds this issue was deepened when the outgoing Taoiseach, Charles Haughey, having failed to be re-elected by the Dáil nevertheless refused at first to resign.

Without pursuing the intricacies of this dilemma any further, I would simply suggest that, now that the monarch has been exorcised from our Constitution for over half a century, we might revert to the more normal international practice under which the name (or possible successive names), coming before Dáil Éireann for nomination would, as in most other democracies be proposed by the Head of State. That would diminish, even if it would not entirely remove, the danger of a continuing deadlock whilst at the same time effecting a clarification of the ambiguity with regard to the issue of dissolution. The President would also by this process be given an enhanced role, which I think would be helpful in increasing respect for the office. On this issue, I disagree with the Constitution Review Group which rejected any increase in the powers of the President in the government formation process and, indeed, proposed the removal of the President's discretionary powers in relation to the dissolution of the Dáil, on the grounds of avoiding his or her involvement in party political issues.

The role of Seanad Éireann in our political system has been questioned from time to time. I have to say that I do not share what is clearly a quite widespread belief that Seanad Éireann is redundant. But then, as one who entered parliament through that chamber, I can hardly claim to be totally objective on this point!

However, as is well known to most members of the Oireachtas (although not to a wider public because of serious inadequacies in the way in which our media address parliamentary matters), there are many bills which are far more fully and effectively debated in the Seanad than in the Dáil, despite the similarity of the composition of the bulk of the membership of the Seanad to that of the Dáil under our present Seanad electoral system.

Indeed governments sometimes select certain bills to be debated first in the Seanad, not just because this may be politically convenient owing to congestion of Dáil business at that particular moment – although that is also a way in which the Seanad helps to make our political system work more efficiently – but because, owing to their particular character, these bills are likely to secure a better debate in the Seanad. I took this course with the National Archives Bill in 1986, and it received a very full and useful hearing in the Seanad, which amended it in significant ways, whereas the Dáil later showed little interest in it.

The reasons for the better legislative performance by the Seanad in relation to some bills are complex. But, one reason is that, despite its largely political composition, the atmosphere in the Seanad is less partisan than the Dáil, and perhaps senators, just because they have less work to do than members of the Dáil, are sometimes inclined to do that work more thoroughly. And, if a Seanad composed as is the Seanad today can be useful in this way – as I believe it is – then one elected in a less political way might be even more useful.

In that connection I recommend a re-reading of the Seanad Electoral Law Commission Report 1959 – with all due modesty, as I was a member of that Commission myself. Largely owing to the strenuous efforts of the late Ralph Sutton SC, whom I abetted, this Commission produced a Report, agreed to by almost all the ten political members of the Committee, which proposed the direct election of twenty-three of its members by the vocational bodies which at present nominate about half the candidates for subsequent election by an exclusively political electorate. This proposal was, however, rejected when it came up for debate in the Seanad, where it was denounced with fervour by, amongst others, two of its principal signatories: the Government and Opposition Leaders of the House. A document that succeeded in getting senior politicians into the position of effectively repudiating their own signatures is surely worthy of further examination!

As a final comment on the Constitution, it is, I believe, interesting to refer back to an article by Mr Justice Declan Costello, then a young barrister, in *Studies* in 1956, on 'The Natural Law and the Irish Constitution'.[7] In it he drew attention to what he saw as a significant difference between the manner in which personal rights in Article 40, including the right to liberty, the right to free expression of opinion, the right to freedom of assembly, the right to freedom of association – rights that were seen as arising from the 'Natural Law' – are limited in the Constitution by being made subject to the provision that they may not be interfered with 'save in accordance with Law'.

He pointed out that this contrasted markedly with other 'Natural Law' rights such as those in Article 41 dealing with the family, Article 42 dealing with education and Article 43 dealing with private property, which are not limited in this way, and in respect of which even forty years ago the courts were already starting to take a tougher view in relation to actions of the Executive and the Legislature.

Mr Justice Costello remarked at the end of that article that 'the desire for uniformity, the wish to be able to point to a Constitution in which human rights are not only safeguarded but correctly defined, must naturally prompt criticism of these distinctions'. At the same time he went on to say that such distinctions 'may have served one very useful purpose. Constitutional experience in Ireland for the past forty years has shown that where constitutional guarantees can be traced to philosophical truths they are not mere empty formulas, they are real safeguards of individual liberty'.

Looking back on this question forty years later, however, and recognizing the perceptiveness of Mr Justice Costello in observing how the courts were making a distinction between these different kinds of rights, some people may be less than happy with the way in which this distinction has since tended to operate. In this, as in other aspects of the Constitution, the inspiration that its authors derived from the particular form that Roman Catholic social teaching had taken in the 1930s can be seen to have been quite profound.

The traditional concern of Roman Catholic teaching with excessive emphasis on individualism has in many ways been a very constructive force in the world. But in the context of the Irish Constitution this concern can be argued to have led in practice to a new imbalance in the other direction, that is to a situation in which the right to property is given a higher value than the right to personal liberty, and in which the ultimate right of the family (defined in a very specific and exclusive way as the family based on marriage), is given a priority over the rights of children. That is a priority which, as the Referendum decision of 1972 showed, the vast majority of our people consider in one respect at least to be unacceptable.

I would not wish to push this point too far, for there are good reasons for introducing the phrase 'save in accordance with Law' in some of the provisions against the deprivation of personal liberty. Without the use of this qualifying phrase the State might in certain instances be deprived of the power to protect the public good, e.g. by way of Special Criminal Courts.

But, in a world in which today the general moral sense of many people attaches more importance to personal rights than to property rights when the two come into conflict with each other, these issues are at least worthy of debate. And that is a debate which many people would be reluctant to see determined on the basis of a dated concept of 'Natural Law' that would appear to give inadequate importance to individual human rights, to the defence of which today the Churches, including in particular the Roman Catholic Church in many parts of the world, are now very strongly committed.

Our constitutional system has come to incorporate a series of checks and balances that in practical terms is almost unique. So far as human rights are concerned, the Executive and Parliament are tightly controlled by the courts. But, if the courts' interpretation of a constitutional provision creates a situation that had not been foreseen, and if that is unacceptable to Parliament and the electorate, acting jointly they can modify that outcome by way of a constitutional amendment.

At the same time it should be noted that the operation of the representative democratic system constrains the electorate from taking constitutional decisions that might be governed by emotion – for the electorate can change the Constitution only on the basis of a proposal adopted by Parliament.

(The Constitution of 1922 had contained a right of popular initiative in relation to referendums, but this was soon removed by an amendment passed by Parliament, which feared that such an initiative might be successfully employed to effect constitutional changes that would be inconsistent with the Anglo-Irish Agreement of 1921, to which the 1922 Constitution was linked.)

Of course, the Constitution of the United States could be said to contain similar checks and balances, but, because theirs is a federal system, it is far more difficult for the US Executive, Legislature and electorate to review and amend decisions of the Supreme Court. Such an amendment requires not only the consent of Congress but also ratification by thirty-six out of fifty-one States.

I think that a particularly interesting feature of the Irish system is the relative frequency with which the courts have struck down laws or parts of laws, or have otherwise constrained the actions of the Executive. However, I do not believe that in most cases this reflects undue interventionism by the judiciary. Nor does it reflect illiberality or lack of sensitivity to human rights issues on the part of Irish

Governments. Indeed the contrary is probably true, at one level because of the nature of Irish history and at quite another level because of the role that the Attorney General plays in vetting draft legislation.

In my view what the Irish experience of relatively frequent successful constitutional challenges demonstrates is how easy it is, even in the most favourable circumstances, for Executive and Parliament, unintentionally and unwittingly to breach or cut across human rights. And this experience shows, I believe, how important it is, therefore, that their actions be effectively policed.

All this having been said, and without any illusions as to its defects, it must be added that our Constitution, enacted under such different circumstances well over half a century ago, has proved to be a remarkably firm bastion of human rights, proving a healthy restraint on the Executive and Legislature in matters of legislation. More generally, it is a document in which most of our people take a certain pride. I believe that significant amendment of some of its provisions is now overdue, but the great bulk of its provisions, many of them dating back to the first Constitution of 1922, should certainly, by general agreement, be retained as serving the public interest well.

4 The Irish party system and the problem of localism

The Irish political system that evolved out of the national revolution in the early decades of the last century has in many ways served the people of Ireland remarkably well.

From the outset our State was one in which all power derived from the people who, by virtue of the 1922 Constitution, ceased to be subjects and became citizens. Under the terms of the Treaty, Griffith and Collins could not avoid the inclusion of some monarchical flummery in the first Constitution. But as was pointed out in the previous chapter, they achieved crucial departures from the practice of other Commonwealth members, as a result of which our Heads of Government would be chosen by Parliament, not nominated by a monarch for approval by Parliament, whilst the Irish Parliament would dissolve itself and make the arrangements for its successor to come into being, thus excluding the nominal monarch from any role in our domestic affairs.

The issue of the role of the monarch was bound to disappear eventually from the political agenda, although it survived long enough to divide the successful revolutionaries between two parties in a way that inhibited the emergence of an ideological division of the Irish political system between socialism, economic liberalism, and conservatism. As the Treaty issue disappeared from the agenda, the two parties which had emerged from this division on constitutional issues were left free to evolve over time in ways that reflected a changing political agenda.

For several decades Cumann na nGaedheal/Fine Gael played a stabilizing and conservative role whilst Fianna Fáil offered a radical alternative, e.g. in terms of its housing and social policies in the 1930s. But through the introduction of industrial protection Fianna Fáil also widened its support base, extending it from small farmers and the property-less, who had little to lose by radicalism, to a newly-created industrial working class and to a new and wealthy group –

the protected industrialists. Fianna Fáil thus moved from being a radical party of the left to becoming a powerful centre party, which in time shifted somewhat towards the centre right, whilst continuing through its rhetorical nationalism to draw on nationalist sentiment in a way that came to make it an important bulwark against extreme republicanism.

From the mid 1960s onwards Fine Gael, for its part, shifted towards a more social democratic, and then in the late 1970s socially liberal, stance, and started to challenge the monocultural Gaelic/ Catholic myth which had for so long impeded any rapprochement or understanding between Northern unionism and nationalism.

From the late 1940s onwards, the polarization of politics around a powerful Fianna Fáil party had led to the emergence of a series of alternative administrations combining Fine Gael and Labour, and sometimes other parties also. And when in the 1980s Fianna Fáil's strength was eroded by a loss of support caused, in part at least, by public fears of a Haughey-led majority Fianna Fáil Government, this Coalition model eventually spread to Fianna Fáil itself.

The absence of a consistent pattern of ideological divisions of the kind common elsewhere in Europe was, of course, frustrating for some people. Nevertheless, throughout most of the period since independence this curiously pragmatic and shifting political structure served Ireland reasonably well. Thus, it protected Ireland against swings to extremes of right and left: by 1934 Fascism had been marginalized in Ireland, and in a country in which a high proportion of the population were farmers or shopkeepers, Communism never had a chance to get a grip on any significant section of public opinion.

As had happened briefly in 1927, and again in the 1940s, the 1980s saw the emergence of some new small political parties. These were:

- Democratic Left (as Sinn Féin/The Workers' Party eventually became), which introduced the left-wing element of Sinn Féin to the parliamentary system, but which has since merged with Labour;
- the Progressive Democrats, who introduced a slightly exotic element of right-wing ideology into Irish politics;
- the Green Party, whose emergence reflected the failure of the main parties, preoccupied with economic development, to address environmental issues.

In a political system noted for its lack of ideological divisions, this recent proliferation of parties, combined with the diversion of support away from Haughey-led Fianna Fáil, has created a situation in which almost any party might and, given the opportunity would, go into government with one or other of the two larger parties – the only excluded combination being a Fianna Fáil–Fine Gael Government.

Leaving aside the Haughey factor and its continuing residual effects, this Fianna Fáil–Fine Gael combination is excluded not, as some people fondly imagine, because of Civil War memories – which so far as most politicians are concerned ceased to be a factor many decades ago – but rather because of the instinctive recognition by politicians in these two parties of the dangers of the mammoth majority that such a combination would enjoy, and would probably continue to enjoy for a disturbingly long period of time.

Our present economic success provides prima facie evidence that over the decades we were quite well served by the curious party structure with which we have been endowed by our singular history. For it cannot be denied that the causes of our high rate of economic growth in the 1990s lay in key political decisions taken by particular governments at various points over the past forty years which were then consistently sustained by their successors. Such decisions were:

- The commitment to low corporate taxation and to an outward re-orientation of our economy towards Europe, which took place under two governments between 1956 and 1959.
- The educational revolution initiated between 1966 and 1968.
- The putting into order of our public finances that was initiated in 1981, and was carried through to a successful outcome by two successive governments between 1982 and 1989.
- The social contract partnership system that was initiated in 1987.

During the quarter of a century between 1973 and 1997 there were no fewer than ten changes of government and ten changes of government leadership (which are not quite the same thing), but despite this political roller-coaster, our political system pursued key economic policies with striking consistency. Few countries have changed their government so often over this period, but I cannot think of any other country in Europe, that has such a remarkably consistent record in the economic policy area.

But the paradox is that, despite all the remarkable economic achievements of our political system, politics is now clearly held in lower esteem by our electorate than at any previous time in our history, including the decades from the 1920s to the late 1950s when we were dogged by economic failure, much of it because of bad political decisions on economic matters.

It seems to me that as we enter the new millennium, this same party system may in its present form be ill-adapted to our future needs.

First of all, so far as the electorate is concerned, if almost any political combination becomes possible, one of the principal factors motivating people to vote for a particular party – a wish to determine the shape of the next government – disappears. Some, at least, of the twelve percentage point decline in electoral turn-out between 1981 and 2002 may derive from this new negative element in our political system.

In turn these developments have spawned an increase in support for Independent candidates, most of whom are locally-focused and whose support for the formation and retention in power of a particular Coalition may depend upon agreement by that Coalition on a deliberate, and potentially damaging and unjust, misallocation of public resources in favour of the constituencies that they represent.

The fact that in 2002 we have six parties in the Dáil, as well as several socialists and a substantial number of Independents, many of them locally-focused rather than issue-focused, may in future make much more difficult the formation of governments with majorities capable of acting effectively in the overall interest of the people as a whole.

With the disappearance of Soviet and Eastern European State socialism, and with the emergence of the market economy as a generally accepted economic model, politics here, as elsewhere, has increasingly come to centre around the single issue of what steps need to be taken to modify the untrammelled operation of the market system in the public interest whilst maintaining the impetus of economic growth.

On the one hand there are the economic liberals who want to minimize interference with the market and reduce taxation on the grounds that economic growth ought to be the main object of political policy and that any interference with the operation of the market will inhibit such growth.

On the other hand social democrats accept the importance of economic growth, but contest the need to give it total priority over everything else, and they also assert that growth will be inhibited by inadequate public investment in infrastructure, including education. They see economic growth not as an end in itself but rather as a means towards a better society, and at the greener end of the social democratic spectrum they also give a high priority to the preservation of the environment, both in Ireland and globally.

In recent years in Ireland this division between economic liberals and social democrats has come to be partially, but incompletely, linked to a more or less parallel division between Eurosceptics and supporters of the European Union.

During the past forty years there have always been divided views in Ireland between those who support membership of the European Community and those who oppose it. In each of the referendums held in 1972, 1987, 1990, 1998 and 2001, the particular Community treaty being put to the electorate was opposed by elements at the left end of the political spectrum.

In 1972 the Labour Party opposed membership, as did Official Sinn Féin, but Labour immediately accepted the decision of the 81% who voted in favour of accession in a 70% poll. And, much later, the successor of Official Sinn Féin, Democratic Left (now merged with Labour), also became supportive of the European Community.

However, more extreme elements of the Left have maintained their opposition and, strikingly, have latterly been joined by some of the small Catholic Right. Moreover, within mainstream politics elements in the Progressive Democrats became increasingly critical of the social orientation of the EU, contrasting European attitudes on social issues with the free market ethos of the United States. This reflected a commitment to high growth for its own sake, a concept strongly supported by Charlie McCreevy, Fianna Fáil Minister for Finance, who in office increasingly behaved and spoke as if he were a member of the Progressive Democrats, rather than of the centrist Fianna Fáil party.

By the time the Nice Treaty was put to the electorate in a referendum for the first time in 2001, these right-wing critics had been joined by the nationalist wing of Fianna Fáil, represented by two ministerial grandchildren of Eamon de Valera, who himself had never been a supporter of the European Community.

At a time when enthusiasm for the European Community has ebbed amongst Irish public opinion, these negative sounds from the right within parliamentary politics reinforced the traditional anti-EU stance of the extra-parliamentary Left and Catholic Right. Apathy amongst supporters of the EU thus made it possible for the opponents to block the Nice Treaty with the votes of only 18% of the electorate.

The structure of the Irish party system does not adequately reflect tensions between social democrats and free marketeers on the one hand or between pro- and anti-Europeans on the other. A certain ambiguity about the stance of Fianna Fáil on these key issues has clouded this whole matter.

When in government with Labour between 1992 and 1994, Fianna Fáil followed a largely social democratic agenda, as formulated by Labour and agreed by Fianna Fáil before that Government was formed. But in government with the Progressive Democrats between 1989 and 1992, and again after 1997, Fianna Fáil pursued, especially in relation to taxation, policies primarily directed towards maximizing economic growth, as propounded by the Progressive Democrats but also strongly advocated by Charlie McCreevy.

Fine Gael, which lost 20% of its votes and by a fluke 42% of its seats in the 2002 general election, has shown less ambivalence on these issues, and has been broadly supportive of a social democratic position on the need for improved public services with correspondingly less emphasis on the need for tax cuts. Fine Gael has also been unequivocally pro-European.

It is now arguable that the party system which was successful in saving Ireland from the ideological battles that tore apart much of the rest of Europe during the greater part of the twentieth century may be less well adapted to the needs of the twenty-first.

Although the socio-economic debate highlighted above is of central importance to Irish politics, it is not the only major issue that has faced and will continue to face our politicians. Two other matters of crucial importance to the Irish people are Northern Ireland and our participation in the European Union, which are addressed in later chapters, 11 and 10 respectively.

At this stage, however, it is fair to point out that, after a period of initial confusion, our political system responded well to the challenge of the breakdown of order in Northern Ireland. The main credit for the progress made towards resolving this problem during the last three decades of the twentieth century must go to the work of successive Irish Governments in persuading successive British Governments on the way forward in Northern Ireland and, of course, to the extraordinary dedication and vision of John Hume's efforts to persuade the IRA to choose belatedly the path of peace.

There are a number of less central but nonetheless important issues in Irish politics that also deserve consideration here. In addition to the problem of localism, considered below, the electoral system, the management of government, the role and power of interest groups, jobbery, political funding and corruption, are dealt with in subsequent chapters.

Localism is a very powerful distorting factor in the Irish political system. Of course within communities strong local loyalties are important and have a very positive role to play. But a problem can arise when citizens have difficulty in combining their local loyalties with a wider commitment to the region within which these localities are to be found or when they take precedence over the good of the people of the whole state. This is what I describe as the phenomenon of localism.

There is much evidence that in Ireland localism can be an impediment to good government. I recall a survey carried out some four decades ago which asked people to react to the possibility of a new industry that would employ 100 workers in their town or village, or alternatively one that would employ 200 people 'some distance away', that distance being defined as six miles or more. Of those polled 96% opted for the lesser number being employed in their town or village; 2% supported the location of an industry employing twice as many people six or more miles away; and 2% expressed no opinion.

I also recall having been asked as a consultant in the mid 1960s if I would prepare a development plan for the town of Castlebar. I said that I was willing to do so, naming a fee, but I queried whether it might not be more effective to prepare a plan for a somewhat wider area of Co. Mayo, incorporating perhaps the three towns of Castlebar, Westport and Ballina. Discussions followed, involving these three towns, but because of local rivalries these proved totally fruitless, and the only consequence of my suggestion was that the project was cancelled – and I lost the fee!

I can give another, and even more local, example. Some years later as TD for Dublin South-East with a 'clinic' in a centre city block of flats, I was phoned and asked to come at once to the parallel Labour Party clinic held in the same room on a different day. The Labour

Party representatives were besieged by angry mothers and wanted me to come and help them deal with the crisis. I came at once, and found that the anger was the result of a Dublin Corporation decision to merge a playgroup in this block of flats with one in an area 250 yards away. This proposal had panicked the mothers who believed that their toddlers' lives would be at risk if they had to go such a distance to an unfamiliar location! I helped to calm this situation by promising that I and my Labour colleagues – whom I got the mothers to release from their siege – would try to get this decision reversed.

Around that time I also found that in nearby Ringsend a mother who had been living there for thirty years, but who had been brought up in South Lotts Road, a couple of hundred yards away, was still regarded by her neighbours as something of an outsider, being described as a 'runner-in'.

No doubt thirty years later horizons have widened somewhat but there can be no doubt that even now, primary loyalties in Ireland can be very localized indeed.

Evidence for this can be found in the concern shown by political parties to select candidates from different parts of a Dáil or local authority constituency. It has also been evident in some of the disputes over the location of hospital facilities, e.g. Cashel versus Clonmel, both in South Tipperary, and Portlaoise versus Tullamore, admittedly in neighbouring counties, Laois and Offaly.

The strong local demand that a member of the government be appointed to 'represent' not just counties but constituencies within a county further demonstrates the intensity of these sub-county loyalties. And recently we have the new phenomenon of Independent TDs being elected to demand preferential treatment for their constituencies in respect of the allocation of public funds, a process which inhibits the allocation of resources on an objectively determined basis of real need.

Moreover, there is ample evidence that ministers do in fact set out to distort resource allocation and decentralization of units of the civil service, thus retrospectively 'justifying' the popular demand that ministries be distributed on a geographical basis.

Localism of this kind not only distorts decisions in relation to resource allocation. In the case of the health service, pressure for the retention of underequipped local hospitals affects the survival prospects of patients needing specialized care that can be provided only in a smaller number of large well-equipped and well-staffed institutions.

And, at quite another level, localism also leads to the exclusion of able politicians from central government in favour of less qualified people. In all such cases there is a loss to the people of the whole state.

One must, of course, accept that, as distinct from transferring civil servants to places outside Dublin, there is a strong case for a greater devolution of administrative functions to local level: Irish local government is exceptionally weak. Why has more not been done in that direction?

One answer is that the devolution of power can work effectively only if it is accompanied by some measure of devolution of tax-raising functions to the same local level: otherwise local government can quickly become quite irresponsible. But in Ireland since the abolition of domestic rates a quarter of a century ago there has been powerful and persistent opposition to the transfer of any tax-raising functions from national to local level. Spurious allegations of 'double taxation' have persistently been deployed by left-wing elements at local level in order to rally opposition, especially from middle-class voters, to charges being raised for the supply of water or for rubbish disposal.

Currently local commercial rates raises only 7% of the amount needed by local councils to run the limited local services they provide, and even when all other local sources of revenue are included only one-quarter of the funds needed are raised locally. Three-quarters of local authority finance comes from central government, which naturally wants to have control of the services it thus funds.

But there is another generally ignored historical reason for the reluctance to devolve more power to local level. Democratically elected County Councils, and Rural District Councils at even more local level, were introduced to Ireland in 1898 by a Conservative British Government which hoped in this way to stave off demand for Home Rule for Ireland as a whole. Despite the unpropitious motivation of their establishment, these County Councils found a fair measure of public acceptance, perhaps partly because the counties had recently been given a new role in the public mind through the activities of the Gaelic Athletic Association (GAA).

Three-quarters of the Council seats were immediately won by nationalists, and during the following two decades the local councils were dominated by the Irish Parliamentary Party. Unfortunately clientelism, jobbery, inefficiency and in some cases actual corruption, became features of the system, as indeed had been the case with some of the urban authorities in Ireland and Britain that had been democratized somewhat earlier in the nineteenth century.

In addition, in the Ulster counties, jobs were awarded by local authorities on a religious basis. Catholics were totally excluded from employment by many Unionist-dominated local authorities whilst in nationalist areas all appointments in the power of the Council – thirty-seven of them in the case of Monaghan – went to Catholics.

The British Local Government Board, whose task it was to supervise the system, failed to control these abuses, possibly because as an appointed agency of the British Government it had doubts about the wisdom of precipitating a head-on collision with democratically elected bodies. However, the revolutionary leaders of Irish separatism in Sinn Féin were not so inhibited, and were vocally critical of the performance of Councils dominated by their rivals in the Irish Parliamentary Party.

The 1920 local elections gave Sinn Féin a controlling position on all but five County Councils, as well as the great majority of urban authorities. These County Councils immediately gave their allegiance to the Dáil Government but the ensuing collapse in local finances as many residents withheld rates led many Councils to contemplate, and in some cases to actually engage in, compromises with the British-appointed Local Government Board. This brought them into conflict with the very efficient underground Dáil Department of Local Government, headed by W. T. Cosgrave and his Assistant Minister, Kevin O'Higgins.

Even Sinn Féin members of a Council like Galway found it difficult to accept the view vigorously conveyed to them by Kevin O'Higgins that 'it would be better a thousand times for the Irish Nation that there should be a financial breakdown here and there amongst the public bodies than that there should be the moral collapse of a surrender to enemy regulations'.[1]

These pre-Truce tensions certainly influenced the attitude of our first government towards local Councils. As soon as the Civil War ended, that Government moved rapidly to abolish the 214 Rural District Councils which had also been established in 1898: these sub-county units had never caught on, partly because the Rural Council areas had been arbitrarily delineated and failed to command local loyalties.

Tensions also arose between the new government and the County Town and County Borough (i.e. City) Councils, centering often on abuses in connection with public appointments. At local as well as national level there was resentment amongst pro-Treaty political supporters because of the refusal of the new government to give job preference to former members of the Volunteers at the expense of the principle of appointment on merit, to which that government was firmly committed. As Mary Daly dryly remarks in her history of Irish local government, to which I owe a good deal of my knowledge of this subject, 'many government supporters under-estimated [the new government's] commitment to a non-partisan recruitment process'.[2]

It was also the case that many local tax officers who had been appointed by the Councils were found to be 'practically illiterate' and incapable of keeping accounts, and there was also an element of bribery of Council members by applicants for jobs. For one dispensary doctor post, bribes equivalent to a 2002 value of 50,000 euro were reportedly offered.

Accordingly, in 1926 a Local Appointments Commission was established so as to ensure that appointments to most local authority posts would be made on merit, although the perhaps inevitable exclusion of manual jobs and of some temporary positions from the Commission's ambit enabled jobbery to survive at that lower level where, however, bribery was unlikely to prove a problem.

Meanwhile, Dublin and Cork Corporations were dissolved and when later restored had many of their powers vested in newly-appointed City Managers. Four County Councils were also dissolved (one of them twice), mainly because of threats of insolvency arising from rates arrears. And a further two dozen subordinate urban local authorities were dissolved, generally because of incompetence or dishonesty that had been allowed to develop during the period of British rule.

Fianna Fáil, in power after 1932, faced similar problems with local authorities in its turn, and took similar action. During its first ten years in power Fianna Fáil had to dissolve six County Councils, and in 1940 it extended to the other cities and to all the counties the City Management system that Cumann na nGaedheal had earlier introduced in Cork and Dublin.

Despite this disturbing background, the enactment of the physical planning legislation in 1963 included a devolution of additional powers in this sensitive area to local authorities, and these powers have been widely abused by a number of Councils, through re-zoning decisions and also by using procedures under Section 4 of the 1963 Planning Act so as to enable individuals to override planning provisions intended to preserve the environment.

The fact is that there has not existed in Ireland sufficient public concern about the preservation of the environment to deter local representatives from inappropriate interventions of this kind. In the absence of such a community environmental concern the deeply-embedded clientelism of Irish politics has led councillors to seek electoral support by backing many individual demands to override planning controls.

Another problem created by the powers that local councils exercise under the planning laws has been the temptation to succumb to pressure from landowners and developers to zone agricultural land for development purposes, whether or not such zoning is in the public interest, and whether or not there is provision for it be serviced. The exercise of this power has always had the capacity to lead to a reintroduction of bribery into the local government system. A consequence of this ill-judged extension of the powers of local authorities has been the perceived need to establish the Flood Tribunal.

My own experience has led me to believe that, contrary to popular belief, our failure to address seriously the need to devolve authority to local bodies lies as much in successive governments' still-remembered unhappy experiences of past local authority misconduct as in an active desire by central government to retain power for its own sake.

However, a general reluctance amongst politicians to voice these concerns for fear of opening old wounds has prevented serious discussion of how it might be possible to set about devolving substantial powers to local level with adequate safeguards against abuse. The absence of such a debate because of this kind of over-sensitivity may be almost as much of a deterrent to progress towards the goal of devolution as the failure of central government to face squarely the issue of the need for local taxation to finance local activities. This is why it has seemed to me desirable to air these aspects of our local government history.

5 Integrity in public life

The Irish State was extraordinarily fortunate in the integrity of those of its revolutionary politicians who subsequently served as ministers, in some individual cases for almost five decades. However, from about 1957 onwards, an increasing number of new faces began to appear in government, a process that accelerated throughout the 1960s. By 1969 all the first generation had left government, although Frank Aiken and Paddy Smith remained in the Dáil until well into the 1970s.

Some of the newcomers in the Fianna Fáil Governments of that period were people whose integrity fully matched that of the revolutionary generation, among them people like Jack Lynch, Erskine Childers, George Colley, Des O'Malley, and Paddy Hillery, to name only the most prominent. But there were others who had fewer scruples, in particular about how funds were to be raised for the party.

Because of the efforts of the first Cumann na nGaedheal government, most public appointments were excluded from political influence, but jobbery had become a feature of Irish politics in relation to the small range of posts that remained outside the purview of the Civil Service Commission and the Local Appointments Commission, posts such as local authority gangers, rate collectors, vocational teachers, government messengers, and – in a genteel way! – judges. But in the 1960s this abuse was extended, most disturbingly, to the appointment of consultants in the construction sector. And in that area it became linked, as other political appointments were not, to financial contributions to the Fianna Fáil party.

In parallel with this development, the 1970s also saw the emergence of growing suspicions about abuses of the planning process, where the scale of the profits to be made from land zoning appeared to be posing too much of a temptation to some landowners and developers. Moreover, a small number of mainly Fianna Fáil politicians at national level began to draw upon themselves suspicions of personal financial misbehaviour, and a 'golden circle' of wealthy businessmen became associated with that element of the party. Elements in business and elements in politics thus began to corrupt each other, encouraging a demoralizing belief amongst many other businessmen that, in some key areas of economic activity in which the Government had a role, success could be secured only by dirtying one's hands.

People of integrity in Fianna Fáil, as well as many politicians in other parties, found this situation increasingly intolerable. Many on both sides of the House came to share a conviction amounting to moral certainty that financial misbehaviour and perhaps actual corruption had come into existence at national as well as local level and on a significant scale. However, in the absence of concrete evidence, there was little that could be done about this most dangerous development. Unfortunately, the majority favouring honest government that certainly existed in the Dáil could not be mobilized across party lines, and efforts within Fianna Fáil itself to purge the party of this element repeatedly failed.

It has to be said that part of the reason for this failure was the existence of a large middle group of Fianna Fáil politicians who, while themselves personally honest, were not sufficiently vigilant about the honesty of some of their colleagues. There were too many who preferred not to know, and who were prepared to ignore the signs and to tolerate the 'low standards in high places' against which George Colley had publicly warned. Had even a few more of these 'middle ground' politicians supported Colley and O'Malley in the late 1970s and early 1980s, this evil could have been rooted out far sooner.

The public reaction evoked by attempts even to hint at these concerns was so passive, even negative, that it became evident that public opinion was markedly unwilling to face this issue, preferring to turn its face away from political malfeasance. All-too-widespread admiration for what was widely seen as political 'cuteness' left little room for healthy moral indignation.

That was a thoroughly depressing period in Irish political life. It was not until the early 1990s that there was any sign of a serious challenge to the wall of silence that seemed to surround this subject. But hopes then raised that a clean-up would take place soon faded again. Before I left the Dáil in 1992, I had heard that fears of the powerful forces ranged against exposure had frightened off people who, it had briefly seemed, might have given evidence on certain matters to the Garda.

The fact that, against all the odds, and largely by chance, exposure of these evils eventually came about was thus for many in politics a huge relief. I know that in the aftermath of these disclosures many of the public have difficulty in distinguishing between the small group who have disgraced politics and the vast majority of decent and honest politicians in all parties. But the short-term damage caused to public confidence in the system by this confusion must in the long run be less than that which was increasingly being inflicted by the apparent immunity of prominent wrongdoers. The persistence of that apparent immunity might have – perhaps even must have – infected our political system much more widely, as has in fact happened in most of the Latin countries of Western Europe.

When the present tribunals and enquiries have finished their work we may once again enjoy a political system where all elements will be free from these distortions. Parties may be able to compete again on equal terms, neither drawing nor repelling support because of improper activities on the part of a very small element amongst their elected representatives.

The past practice of financing parties and elections by means of contributions from business, given without expectation of receiving improper favours in return, has come to be seriously questioned in recent years because, in some important instances, it clearly was abused. But the reforms thus far introduced have not yet gone far enough to replace that system by what I have become convinced needs to be a system of virtually exclusive State financing of political activities.

The argument that this would be unconstitutional is frankly not credible. Even if it might be unconstitutional to ban people from giving money to political parties, it beggars belief that it would be unconstitutional to forbid parties taking such money.

It is difficult to see why political parties should want to retain their dependence on financing of this kind, which has given them nothing but grief in recent times. But perhaps those political parties which have refused to face the urgent need to purge the system of this dubious element feel that they are more likely than their rivals to receive substantial sums from the business community. If true, that would be a most worrying reason for not reforming the financing of politics more drastically.

The total elimination of business contributions to parties would not merely exclude the buying of favours for individual business projects: it would also remove the source of what can be subtle 'pro-business' bias against socially necessary redistributive policies. Such improper constraints on redistribution will need to be tackled if we are ever to succeed in mobilizing growth to achieve the effective elimination of poverty in Ireland. In relation to this matter of political funding, there are really three quite distinct issues:

- First, the need for limits on party spending at election times. Most disturbingly, the limits re-imposed a few years ago were subsequently arbitrarily increased by 50% prior to the 2002 election;
- second, the actual sources of party finance;
- third, the evidence that some senior Fianna Fáil ministers used political donations to enrich themselves personally.

Until 1963 there had been no legal recognition in Ireland of the existence of political parties. This was partly a carry-over from British constitutional theory and partly a reflection of a utopian and totally unrealistic belief by the founders of our State that we could avoid the emergence of party politics here. The Civil War, together with the re-emergence of the Labour Party in the aftermath of the struggle for independence, put paid to that particular illusion.

Nevertheless, for forty years after Independence candidates in Irish elections in theory stood as individuals rather than as party members: party labels did not appear on election ballot papers until this was authorized by legislation enacted in 1963. All limits on party spending disappeared at that time perhaps because limits on spending by individual candidates in constituencies seemed anachronistic with formal recognition of political parties, and perhaps also because control on party spending at a national level appeared difficult to organize and, given the relatively small amounts then being subscribed, scarcely worth the effort.

This happened to favour Fianna Fáil, then in government, because that party's introduction of industrial protection had left it better placed than others to secure financial support from Irish business. Moreover, around that time Fianna Fáil was moving towards a new stage in party funding, through the highly-organized Taca system of fundraising from business interests that had been established by Neil Blaney.

It was not until the 1981 election that Fine Gael seriously matched Fianna Fáil's fundraising efforts, enabling it for the first time to challenge that party on something approaching equal financial terms in the three elections of 1981–82. Fine Gael's emergence at that time as a serious challenger to Fianna Fáil led to a gradual shift by business people away from contributions being based solely upon the party loyalties of individual businessmen and towards a new system under which in most cases contributions were made by businesses to all the main parties, more or less proportionately to the size of those parties' Dáil membership.

At least in the case of Fine Gael the danger of government decisions being influenced by contributions to parties was obviated by establishing a Chinese wall between contributors and ministers. But the trouble about this was that the effectiveness of such voluntary policing of the funding system depends upon all parties sharing, and maintaining, the same standards in this matter, which did not prove to be the case.

Two distorting factors, which ultimately devalued and eventually undermined the more or less proportionate contribution system that had then emerged, were: first, the appearance of a small group of contributors – the Golden Circle – who apparently saw a possibility of benefits to their businesses arising from major contributions to Fianna Fáil, and second, the emergence of a new and alarming phenomenon, where contributions were given not to parties but to individual politicians, several of whom, encouraged by the example of their leader, Charles Haughey, seem to have retained certain sums for their own personal benefit.

This latter abuse derived from a general breakdown in party discipline from the late 1980s onwards, a breakdown reflected in the emergence of personal campaigns in constituencies by candidates of both main parties in contention with colleagues of their own party.

Of course the multi-seat electoral system had always sparked sporadic outbreaks of rivalry between candidates of the same party at election times, but these rivalries had until then been largely contained. Indeed, in the case of Fine Gael, a combination of tight discipline and remarkable unselfishness by some candidates, involving vote-splitting agreements in key constituencies, actually enabled that party in November 1982 to win with fewer votes than Fianna Fáil the three or four extra seats needed to put them in government for a period of over four years.

But after 1987 this kind of discipline seems to have broken down in both main parties. Increasingly, party campaigns at constituency level were paralleled by personal campaigns, for which an increasing number of candidates sought financial support. And substantial sums channelled through individuals to the Fianna Fáil party sometimes failed to reach their intended destination.

In the past, individual candidates sometimes had to provide part of the finance for party campaigns in their constituencies, a practice I sought to eliminate in Fine Gael because it could militate against people of slender means standing for election. But, in this recent period, our political system eventually reached the stage where elections actually became a potential source of personal profit for a small handful of politicians willing effectively to embezzle party funds, and powerful enough to prevent this abuse being exposed.

Revelations about these malpractices, and suspicions that government decisions might have been influenced by payments to the party or to individual politicians, ultimately gave rise to deep public concern about the influence of business on politics. But the reaction of the party system to these concerns was less than wholehearted. The Progressive Democrats were the first to resist the idea of substituting private party funding by public funding and Fianna Fáil has remained reluctant to ban business funding of politics, although willing to limit the amounts permitted to be paid.

The truth is that private, and in particular business, funding was always a dubious way to finance parties or elections. We deluded ourselves into thinking that safeguards could protect us against abuses of the system. We now know that we were wrong in that belief. The political parties should now have the wit to respond to deep public concern on this score. That is the very least that needs to be done in an effort to restore some measure of confidence in our political system.

It is true, of course, that only a very small number of politicians have abused their trust. But the vast majority of honest politicians should have the good sense to realize that all of them are suffering from the misdeeds of that few and that there is a need to take effective action to recover lost ground.

There are lessons to be learnt from our experience of recent years in relation to tribunals investigating abuses of this kind, and some of the possible lessons have, in fact, been identified in an article in the *Bar Review* by Rory Brady SC, who became Attorney General in 2002. He traces back the origins of the decision of the United Kingdom Parliament to enact the Tribunals Act of 1921, from which our tribunals derive their origin, to unsatisfactory aspects of the previous system of Select Parliamentary Committees or Commissions of Enquiry, which were both open to political bias.

While there are a variety of bodies that can conduct investigations – the Dáil and Seanad, the Garda, the Revenue Commissioners, and 'a vigilant media' – he has pointed out that 'to date such bodies appear not to have satisfied the requirements of certain situations . . . the plain fact is that it was only through a Tribunal that facts of cardinal importance relating to the BTSB Inquiry and the Dunnes Payments Inquiry were revealed to the public'.

In a measured analysis Rory Brady then goes on to draw some lessons from this experience of the working of tribunals, pointing out that once people have learnt from experience that no one can escape the vigilance of a tribunal, 'only a fool would fail to co-operate with a preliminary investigation carried out on behalf of a Government', by a suitably appointed person whose report would be published when completed. He has, therefore, proposed that statutory bodies and financial institutions should have a legal obligation to cooperate with such preliminary investigations and to discover documents sought by them.

He has also gone on to point out that, if such a system of preliminary investigations were to be introduced now, a costly tribunal would, henceforth, be required only when an investigated person did, in fact, behave like a fool. And, if such a person were to be found by a tribunal to have engaged in misconduct in public affairs or in matters of public interest, he or she should then be required to pay all, or part, of its costs.

Rory Brady has also proposed that in order better to control the costs of any tribunals that may still need to be appointed from time to time, these bodies should be required to report on the state of their investigations to the Houses of the Oireachtas at the expiry of a limited period of time, adding that the Oireachtas should have an express power to suspend a tribunal if the costs become disproportionate to the issues involved.

Another valid point he makes is that the terms of reference given to a tribunal should be precise, and if it has difficulty in interpreting them, then it should have power to seek further guidance from the

Oireachtas. He has also suggested that any future legislation giving effect to such proposals should specifically confine membership of tribunals to the judiciary, which is not the case at present. Finally, he proposes that the issue of tribunals might usefully be referred to the Law Reform Commission, which could study these and other related ideas.

Meanwhile, the material that has already emerged from the work of the tribunals has made it clear that the health of our society certainly requires systems of enquiry and investigation that are outside the political arena. This is not in any way to denigrate or devalue the remarkable work done by the Public Accounts Committee under Jim Mitchell's chairmanship. For matters not involving politicians, that Committee showed that it could do as good a job as any tribunal, and at much lower cost. But the Committee's decision to delegate to its lawyers the questioning of ministers showed its appreciation of its own limitations when the actions of politicians came to be at issue.

There remains the sore subject of the cost of lawyers employed to represent the public interest and the interests of involved parties during the course of tribunal hearings. It is, of course, only when our attention is drawn to particular instances of what we regard as excessive rates of pay that our irritation really surfaces. And, in general, rates of pay of professional and business people come into the public view only when these emerge from parliamentary questions about professional people employed by the State or when, on the occasion of the AGMs of public companies, the amounts paid to a small group of directors, executive and non-executive, are published. For the rest, we generally remain in ignorance of the pay rates of people with high skills, but because of the tribunals, the rates paid to top lawyers have been heavily publicized in recent years. A lot more has been made of their remuneration than of the amounts paid to accountants, for example, although these, I believe, charge much the same hourly rate.

A relevant point that is not, perhaps, sufficiently widely recognized is that our citizens have a constitutional right to be represented by lawyers in court or at a tribunal. And, many companies, as well some individuals (including people whose activities are being investigated by one or other of the tribunals), are prepared to hire the services of solicitors and/or barristers with particular skills, and are prepared to pay the cost of doing so.

Now, where the State is involved in litigation with such people, or where the Oireachtas has established a tribunal, it would be totally counterproductive for it to be represented in court by lawyers with lesser skills than those representing the people it is investigating. So, the State has to pay broadly similar rates.

However, although some people will choke on their soup on having this drawn to their attention, lawyers are unusual amongst the professions in that their rates of pay are, in fact, subject to control. First of all, in the case of barristers employed by the State, a key role in this process is undertaken by a Cost Drawer in the Attorney General's Office. Moreover, if anyone questions the bills submitted by solicitors or barristers for their work, these bills are then examined meticulously by the Taxing Master, who can, and often does, cut them by substantial amounts. And if someone still thinks they are too high (or, of course, if the lawyer in question thinks that they have been cut excessively!) an appeal can be made to a High Court judge.

Now, many will regard the outcome of all these controls as unsatisfactory, feeling that the fees received by the minority of the 1,700 practising barristers at the top of their profession are too high. But, so far as I am aware, lawyers are the only group of people whose charges are subjected to control of this kind. Any proposals for further controls – and I have yet to hear of concrete proposals of this kind that would be workable – should, of course, also address the rates of pay of other professionals who are not subject to any system of regulation similar to that applied to barristers.

Having said all that, I should add that I would, of course, share the concern that has been widely expressed over the scale of fees agreed by the State with lawyers engaged by tribunals of enquiry which continue their work for very long periods of time, even allowing for the fact that lawyers undertaking work of this kind need to be compensated for the fact that their earnings after the end of the life of such tribunals' work could be affected by their long absence from their normal activities at the Bar.

(I should, perhaps, add at this point that, although I qualified at the King's Inns in an undistinguished way fifty-five years ago, I have never practised at the Bar and thus, in this matter, have no financial interest to declare!)

The vast majority of public appointments are made independently by the Civil Service Commission or the Local Appointments Commission, which were both established by the first Government in the 1920s. Appointments over which politicians retain control are relatively few. Some are low-paid posts, such as messengers in government departments. But they also include some high profile appointments such as judges, Secretaries-General of government departments, temporary advisers to ministers, directors of State bodies, and of course appointments to top posts in European institutions. Quite different considerations apply to each of these categories.

In a number of these cases governments have introduced voluntary constraints on their range of choice which effectively limit, or at any rate reduce considerably, the possibility of using these appointments to reward party supporters. But in other cases the government's discretion remains unfettered. Moreover, and even where independent pre-listing of possible candidates has been introduced, the number of names put forward in the pre-listing process is sometimes so large as still to leave the way open to political favouritism.

This is the case, for example, with the vetting procedure introduced some time ago for the appointment of judges. This involves the submission by an independent body of a large number of names to government, which then exercises its constitutional prerogative by choosing from this list.

Now, it would be surprising if amongst, say, seven suitable lawyers there were not some supporters of whatever government might be in office, although this can happen. Indeed, one case of reported inaction by government over many months in relation to a judicial appointment was attributed by some to the absence of any government supporters from the list in question!

Thus, this recommendation mechanism does not normally eliminate political considerations from such appointments. However, it does offer protection against unsuitable political appointments and, if these lists were to be cut, say, to three names, the political factor would be considerably reduced.

Another approach, suitable in certain cases only, would be to delegate the making of certain appointments to outside bodies. Thus, in early 1983, Dick Spring, as Minister for the Environment, dismissed a number of ill-qualified supporters of Ray Burke who had been given effective control of An Bord Pleanála after the two dissolutions of the Dáil in June 1981 and November 1982. He did this by introducing a bill reconstituting An Bord Pleanála which provided for the nomination of members other than the Chairman by groups of organizations concerned about environmental and planning issues. This was designed to safeguard this crucially important body against efforts to politicize its work, which could have ended in corruption of its processes.

Ruairi Quinn, the leader of the Labour Party, has pointed out that governments sometimes have difficulty in finding suitable people to fill posts at their disposal, a point that I can endorse from personal experience, and he has suggested that a national 'Talent Bank' be established with which individual citizens who wish to serve in public positions could register so as to be available for selection. Such an arrangement could certainly widen the range of choice of governments, but if the process were restricted to self-selection without subsequent independent vetting, it could lead to some very odd appointments indeed. To vet such a list we would clearly need an independent commission of the kind that exists in New Zealand, and Labour might usefully add that additional element to its talent bank idea.

Another method of ensuring the quality of public appointments, which has received the support of both main opposition parties, is the vetting by a Dáil Committee of certain appointments. Ruairi Quinn has suggested that potential nominees for key positions be required to give evidence to such a Committee as to their suitability for the position proposed for them. Clearly this could not be applied to all of the hundreds of public appointments in the discretion of the government of the day, but it could, as John Bruton, the former Fine Gael leader, has suggested, be used for 'all major national and international appointments'.

It has been suggested that such a parliamentary vetting system might be abused by Opposition parties to engage in 'mud-slinging'. But, whatever about debates in the Dáil chamber, that would be contrary to the tradition of most Committees of the House and the introduction of such a system would be likely to deter governments from proposing names of unsuitable political supporters for important posts.

Why is there such a demand by a significant minority of party supporters for public positions of this kind?

In most cases the payments made to holders of such positions are either confined to expenses or, if a fee or salary is involved, the amounts paid are small by comparison with similar positions in the private sector. Some of those who nevertheless seek such appointments are people genuinely concerned with public service which in very many cases is the factor that brought them into politics in the first instance. The prevailing cynicism about party politics has made it fashionable to deride or dismiss the possibility of such motivation, but that cynical attitude is shared by few who have any real knowledge of the political scene.

Nevertheless, it would be starry-eyed to suggest that no other factors influence the approach to public appointments by some of the people engaged in party political activity. One cannot exclude less worthy motivations, such as a desire for recognition and prestige, and it is of course possible that in some cases financial gain, even if on a small scale, may also be a factor.

Even on boards or committees where no fee or salary is paid, there can be a mercenary element, for the payment of the Civil Service mileage and subsistence rate for attendance at meetings some distance away from an appointee's home can be a source of additional tax-free income – a factor that may explain the disturbing fact that members of prison-visiting committees, many of whom are associated with political parties, are often appointed to prisons far distant from where they live. To be blunt about it, that is a clear abuse of public funds.

At the time of writing, the Monday–Friday return rail fare from Cork to Dublin is €44.40, or €62.70 first class. But the mileage payment for a 320-mile return journey from Cork to Dublin is €355.23, in addition to which this Civil Service expenses system provides for additional payments, not just for overnighting (€112.88), but also lesser sums for day trips of three or more hours. For some of those concerned the temptation to take the train while charging the car mileage rate must be very strong.

In other cases, there may be privileges attached to appointments. The exceptional political demand for positions on the board of Aer Lingus (which I am convinced contributed significantly to the poor performance of that company at various periods of its history) was certainly not unconnected with the privilege of free air travel enjoyed by its directors.

Most party politicians support the present practice of political appointments and see nothing untoward about favouring their supporters in this way, whether or not those concerned have much to contribute to the board or committee to which they are appointed. Politicians generally seem to be blissfully unaware of the damage being done to the reputation of politics by these abuses in the present system or of the damage sometimes done to the public bodies concerned by some of their appointments.

That is why as Taoiseach I insisted that, together with the Tánaiste Dick Spring, I see such nominations before they were submitted to government. He and I sought to keep the number of appointments of political supporters down to one such appointment per board, and also to ensure that all of these would be people capable of making a serious contribution to the work of the body concerned. I believe that we achieved our objective in all but two instances, Aer Lingus and Bord na gCon.

It is up to the leaders of our political parties to persuade their deputies to accept the urgent need for reforms that will prevent an erosion of confidence in our democratic system on the part of an electorate who have been belatedly aroused by recent events to an unwonted distaste for political malpractices that they had previously been content to tolerate or ignore.

A different but related issue is the manner in which different interest groups impact on political policy-making.

There is an evident imbalance in the scale of influence of different groups in society upon the political system. This power imbalance takes a form quite different from that which had been envisaged when democracy in the shape of universal suffrage was being sought in the latter part of the nineteenth century, or even more recently in some countries.

Many of those who then held power within systems of government involving elections with restricted suffrage believed that universal suffrage would bring in its train the rapid overthrow of the existing stratified societies. The masses, once enfranchised, would, it was feared, take power into their own hands and use it to redistribute resources amongst themselves.

In the event, nothing like this happened in any democracy following the arrival of universal suffrage. Although during the past century there was undoubtedly a measure of redistribution that narrowed income differentials significantly up to the end of the 1970s, and although the extreme misery of the very poor has certainly been alleviated by social welfare measures in all democracies, this process has been gradual, and remains, to say the least, incomplete.

Moreover, such redistribution as has been effected through the democratic system has generally not been carried out by mass parties sustained by the votes of a proletarian majority but, most often, by middle-class leaders of reformist parties. And, since about 1980, this process of gradually narrowing income differentials has, of course, been reversed in many countries, including Ireland, where the spread of incomes is now more unequal than almost anywhere else in Europe.

Why, when they were given the vote, did the masses not take over power and redistribute wealth in a significant way?

Part of the explanation may lie in the fact that at the time when universal suffrage was being introduced many of these societies were still predominantly rural, land reform in some cases offering a prospect of peasant proprietorship and thus operating as a stabilizing and conservative factor.

But another reason may have been that in most democracies the gradual extension of the suffrage to the whole population more or less coincided with, or was at any rate closely followed by, a growth in general prosperity. And this growth in prosperity was gradually transforming the shape of society from the pyramidal structure that had prevailed throughout history – with a small group of rich at the top and a huge mass of poor at the bottom – to a quite different kind of shape: still a pyramid at the *top*, but with a *narrowing base*. In other words, the poor were in process of ceasing to be the majority and were becoming a minority, with the bulk of the population now concentrated in a bulge somewhat higher up, and thus having an interest in holding on to their gains.

The weight of numbers thus became concentrated at a point somewhat above the bottom of the heap, the semi-skilled and skilled working class and clerical workers. By virtue of *not* being at the bottom of the heap as unskilled workers or unemployed, all of these other groups, despite their limited means, were becoming in some measure ‘haves’ in society, with something to lose, and therefore with an interest in preserving the broad structure of the status quo as well perhaps as having an aspiration to rise to a higher status amongst the ‘haves’.

Earlier in the twentieth century there were probably moments in certain countries at which an alienated mass did have a voting majority in democratic elections and could have used this to overturn the existing balance of power favouring the better-off minority of the population. Leaving on one side the obvious case of Russia, in the early 1930s something of the kind did happen in a very messy way in Spain, but was pre-empted by the right-wing rebellion of July 1936. Some would argue that a similar pattern is to be seen in events in Chile in 1973, although in that instance the share of the popular vote secured by Allende, the Socialist candidate for the presidency who was subsequently overthrown, was still well under 40%. And Chavez in Venezuela provides another example.

But, even if one accepts these events as having represented attempts by the alienated masses to secure power through the operation of the democratic system that were blocked or had attempts made to block them by right-wing coups, what is striking is that these would seem to be the only examples of the democratic process having operated in this way. By and large in most countries such developments seem to have been pre-empted by a combination of what might be described as a persistence of traditional 'deference' on the part of the alienated masses during the early stages of universal suffrage, and the gradual shift in the shape of the societal pyramid that coincided with the introduction of this franchise, itself a consequence of a combination of economic growth and of the introduction of extensive social welfare provisions.

Thus, the power balance in democratic societies did not take the shape feared by the nineteenth-century upper class and bourgeoisie – namely a majority of less-well-off people dominating a minority of better-off – but emerged instead as a majority of people with jobs or property, usually grouped in or represented by, bodies such as farming and industrial organizations or trade unions on one side, and a minority of unemployed, and young and retired people on the other, effectively without representation and remaining dependent on the majority of 'haves' for their quality of life. The organized groups have proved well equipped to protect their interests and advantages from unorganized, disadvantaged minority groups.

While, as has already been pointed out, it is simplistic to equate democracy with majority rule in the arithmetic sense, nevertheless even in societies without ethnic or religious minorities, a problem exists in relation to the exercise of power by a broad majority coalition of organized interest groups which, whatever their differences with regard to each other, have a common interest, at least in the medium term, in protecting their jobs/incomes/property from a disadvantaged and poorer minority.

Given the relative numerical strength and disparity of organizational capacity of these two groups how can the democratic system cope with this inherent imbalance within our society? The correction of this imbalance seems to me to depend upon two motivating forces which may modify the selfish exercise of power by the 'haves': social concern, and fear.

Social concern, for its part, is a factor that varies between societies, Scandinavian societies generally being visibly more socially concerned than many others in Europe, and American society being clearly much less so. Within a given society social concern may also fluctuate over time in conjunction with ideological swings between right and left.

In this respect, Irish society has in the past probably been nearer to the Scandinavian end of the spectrum. As discussed in chapter 2, within the resources then available all governments during the 1960s and 1970s made relatively generous social welfare, health, and education provision, despite the fact that it was only in the 1990s that Ireland became a country with a level of income per head close to that of its near neighbours.

But, as also happened in Britain and elsewhere, this social progress ceased in Ireland in the mid 1980s. For much of the last fifteen years the purchasing power of social benefits in Ireland was deliberately held down, being allowed for much of this period to fall behind industrial earnings, and recent real increases in social payments have done no more than restore belatedly the earlier ratio between these two types of income.

The other motivating force that might stimulate transfers by 'haves' to 'have-nots' is, of course, fear. But, in most democratic societies the relative quiescence of the unemployed, even when, as in Ireland and Spain in the 1980s their numbers approached 20% of the labour force, has prevented this factor from having any perceptible effect.

It is, thus, difficult to avoid the conclusion that in modern democratic societies the social gap between a majority of 'haves' and a minority of 'have nots' is very difficult to remedy. For it depends upon the social commitment of members of the political class being strong enough to counteract the now very powerful forces of materialistic self-interest, extracting a mandate from the 'haves' for social reform, which in some measure has to be carried out at their expense.

While one may hope for some revival and strengthening of this altruistic element amongst politicians and people generally, the negative impact of the growing selfish individualism that became such a striking, and deeply depressing, feature of the 1980s remains today in many countries a powerful force. Our societies are finding it very difficult to free themselves from this negative factor.

6 The Electoral System

Democracy has been variously defined, but, at the least, it involves government with the consent of the governed. Most people would regard this, however, as much too minimalist a definition, and would, I think, insist that democracy must involve the people having a right to choose its government, together with the right, at reasonable intervals, to reject and replace it. Many, indeed, see as implicit in this concept the idea of *majority* rule, for how else, they will ask, can government be chosen, and from time to time replaced, save by a majority vote of the people?

Would that it were that simple! There are, in fact, relatively few democracies where some component of the government is chosen *directly* by a majority of the people – the popular election of the French President is one such example. Even in the case of the United States, as was made clear in 2000, the President is not popularly elected but is chosen by an Electoral College the majority within which may not in fact correspond to the majority of votes cast for the different candidates. Furthermore, contrary to popular assumptions, the systems by which legislatures are elected very often fail to yield what can be described as governments chosen by a majority of the people.

A very small number of democracies, most notably the United States, have clear-cut two-party structures permitting in theory a direct popular choice of a legislative majority. But, the reason why the United States has preserved its two-party structure and why Britain continues to have a two-and-a-half party structure at national level, laced with some regional representation, is that in these countries the pre-literate X-vote electoral system is maintained in single-seat constituencies.

This system can, and does from time to time, yield perverse results in the form of majorities in Congress, or in Parliament, for a party that has received fewer popular votes than its principal opponent. In the British case, moreover, because of the ineffectiveness of most of the votes cast for the third party, this system can produce governments supported by less than 40% of the voters, and in some cases these governments will not be the ones that would have emerged if the electorate had been given a straight choice between the party thus elected to government and the principal alternative.

This British/American electoral system has a very limited application, surviving only in a small number of democratic countries, mainly ones that have been British colonies at some time in the past and also have a federal structure, e.g. the United States, Canada and, partially, Australia.

The abandonment by most countries of the system of placing an X after a single name must, I feel, have been influenced by the fact that this system – even when, as in France, it is modified by a second round of voting – can lead to overwhelming majorities for one party, majorities quite disproportionate to the actual votes cast, as well as to vast swings in parliamentary representation at elections. Indeed, in the extreme case – that is in a case where each party has the *same* support in *all* constituencies – the party with the greatest support would win *every* seat in parliament.

So long as there were rotten boroughs 'owned' by patrons of different parties this danger was avoided, but with the advent of the secret ballot and universal suffrage in the late nineteenth century and the early decades of the twentieth century most countries abandoned an electoral system that was so arbitrary and unstable in its outcome.

In Britain, however, despite it being a unitary state, the geographically uneven spread of political allegiance (which may in some measure have been a function of the religious divisions within Protestantism in the sixteenth and seventeenth centuries) ensured that the defeated party at each election always retained a substantial minority of seats throughout the centuries. And because this system, until recently at least, has seemed to serve the interests of the two large parties in Britain, it has survived to date.

In most democratic countries, however, some form of proportional representation was introduced, in many cases in the early part of the last century. Even where a threshold is applied to exclude very small parties, electoral systems of this type make possible the representation in parliament of a spectrum of groups. As a result, with proportional representation it is only rarely that the electorate is faced with a clear-cut pre-election choice between two blocs of parties. In many such cases parties negotiate the formation of a government *after* the election, when their relative strengths have been determined by the electorate. It is largely a matter of chance whether the government that then emerges reflects the choice that the electorate would have made if it had been faced at the time of the election with the alternative of that particular combination of parties, rather than one, for example, comprising all or most of the remaining parties that the people have chosen to return to parliament.

The emergence in Ireland in the 1990s of this type of ad hoc post-election government formation – replacing the earlier de facto clear choice between a Fianna Fáil Government on the one hand or a Coalition involving Fine Gael and Labour on the other – may have contributed to the decline of over one-sixth between 1987 and 2002 in the percentage of the electorate voting in Irish general elections. When people come to realize that the votes they cast for party candidates no longer decide the shape of their future government, some of them are bound to lose interest in voting at a general election.

The democratic principle is seen by most people in Ireland as requiring that a parliament should be broadly representative of the spectrum of political views and party allegiances of the electorate, a view which I share. There are other electoral considerations to which weight is given in different societies: the discouraging of a proliferation of small groups the existence of which might make it difficult to form stable governments; the maximizing of party control of parliamentary representation; or the maximizing of the electorate's choice of representatives so that they may provide a strong personal link between parliament and electors at local level.

No electoral system can meet all four of these requirements in equal measure – each of them being to a significant degree incompatible with some of the others. Examples of countries that give primacy to one of these considerations, to the effective exclusion of at least one other, are Israel, Britain, Italy and Ireland. And a country that seeks to achieve some kind of balance between the different criteria is Germany.

Israel demonstrates the consequences of giving absolute preference to proportional representation in parliament at the expense of a coherent party system capable of yielding stable governments.

The United Kingdom could be said to illustrate the consequences of giving precedence to limiting the proliferation of parties with a view to ensuring stable government, but at the expense of any kind of reasonably proportional representation in parliament of the preferences of the electorate.

Italy, like many other Continental countries, has at times sought to maximize party control through a list system.

And Ireland illustrates the consequence of giving priority to the electorate's choice of representatives.

The Irish system of proportional representation in multi-member constituencies ensures reasonable, but imperfect and, as was seen in the 2002 general election, sometimes unstable, proportionality of representation in parliament (albeit usually with a bias towards the two larger parties), with, however, a de facto – but not excessively severe – constraint on the number of parties. During the 1920s and 1930s a reduction in the number of parties was actively sought and secured through a gradual process of reducing the size of constituencies down from a maximum of nine to a maximum of five seats. This limitation has operated to inhibit the proliferation of small groups, many of which have normally failed to get enough votes in any constituency to secure one of the available seats.

But what is unique about the Irish system is that the electorate, who vote for individual candidates rather than for parties, can choose *between* different members of the same party. As a result of this the chance of members losing their seats is approximately doubled, indeed trebled in the case of Fianna Fáil. For overall, approximately half of the seats lost by members of the two larger parties are lost to other members of their own group rather than to candidates of other parties.

The result of this is that members of the Irish Parliament understandably feel it necessary to give a disproportionate amount of their time to constituency work in order to protect their seats from ambitious colleagues as well as from their opponents in their own party, and in my view this adversely affects Parliament's legislative role. In addition, the very high turnover of members also discourages potential candidates and thus restricts the range of talent available in the Oireachtas.

The impact of this system on members of Irish governments is particularly severe. I know of no other country in the world where ministers are required, by a combination of constitutional provisions and public attitudes, to carry the kind of burden of work which the members of Irish Governments have to carry.

First of all, members of our Government are constitutionally required to be members of our Parliament. This is, of course, the case in a number of other parliamentary democracies, although not in the Netherlands or France, where ministers are actually forbidden to be members of the legislature during their term of ministerial office – nor, of course, in the United States where, however, the system of government is not a parliamentary one.

But, in all the parliamentary democracies where ministers are required to be members of parliament they are elected either by a list system, under which their re-election can be assured by placing them high on the party list, or, in the case of Britain and most of the 'white' dominions of the Commonwealth, they can be facilitated in the matter of re-election – although not, of course, guaranteed it – by a single-seat parliamentary electoral system. For, in these countries, many members of government have 'safe' seats, and, for the rest, the actual working of the system does not require them, as in Ireland, to spend such a large part of their time 'nursing' their constituencies.

We have to recognize, moreover, that in Ireland where the political system is so deeply rooted at the local level, and where the vast majority of the members of the Dáil are also members of local councils – between two-thirds and seven-eighths of them in latter times having made their way into the Dáil through that channel – the pressure of demands by constituents upon ministers, as upon other TDs, is far more acute than in any other developed democracy.

Thus, the genius of Irish people for personal relations has its negative side, for it means that TDs, including, of course, ministers, must in most cases satisfy their constituents by constant personal attention to their individual problems, a role that they can rarely, or only partially, delegate.

The result of this system is that the process of securing a reasonable prospect of re-election requires members of the Dáil to spend an inordinate amount of time on constituency business. This is more particularly the case for rural ministers, although the problem exists in quite an acute form also for some ministers representing disadvantaged parts of the larger cities.

In practice, ministers, especially from rural areas outside the Dublin region, have to spend the greater part of an extended weekend attending to these duties. Some rural ministers in this position have been known to devote only four days of the week to ministerial duties during that half of the calendar year when for the greater part of this mid-week period they are required to be in attendance in parliament rather than in their ministries. Added to this, whilst the Dáil is in session ministers have to devote a large part of their time in Leinster House to meeting backbenchers and to delegations from every part of the country raising local issues.

Even when, as many ministers normally do, they work at one or other of their roles for something like a fifteen-hour day, six days a week – and often for part of Sunday as well – the actual amount of time during which they can carry out their governmental functions is quite limited, and part of that time is taken up by Cabinet and other Government Committee meetings.

In my view, the astonishing thing is that, against this background, the quality of government in Ireland has been as high as it has been. The dedication of most ministers, of whatever party, to their careers – if not always to their ministerial roles – regardless of the strain on themselves and their families, has kept the system going, despite the increasingly intolerable demands that it makes in human terms. But I do not think that this can, or will, continue indefinitely.

Nor do I believe that the intellectual capacity of Irish politicians, which, objectively, has risen significantly in the last few decades, can be maintained indefinitely in the face of the pressures that the present system now places upon backbenchers as well as on members of the government.

It was for this reason that I proposed in my party's manifesto at the 1987 election a fundamental review of the electoral system. The purpose of that proposal was to find some way of reducing the pressure created under Irish conditions by multi-seat constituencies, whilst at the same time maintaining full proportionality between votes and seats in the Dáil.

My proposal would have involved a German-type system, with a majority of members elected in single-seat constituencies but with a large minority elected by some other system that would be deployed to compensate for the disproportionate results of such a single-seat electoral system.

In these single-seat constituencies the present preferential voting system would be used – 1, 2, 3 etc., in order of the voter's choice, rather than a single X – thus ensuring that the most popular candidate in each constituency, rather than the one with the largest first-preference vote, would be chosen.

Because this single-seat system on its own would inevitably yield a result disproportionately favourable to the largest party, proportionality in the strength of the parties in parliament would be secured by adding to each party's Dáil strength an appropriate number of additional members. These additional members could be elected either from regional or national party lists.

Research I have undertaken during the past decade has shown that in the Irish State, in order to ensure that the number of seats won by the largest party in the single-seat constituency part of the election would not exceed the number to which its national vote would entitle it in the fully-constituted Dáil, the proportion chosen by the list system would need to be at least 40% of the total.

I have also suggested that if doubts amongst existing deputies about their chances of being placed high enough on a party list to have a good chance of re-election under such a new system were to involve resistance to such a reform, some or even most of each party list could be constituted retrospectively by those most narrowly defeated in the single-seat election, ordered in terms of the narrowness of their defeat, determined by reference to the proportion of the quota achieved in the final count.

This proposal has been criticized as an attempt to 'squeeze out the smaller parties'. In fact one of its defects – possibly even a fatal defect in terms of getting it accepted by the major parties in present circumstances – is the fact that my proposal would require more strict proportionality between votes and seats than exists with the present electoral system. This alternative system would accordingly give the smaller parties more seats in the Dáil than they generally secure at present.

In this connection it should be remembered that when they first entered the Dáil in 1987 the Progressive Democrats, like Clann na Poblachta before them in 1948, won only 7–8% of the Dáil seats despite securing 13–14% of the votes in these first elections that they contested. Thus a revision of the electoral system that would involve strict proportionality might not be popular with the existing larger parties because it would favour small, and especially new, parties.

A reform along the lines suggested above has, in fact, been suggested by Noel Dempsey, Minister for the Environment and Local Government in the 1997–2002 Government, but the critical reception he and I received when together we presented this concept to a Dáil Committee in 2000 does not suggest that it is likely to be adopted in the near future.

Nevertheless, I still believe that this whole problem of the electoral system and the pressure it places on TDs and ministers needs to be tackled objectively, and soon. An examination of this problem should extend not only to the electoral system but also to the question as to whether under Irish conditions we can continue much longer with a system that imposes on ministers all the burdens of constituency representation simultaneously with the burdens of office.

Some may, of course, think that I have devoted an undue amount of time to these issues of effective government, including the electoral system. But I have dwelt upon it at some length because I am convinced that there is a serious hidden problem here, one which has received far too little public attention. It is a problem that has, I believe, tended to be obscured by overconcentration by the media on issues such as the length of parliamentary recesses and allegations that politicians are lazy and underworked, whereas the real problem is the exact opposite.

It is, of course, true that our parliamentary sessions are shorter than in many other countries and it is also true that our legislation has tended to lag behind our needs, leaving untackled many problems which require urgent legislative action. But the cause and effect relationship suggested in the media – that this is due to the laziness of parliamentarians who will not work in Leinster House for a sufficient number of weeks in the year but insist on long holidays – totally misses, and indeed turns on its head, the real point. This is the fact that under the present system the amount of time available to most ministers to spend in their departments preparing legislation and carrying out their administrative duties is restricted to a fraction of what is actually needed.

This is due to the combination, already alluded to, of the need to be present in Leinster House and accessible there to backbenchers and delegations; the need to attend Government meetings and Government Committees; and pressure of constituency duties on ministers. Together these demands have created a bottleneck at Government level, which cannot be cleared without constitutional reform.

To those who say that ministers should ignore the pressures of representations, delegations and constituency work, and should concentrate solely on the task of government and their Dáil duties for five or six days a week, I would reply that this would require an unrealistic and indeed suicidal level of self-sacrifice, with such a high prospect of loss of tenure as a member of the Oireachtas that the suggestion implies a remarkably quixotic view of politicians, somewhat at odds with that which has been propagated by the media in recent years.

The reality is that politicians are neither angels of light, who can be relied on to disregard totally the future interest of themselves and their families, nor lazy good-for-nothings on the make. They are simply human beings like everyone else, and our political structures need to be devised in a way that will recognize this fact.

One of the – understandable – human failings of politicians is concern about how they are seen by the electorate: in other words preoccupation with public relations.

Events in Britain in recent years have demonstrated the dangers at government level of too much ministerial, as distinct from governmental, public relations. In 2000 the infighting between Peter Mandelson and Gordon Brown's PR man, Charlie Whelan, eventually contributed to the departure of both of them from the Government team.

We in Ireland have not experienced a political problem of that magnitude but I have the impression that, in the case of some recent Irish governments, the employment by a number of ministers of what have effectively been personal public relations officers may have created some unhelpful tensions, which could ultimately carry the risk of undermining Cabinet responsibility.

I have to say that I have always favoured the employment by ministers of 'Chefs de Cabinet' on the Continental European model, or Special Advisers as they used to be called here, before they were rechristened 'Programme Managers' by the government that came to power in 1992. But the role that I have seen for such appointees would involve no relationship whatever with the media or the public. It would exclusively be one of assisting ministers to operate effectively at Cabinet level, as well as helping to give a political impetus to the implementation at Civil Service level of the government's programme.

The first of these roles is important because ministers are not merely political heads of government departments but are also members of a Cabinet that collectively decides on policies. And many of these policies involve complex economic and social, and sometimes also cultural, issues. How are busy ministers to address these issues, for which they will be collectively responsible, but in respect of which neither they nor the Civil Servants in their own department will have any special knowledge?

It should, perhaps, be explained that when a policy is initiated, a memorandum from the originating department makes the case for the proposal being put forward, which often, but not always, involves legislation. However, this originating memorandum may not give a full account of all the counterarguments against the proposed initiative, nor of possible variations on what is proposed. Its purpose, after all, is to persuade the government to adopt the policy proposed, not to offer an academic treatise on the issue involved.

Of course the Department of Finance can be relied on for critical comments of almost any departmental proposal, which, however, will normally be directed exclusively towards minimizing costs, or possibly even blocking the proposal on cost grounds. Where other departments have different interests to defend, or to promote, their Civil Servants will also submit critical comments.

However, these Civil Servant comments may not – indeed normally will not – address some of the key policy issues that are the proper concern of politicians. And the capacity of busy politicians in government to undertake the kind of study – in some cases requiring actual research into legislation proposed by their colleagues – that would be needed to ensure an adequate discussion in Cabinet of such measures is strictly limited.

Nor can a minister reasonably expect Civil Servants in his or her own department, who are properly concerned only with matters for which their department has direct responsibility, to have the skills or the time or the necessary political sensitivity, to undertake the research work required to provide their minister with the kind of material he or she may need to contribute effectively to Cabinet discussion of many of the proposals their colleagues will bring forward. That is why, during the lifetime of the 1973–77 Government, most Labour ministers, and I as Minister for Foreign Affairs, employed economic advisers as I also did later when I was Taoiseach.

Such an expert adviser to the Taoiseach – whether he or she is called Special Adviser, Chef de Cabinet, or Programme Manager – also has another potentially important role, that is to steer the government's programme through the legislative process, keeping up pressure on the

Civil Servants (whose idea of elapsed time sometimes falls well short of the tempo at which politicians have to work!) and on the Attorney General's Office and that of the Parliamentary Draftsman. More generally, such appointees can provide a valuable supplementary level of general coordination of government policy, a role for which the departmentalized Civil Service is, I believe, imperfectly equipped.

It is, however, most important that such appointees to posts as Special Advisers or Programme Managers be genuine experts, well qualified to undertake this kind of work, and not just pals of a minister, brought in to give moral support, or to promote his or her public image – both of which have clearly happened in quite a number of instances in recent years. I am particularly doubtful about a proliferation of such dubious PR appointments to ministerial private offices, because the more such appointments are made, the more the temptation for idle hands to dabble in matters best left alone, in particular, public relations on behalf of their minister.

A curse of modern governments is the over-preoccupation of many politicians with their 'image', a preoccupation sometimes indulged at the expense of the job they are actually supposed to be doing. And when this overflows into competitive self-promotion by ministers, or by PR people employed by them, the consequences for the cohesion of a government can be quite serious.

Even worse may be the impact of an overloyal, overenthusiastic adviser, who may be tempted to boost his or her minister's image so blatantly as actually to damage that minister in the eyes of his colleagues, and ultimately also in those of the public, as has happened in Britain in recent times.

In our political system, the task of handling the presentation of the activities of the government is undertaken by the Government Press Secretary, who in the case of what has become our normal Coalition-type government will be assisted by a colleague or colleagues appointed by the leader(s) of the other party, or parties, in government.

Much will, of course, depend upon the cohesion of this Government Press Office team – on the willingness of the members of the team to work for the *government*, rather than for the parties that compose it – but in recent governments this system seems to have worked reasonably well.

More generally, it has to be said that the overall efficiency of our process of government has improved greatly over recent decades, and the Strategic Management Initiative may deliver even further improvements in the period ahead, although the Mission Statements for departments that are part of this process appear to me to be very anodyne.

A reform of the higher level Civil Service promotion system that John Boland, Minister for Public Service, and I introduced almost twenty years ago has, I believe, had a visible impact on the quality of our higher Civil Servants. We created a system, known as TLAC (The Higher Level Appointments Committee), under which the Secretaries of the Taoiseach's and public service departments, and of two other rotating departments, interviewed candidates for Secretary and Assistant Secretary posts, and recommended a single name to the relevant minister. The minister could reject this name, but in practice ministers did not do so.

Whereas previously Civil Servants chosen for these posts almost always came from their own departments, under this new system promotions by merit, especially to the Secretary grade, tended to come from other departments. This introduced into the higher level of the Civil Service a badly-needed, long-overdue, and very valuable element of interdepartmental mobility.

Unfortunately, the effect of this reform was subsequently significantly diluted by a change in the appointment system for departmental Secretaries-General – although not in that for Assistant Secretaries – that was made by Charles Haughey after the change of government in 1987. Since then, instead of one name being put forward for Secretary-General posts, three have been offered. As one of these is normally that of an Assistant Secretary in the department in question, and as ministers almost always choose this internal candidate (either preferring the familiar or, perhaps, fearing the consequence of rejecting an internal candidate), mobility at the Secretary-General level effectively disappeared again.

This diminution of mobility has been partly mitigated by the fact that some of the internal candidates appointed to the Secretary-General post are Assistant Secretaries who were appointed to that grade from another department and thus have external experience. Nevertheless, a reform that might usefully be considered would be the restoration of the single nomination to Secretary-General positions. The enhanced mobility that this would secure at the top level would be of long-term benefit to our system of government.

A striking feature of recruitment to the highest level of the Civil Service has been the absence of external recruitment. It had been my hope that under the TLAC system a significant proportion of heads of departments would be drawn from outside Civil Service, bringing new skills and perhaps new dynamism into the system, but nothing of the kind has, in fact, happened. Indeed, the opposite has occurred; not only have no such outside appointments been made but the past two decades have seen the emergence of a serious brain drain from the Civil Service, not only from the highest level but also from key grades further down the hierarchy.

As a result, there is now a most serious shortage of skills, especially of economic skills at the Assistant Principal level where much research and policy analysis takes place. This may, perhaps, account for the recent stark deterioration in the quality of revenue forecasts and perhaps also in the control of public spending. The error of €2bn. in the calculation of the tax revenue that the correctly estimated GNP figure would yield in 2001 is horrifying, and the failure either to explain why this happened or to announce any action to prevent a recurrence is simply unacceptable.

Whilst it will, of course, always be necessary for the Civil Service to draw on outside talent for some very specialized tasks, the extent to which almost all departmental economic analysis, even of a relatively straightforward character, is now shipped out to enormously expensive consultants is very disturbing, and adds hugely to the cost of administration, as well as slowing down greatly the decision-making process.

This may well reflect the rigidity and inflexibility of the hierarchical grading system and pay scales of the Civil Service, which makes the recruitment and retention of highly skilled professionals extremely difficult. If the public administration is to be carried on efficiently under modern conditions, holding its own in the face of the vast resources available to the private sector, a quite radical reform of the whole recruitment and remuneration system is now required.

For their part, in the 1990s, the Revenue Commissioners spectacularly failed to maintain public confidence in their capacity to carry out their task with visible even-handedness as between rich and less well off. They would, no doubt, contest such a comment and, in relation to the issue of tax evasion would probably claim lack of support on tax evasion from politicians and from officials in the Department of Finance, both of whom seem to have been over-fearful of 'frightening away' capital by strict enforcement of taxation law. But these factors can excuse only a small part of the Commissioners' failures of recent times, including the disgraceful instruction by an official, who we are told 'cannot be identified', which effectively overruled the decision I initiated as Taoiseach on the recommendation of my Economic Adviser, Patrick Honohan, to catch tax evaders by introducing the Deposit Interest Retention Tax (DIRT).

These developments, together with many other cases of maladministration, reported annually by the Auditor and Comptroller General but which never seem to have any negative consequences for those involved, seem to me to raise a question about the adequacy of the present disciplinary arrangements within the public service. Given what appears to be an absence of adequate self-policing within the system, and the necessary constraints on disciplinary action being undertaken by their political chiefs, I feel that, if we are to avoid a deterioration in previously high standards of performance within the public service, we may now need some kind of Inspector-General to investigate and, where appropriate, penalize cases of gross misadministration.

7 Irish demography

Demography is about people: such matters as how many are born, how long they live, whether and at what age they marry and have children; whether they stay put where they are born and brought up, or migrate elsewhere.

We happen to live in a country which over the past couple of centuries has had one of the most unstable demographies in the world, with more ups and downs, and twists and turns than, I believe, any other. We are above all a land of demographic extremes: at one or other time the lowest in the world in one way, or the highest in another.

For example, although this is not generally realized, in the 1840s Ireland was one of the most densely populated territories of the part of Europe now comprising the European Union. I have calculated that at that time Ireland's population density was almost twice the average for the rest of this area. Only Belgium and a couple of tiny Italian city-states then had a higher population density than Ireland.

Today, 160 years later, our population density is only two-fifths of the European average. And from having had, 160 years ago, one twenty-fifth (4%) of the population of the area now comprised by the EU, today we have only one-hundredth of the Union's population, i.e. 1%.

Since the 1840s – which to me at least is not so very long ago, for in my childhood I knew several people born in that decade as, indeed, were three of my four grandparents – there have been no fewer than four absolute reversals of our marriage rate. Another example of the instability of Irish demography is the fact that since the 1880s the Irish non-marital birth rate doubled, then more than halved, and finally increased over twenty-fold. Again, infantile mortality at first declined, rose again during the Second World War – to over 10% in Dublin – and then fell once more to a rate of less than 0.5%.

As for migration, whilst we are now a country of immigration, up to the end of the 1950s we were losing one-third of our young people to emigration. This deeply depressing Irish picture of the first half of the last century was radically transformed by the economic growth that we began to achieve in the 1960s. Indeed, throughout the 1970s we actually enjoyed net immigration, as we are again doing today.

The interaction between these extraordinary switches in so many elements of Irish demography, together with, in recent decades, the quite astonishing pace of demographic change, underlies and helps to explain some of the remarkable economic and social changes of the past forty years in Ireland.

During most of the first two-thirds of the twentieth century marriage and birth rates in Ireland had in fact temporarily stabilized, albeit at levels that diverged markedly from the European norm. The Irish marriage rate was then abnormally low (averaging just under 5.5 per thousand population), primarily because the proportion of those surviving in Ireland who never married was abnormally high, at about 25%. Moreover those who did marry, tended to marry late.

Nevertheless, an exceptional rate of marital fertility provided Ireland with a high marital birth rate up to the 1960s, substantially above that of the rest of Europe. By contrast the Irish non-marital birth rate was very low, the proportion of births in this category having dropped by the middle decades of the last century from 3.5% to a phenomenally low 1.5%. In addition, because artificial contraceptives were not then available (around the time when they might have come into use on a significant scale in Ireland, i.e. the mid 1930s, they were banned by law) and because abortion is not available in Ireland, and at that time few seem to have gone to Britain for this purpose, this extraordinarily low non-marital birth rate has to be taken as reflecting a genuinely low level of full sexual intercourse amongst single people.

The potential impact of a very high marital fertility rate upon the Irish population level was more than offset not just by the low marriage rate but even more so by the exceptionally high rate of emigration, combined with a poor survival rate amongst the younger generation, attributable to a high rate of infantile mortality combined with heavy mortality from TB amongst young people in their teens and twenties.

This high death rate amongst the young, which continued, albeit to a diminishing extent until after the middle of the twentieth century, has been persistently underestimated as a factor contributing to the decline in the Irish population. Amongst those born even as late as the 1930s the proportion of these remaining in Ireland who died before the age of 35 was almost one in six. When combined with the emigration of one-third or more of each generation, this high death rate amongst the young ensured that, despite exceptionally high marital fertility, the decline in the Irish population that had begun in the late 1840s persisted in the Irish State until the start of the 1960s.

To a considerable extent this abnormal demography was a consequence of slow economic growth, a phenomenon which, as was mentioned in chapter 2, persisted throughout the first four decades of Irish independence. The post-1960 shift of the Irish economy from virtual economic stagnation, unique in the Europe of its time, to a growth rate which, as early as the mid 1970s had already come to exceed that of the remainder of the EU, was bound to have huge consequences for Irish society.

The exceptional speed of the demographic and social changes of the past three or four decades has reflected not merely the radical character of the change in the pace of economic growth that occurred at the end of the 1950s but also the extraordinary extent to which Ireland had for so long been sheltered by the conservative influence of the Roman Catholic Church from changes that had occurred elsewhere, over a long period. For this combination of reasons, social changes that elsewhere had been taking place gradually throughout the twentieth century have, in the Irish case, been compressed into a fraction of that time.

A consequence of the shift from virtual economic stagnation in the 1950s to a 4.25% average growth rate thereafter was a drop of over three-fifths in net emigration. During the 1970s, indeed, the economic recovery led to an actual reversal of the net outflow from Ireland as 30,000 former emigrants in the 25–40 age group returned, bringing with them in many cases wives and children whose numbers swelled this inflow to about 100,000, a figure large enough to outweigh the continued outflow of younger emigrants.

The impact of this change in the Irish migration pattern, together with the mid-century fall in the death rate of young people, was such that whereas in 1970 only 49% of those born in Ireland thirty-five years earlier were still alive here, no less than 85% of those born a quarter of a century later, i.e. in 1960, were alive in Ireland in 1995.

The effect of this was that within a period of two decades the number of young people in Ireland rose by almost three-quarters, a population development that can have had few, if any, parallels elsewhere in the world.

The two birth years just mentioned – 1935 and 1960 – represent the extremes of this comparison, and it has to be said that those born in the years immediately following 1960 were hard hit by the recession of the early 1980s which led to a temporary recurrence of large-scale net emigration in the latter part of that decade, averaging 30,000 a year for six years. However, some of this age cohort subsequently benefited from the employment boom of the 1990s, which brought back to Ireland in the second half of that decade many who had had to leave in the late 1980s.

It is a measure of the extraordinary oscillations in Irish economic performance over the past half century that a number of those who have recently returned to work in Ireland after having had to emigrate in the late 1980s had as children been brought back to Ireland by parents who returned here in the 1970s after themselves having had to emigrate in the 1950s or early 1960s!

One effect of our quite abnormal demographic history has been that our retired population is today exceptionally small. This is because those aged 65 and over in Ireland belong to a generation whose numbers were halved by early deaths and emigration. By contrast, our younger working population – those aged 20 to 35 – come from a relatively large age cohort that was born at a time when the birth rate was high, and most of this age group did not experience large-scale emigration, which finally came to an end in 1990. Their numbers have further been supplemented by some 50,000 children brought here in the 1970s by parents returning to work here.

Consequently the size of the 65+ age group in Ireland today is only 45% of that of the 20–35 age group, whereas in the rest of the EU this ratio is around 70%. Of course, as decades hence our present large young age group moves towards retirement, the cost of supporting our older population will grow, reaching a peak between 2030 and 2050. However, by setting aside 1% of our GNP annually to build up a fund out of which to supplement future pension payments from taxes to be paid by the working population of that future period, we are currently making earlier and better provision than other countries for this long-term contingency.

There is, however, a more immediate consequence of our demography to which I want to draw attention, that is, the impact of demographic factors upon the future growth of our labour force.

Part of the good side of our demographic turmoil has been the fact that because our birth rate peaked in 1980, several decades later than in the rest of Europe, we have been enabled in recent years to increase our workforce far more rapidly than anywhere else in the industrialized world. Because of this fact, the flow of people from our educational system into our workforce in the 1990s has been adding to employment at a rate half as great again as such flows were doing in the rest of Europe.

Unfortunately, much of this advantage is now about to disappear because between 1980 and 1995 our birth rate fell by over one-third. The bulk of this decline in our young working population is going to hit us during the first decade of the twenty-first century, eventually reducing by almost 30% the number of Irish-born entrants to the labour force. Nor can we any longer draw down workers from the pool of unemployed that had been crested by the recession of the 1980s, for between 1993 and 2001 unemployment was reduced from 16% to less than 4%.

This drying-up of the flow of young people from our education system, and from unemployment, into the labour market is bound to have significant effects upon our economic growth rate in the first decade of the new century.

There are two other sources of extra workers in addition to school leavers and the unemployed; these are the movement of women from work at home to paid work, and immigration, but both of these are also going to come under pressure in the years ahead.

It may not be generally realized that, at the price of postponement of family creation by young women, Ireland now has the highest employment participation rate in Europe for women in their twenties. Consequently if we are to increase female employment further, we shall have to depend largely upon the return to work of older women, many of whom left the labour force in earlier decades in order to undertake childcare. Over the years ahead the pool of women working at home must inevitably also become a diminishing source of new labour supply.

As for immigrant workers, the inflow of such workers during the 1990s added to housing demand on a scale that must have accounted for a good deal of the huge pressure on house prices here. And, to the extent that house prices remain high, this could in turn slow the growth of this type of immigration in future, after our recovery from the recession of the year 2001.

The truth is that three-fifths of our economic growth between 1993 and 2001 came about through more people being at work, the remaining two-fifths being, of course, the outcome of improvements in labour productivity, mainly attributable to the character of so much of recent foreign investment here. An increased labour supply on this scale is simply no longer available to us, and even if we had not faced the impact of a global recession in 2001, we certainly could not have gone on expanding our economy at 8% a year, as we did throughout the whole period from 1993 to 2000.

I have mentioned that between 1961 and 1981 our economic recovery had the effect of increasing, by an astonishing 72%, the number of young people in their twenties living in the state. During much of that initial period of economic growth, whilst economic conditions were accelerating the shift from a late-marrying rural society to an earlier-marrying urban one, social attitudes towards marriage remained largely unchanged. Furthermore, within urban society, employment at reasonable pay rates was, at that period, fairly readily available (*vide* the temporary emergence of net immigration in the 1970s), and house prices remained low in real terms owing to the ready availability of privately-owned housing as a result of the earlier population decline.

In these favourable conditions, the annual number of marriages increased by one-half between 1961 and 1974, and by 1981 the number of married women aged 20–24 had jumped by an astonishing 160%, whilst the number aged 25–29 who were married had more than doubled. This huge increase in the number of young married couples had evident potential implications for the number of marital births, despite a counterbalancing element in the form of the emergence of contraception as a significant demographic factor from the mid 1960s onwards. Initially, this development took the form of quite widespread use of the contraceptive pill, but during the 1970s other contraceptives came increasingly into use. As a result, by 1981 marital fertility had declined by about one-third, so that instead of the total number of marital births rising from under 60,000 to over 100,000 during this period – as would have happened had marital fertility remained at the level of the mid 1960s – the increase in such births following this very large increase in the number of young married couples, was less than 10,000.

By 1981, the number of young married couples had levelled off, and thereafter a combination of a sharp drop in the marriage rate, which had peaked in the early 1970s, and an acceleration of the decline in marital fertility led, within fourteen years, to a virtual halving of the number of marital births. This was, however, accompanied by a very large increase in non-marital births. As mentioned on p. 104, the proportion of births that were non-marital had fallen from around 3.5% in the 1930s and 1940s to 1.5% in 1961 – i.e. to under 1,000 a year – but by 1981 it had risen to 5%. Given that the number of young single women had also increased in this period by almost one-quarter, this represented rather more than a doubling of the ratio of such births to the numbers in the relevant single female age group (15–39). However, the proportion of single women in that age group giving birth to a child in the year 1981 was still only 1.25% of the women in that age cohort.

Despite the dramatic impact of contraception upon marital fertility during the late 1960s and the 1970s, and despite the emergence in the 1970s of a growing flow of women to Britain in search of abortions, during that initial period of economic growth up to around 1980 the ethos of Irish society, in terms of the maintenance of traditional family structures, did not appear to most contemporaries to have been seriously modified. Despite the fact that the origins of these developments lay back in the early 1970s – the marriage rate had peaked in 1971 – it was only during the 1980s that the reality of these potentially destabilizing developments in our demography began to impinge upon public consciousness.

A key element of the demographic revolution that has since taken place has been a huge reduction in the number of people marrying and having children in their twenties, a development that clearly reflects some as yet undefined combination of postponement and abandonment of marriage.

More recently there has, however, been a cessation, for a period at least, of the post-1980 decline in marital births, the number of which had virtually halved by 1995, having fallen from over 70,000 to just under 38,000. In mid 1996 the number of marital births effectively levelled off for a period, but although there was a further small decline during 1999, a recovery in the number thereafter, which by 2001 had risen to almost 40,000, may have owed a good deal to births to non-nationals. The number of marital births to Irish women seems to have more or less stabilized, but because the number of married women of childbearing age fell by about 15% between 1996 and 2001, there has been a rise in marital fertility, not all of which may be attributable to immigration.

Table 4: Births 1965–2001 (thousands)

		1965	*1980*	*1995*	*1999*	*2001*
Marital	First	13.6	18.5	11.0	11.6	NA
	Other	48.5	51.9	26.9	25.4	NA
	Total	62.1	70.3	37.9	37.1	39.9
Non-marital	First	1.3	3.1	6.7	10.2	NA
	Other	0.1	0.6	4.1	6.6	NA
	Total	1.4	3.7	10.9	16.8	18
Total	First	14.9	21.6	17.8	21.8	NA
	Other	48.6	52.5	31.0	32.1	NA
	Total	63.5	74.1	48.8	53.9	57.9

The trend towards much later marriages has been reflected in the age distribution of married women giving birth. Between 1984 and 1999, the proportion of such births to women aged 23–26 fell from 23% of the total to less than 10%, whilst the proportion of births to women aged 31–38 rose from 33% of the total to 54%.

After 1995, when the decline in marital births was almost halted, the number of first marital births actually rose slightly: an increase of almost one-quarter in the number of first marital births to women in their thirties more than offset a further drop of almost one-third in the number of first births to married women under the age of 27. This provides clear evidence of an accelerating first-birth postponement phenomenon, which has been pushing a growing number of first pregnancies from the twenties into the thirties.

Table 5: First marital births, age of mother, 1965–99 (thousands)

Age of Mother	*1965*	*1980*	*1995*	*1999*
15–26	8.2	12.4	2.8	2.0
27–29	2.3	3.2	3.3	3.2
30–34	2.0	2.0	3.8	4.7
35–39	0.8	0.5	1.0	1.4
40+	0.2	0.1	0.1	0.2
Total (incl. not stated)	13.6	18.5	11.0	11.5

Since the early 1980s, the combined effect of the decline in the marriage rate and the postponement of marriage has been such that the married proportion of the 15–29 age group, which had risen from 22% to 32% between 1961 and 1981, has since fallen to 10%. And, whereas in 1981 almost one-third of women aged 20–24 were already married, by 2001 this proportion had fallen to 2%.

Table 6: Marital status of women aged 15–39, 1965–2001 (thousands)

Age Group	*Status*	*1961*	*1981*	*1996*	*2001*
15–29	Single	205.9	282.8	375.7	433.6
	Ever-married	58.4	134.2	63.8	48.2
	Total	264.2	417.1	439.5	481.8
30–39	Single	43.0	27.1	56.2	75.1
	Ever-married	119.7	181.1	206.5	200.2
	Total	162.7	208.2	262.7	275.1

It is still not clear to what extent these radical changes in Irish marriage practice have reflected a postponement of marriage rather than an actual abandonment of this institution. However, a significant element of postponement has certainly been involved, reflected in the fact that whilst in the twelve-year period between 1984 and 1996 the proportion of marriages that involved women at ages under 26 fell by over 65%, the proportion involving women over 26 rose during this period by 130%.

Of its nature, postponement of marriage must involve an initial quite prolonged drop in the marriage rate, followed in time by a recovery as those concerned finally take the plunge. There must be considerable significance in the fact that following a drop of over 30% in the number of marriages between September 1980 and September 1995, by 2001 this figure had risen again by as much as 23%.

It should be said that, for some time past, this trend towards later marriages and first births has been almost universal in Europe. Up to the mid 1970s contraception had been reducing the birth rates for women over 35 throughout Europe, but from the mid 1970s onwards in Scandinavia and Britain, and since the late 1980s in most other EU countries including Ireland, the mean age at childbearing has been rising. By 1995 the Irish birth rate for the 35–39 age group in some countries had actually doubled.

Where Ireland is unique, however, is in the fact that, even at its lowest point in 1987, the number of births to women over 35 was higher than anywhere else in the EU, and the subsequent increase in this rate has kept it above the level of any other EU country, to an extent that must surely be worrying from a health point of view.

There are also some indications that, in addition to the postponement factor, marriage is actually being abandoned by at least some proportion of the new generation in Ireland. The big increase in the number of non-marital births to older mothers may in part at least reflect a growth of cohabitation. Whereas in 1981 only 7% of non-marital births were to women in their thirties, by 1999 this proportion had risen to 17%. The proportion of such births to women aged 25–29 also doubled during this period, rising from 12% to 24%.

Table 7: Non-marital births 1981 and 1999 (thousands)

Age of mother	*1981* No.	*1981* %	*1999* No.	*1999* %
Under 20	1.5	38	3.2	19
20–24	1.6	41	5.9	36
25–29	0.5	12	4.0	24
30–34	0.2	5	2.0	12
35–39	1.0	2	1.0	6
40+	0.0	0	0.2	1
Total	3.9		16.5	

The proportion of second or later non-marital births to women over age 25 rose sharply during this period, from under 40% to about 60%, and, whilst a first non-marital birth may often be the unintended result of a casual encounter, second and later non-marital births are more likely to take place within an established relationship.

In the absence of research into cohabitation in Ireland it is not possible at present to assess the precise extent to which by the end of the 1990s it had become common for non-marital relationships not only to precede marriage but to be maintained without recourse to marriage even after the birth of a child. Whilst in some cases where this happens an undissolved marriage of one or other of the partners could account for this situation, in other cases it may perhaps reflect an actual parental preference for an unrecognized union.

It is even more difficult to get a fix on the number of people who now choose initially to cohabit with a view to marrying when, whether by intent or otherwise, they later become parents. Nor do we

Table 8: Irish births and abortions, 1998 (thousands)

	Marital	Non-Marital	Total
Total births	38.4	15.1	53.6
Abortions*	0.7#	5.2#	5.9
Total pregnancies	39.1	20.3	59.4
Percentage aborted	1.8%	25.5%	9.9%
First Births	11.2	8.0	20.2
Abortions*	0.6+	4.7+	5.4+
Total pregnancies	11.9	12.7	24.6
Percentage aborted	5.40%	37.20%	21.40%
Other Births	27.2	7.1	34.3
Abortions*	0.1	0.5	0.5
Total pregnancies	27.3	7.6	34.9
Percentage aborted	0.2%	6.1%	1.5%

* Abortions in England and Wales to women giving addresses in the Irish State.
# These figures are based on the fact that in 1996 only 11.9% of these abortions were to married women (Green Paper on Abortion, Sept. 1999, Appendix 2, Table 2).
+90%–92% of abortions are first abortions (Green Paper Par. 6.07).

For the pupose of this table it is assumed that, in 1998, 91% of both marital and non-marital abortions were first abortions.

know anything about the proportion who engage in casual premarital sex unrelated to cohabitation.

What we do know is that, in the past two decades, there has been an explosion in the total number of non-marital births. Since 1981 the number of non-marital births has almost quadrupled from just under 4,000 to over 18,000. Non-marital births now constitute 31% of all births, and about 40% of first births. Given that 88% of Irish abortions in England and Wales involve single women, and that only 8%–10% are second abortions,[1] it is clear that just over half of all first pregnancies are now non-marital. Finally, over 35% of first non-marital pregnancies are now aborted in England or Wales.

All these figures ignore the possibility of understatement of abortions in England and Wales to Irish residents, some of whom may give British addresses, as well as leaving out of account abortions to Irish residents in Scotland or Continental countries.

In interpreting these figures account must, however, be taken of several factors. First, there has been the impact of the post-1960 rise in the birth rate and of the drop in emigration upon the *number* of young people in their twenties. And, second, there has been the decline in marriage amongst that age group.

In combination, these factors have since 1981 contributed to a doubling of the number of single people aged 20–39, from 370,000 to 750,000. Consequently the quadrupling of non-marital births since that year has involved a doubling rather than a quadrupling of the *ratio* of non-marital births to the number of single young people.

In the year 2001, the 18,000 non-marital births involved 3.5 births per 100 single women in the 15–39 age cohort, and the pregnancy rate for this cohort was about 4.6 per 100. By contrast, the marital fertility rate for this cohort in that year was 17 per 100. However, this four-fold differential between marital and non-marital birth rates is much lower in older age groups; indeed, for women over 40 the non-marital birth rate is now higher than that for married women.

Within the EU, only the three Scandinavian members, plus Britain, France and Austria appear to have higher proportions of non-marital births than Ireland. However, because of the phenomenon of cross-border abortions, as well as uncertainty as to the proportion of abortions that are marital in different countries, international comparisons of the proportion of non-marital *pregnancies* are not available. Nevertheless, although abortion rates are higher for women in many other countries than for Irish women, it may be doubted whether the inclusion of this abortion factor would bring the non-marital pregnancy rate of the other eight EU countries above the Irish figure.

It should perhaps also be noted that there is other more concrete evidence that a significant proportion of single mothers are in stable relationships with the natural fathers at the time of the births: as long ago as 1986–88 this was the case with 50% of non-marital births in Holles Street Hospital.[2] Moreover, the Irish experience has been that one-quarter of natural fathers spend some of each day with their child, while over half of such fathers share some of the parenting role with the mother, two-thirds of whom were living with their family a year later.[3]

Finally, it may be noted that, despite the temptation to deny cohabitation because of the social welfare provision for lone parents, claims by mothers for lone parent allowances in 1996 related to only 80,000 children, despite the fact that there had been 120,000 non-marital births in the preceding sixteen years. This suggests that at least one-third of mothers of non-marital children either marry later or enter into a stable relationship with a supportive partner, although not necessarily with the father of their child.

It is well known that marriage breakdowns are increasingly common. The 1996 Census showed that 9% of couples within the age range 33–42, which is the cohort most affected by the rising trend of marriage breakdown, were separated in that year, which represented an increase of three percentage points by comparison with the separation rate for this group five years earlier.

At the time of the second divorce referendum, I expressed the view that the Irish divorce rate would probably end up within the range of 15–20%, a good deal higher than in Italy, and perhaps somewhat higher than in Spain, but somewhat lower than the divorce rate for Catholics in Northern Ireland and barely one-third of the level in Britain. Allowing for the fact that the current divorce rate may still contain something of a back-log element, the fact that in 1999–2000 the ratio between divorce applications and divorces granted and the average annual number of marriages in the period 1960–1989 were respectively 17% and 13%, suggests that my estimate may turn out to be about right. It may be worth noting, incidentally, that the number of legal separations has fallen by one-third since the introduction of divorce.

Such are the basic facts about the changes that have taken place in Irish social mores during the 1980s and 1990s. The picture is disturbing in several respects. The speed with which such huge changes have taken place has been quite extraordinary in a society that had for long been stable to the point of being in some respects unhealthily stagnant. It is difficult indeed to think of any other country within which so many and so great social changes have occurred within such a short period.

Clearly, against a background of gradually changing mores throughout the industrial world as a whole, the sudden shift from economic stagnation in Ireland forty years ago to quite rapid economic growth in most of the subsequent period, set forces in motion underneath the surface of our society the full effects of which have become evident only after a delay of several decades.

As late as 1981, twenty years after the start of this growth cycle, most people still saw the social effects of the preceding period of economic growth in quite a positive light. This was because the marriage boom and the increase in births that had marked the two preceding decades seemed at that time to offer a positive prospect of social stability combined with a renewed social dynamic, whilst a rise in non-marital births and the emergence of a significant level of Irish abortions in Britain had not yet attracted much attention.

For my own part, I can recall the exhilaration I experienced at the crowds of young couples with their families that thronged the streets as I campaigned in the June 1981 election – something that seemed to bode well for the future of our society.

What were the precipitating elements in the process of radical social change which started imperceptibly in the 1970s and became increasingly apparent as we moved through the 1980s? Although there are several specifically Irish aspects, most of the forces at work have been operating in all industrial societies over many decades. In the Irish case they simply started later than elsewhere and were compressed into a shorter period.

These factors can, I believe, be summarized under six main headings: the growth of individualism; the much wider use of contraception; the expansion of female employment; the rapid increase in the level of education attained by young women; the decline in religious belief; and practice; and what seems like a reversal of social pressures that previously operated against premarital sex.

First, and perhaps most fundamental, has been the growth of individualism in Western society. The culture of earlier periods was marked by, and required for the stability of society, strong social constraints: individuals had to conform to social norms, and there were limited opportunities for pursuing personal goals. Moreover, traditional Christian teaching in Europe blended respect for the individual, made in the image of God, with a strong social ethic that was designed to ensure social stability and, even more fundamental, the successful survival of the human race. Under conditions in which a high proportion of children failed to survive to maturity, this latter objective was seen as best achieved by unconstrained procreation taking place within the shelter of a two-parent nuclear family.

However, during the nineteenth and twentieth centuries, humanity, especially in industrialized countries, increasingly came to master its environment, and some of the social constraints previously needed for human survival thus became less necessary, leaving room for the development of an individualism which has expressed itself through – and in turn has been intensified by – the rapid development of urbanization and of the market system and capitalism.

Childbearing, which had previously been an inevitable consequence of marriage for all but a small proportion of infertile couples, ceased to be inevitable, and, with much improved health conditions, could, without risk to the survival of the human race, be constrained. Indeed the risk to human survival shifted rapidly from a danger of too few children to a danger of too many, namely overpopulation.

This radical and almost overnight change in the evolutionary conditions of the human race served to undermine the rationale of the social constraints within which it had previously to operate, and opened up a much wider range of human choices than before. And this in turn paved the way for the release of an individualism which, until and unless constrained by modified social norms appropriate to this changed human condition, may prove to have a socially destructive potential.

In the second place, an associated development that greatly enlarged the scope for uninhibited individualism has been the emergence and wide availability of forms of contraception. On the one hand, this has provided parents with a means of limiting family size to compensate for the huge increase in child survival rates, whilst also making it possible for women to avoid late pregnancies that are both dangerous for them and are more liable to produce children with mental or physical defects, a possibility of which, because of workforce pressures, they are currently tending to ignore. But, at the same time, contraception has also greatly weakened the constraints on extra-marital sexual relations, thus removing what had formerly offered something of an incentive to early marriage.

One of the effects of these developments seems to have been a significant shift in motivation amongst young people, involving a new emphasis on self-fulfilment at the expense of fulfilment through procreation. 'Child-bearing is becoming a transient rather than a central activity for many parents.'[4] The priority previously accorded to having children and successfully raising them has been replaced by a priority in favour of what is seen as the achievement of personal fulfilment. The rapid growth of marriage breakdown has derived largely from this aspect of individualism.

Associated with this individualist factor has been the emergence of a reluctance by young people to commit themselves to the kind of long-term relationship that is involved in marriage. This is an understandable reaction in the case of children of broken, or troubled, marriages but, to what appears a puzzling extent, it seems to be shared by most children of successful marriages, who in the past would have been encouraged by their parents' example to find a life-partner early in their own lives.

The explanation sometimes given for this – that it is due to concern with the increase in the average lifespan – is in my view unconvincing, because the scale of the increase in the human lifespan that has taken place within the period during which young people have 'decommitted' – in the case of Ireland no longer than a quarter of a century – has been much too short to have had such an impact.

The third factor contributing to radical changes affecting the family has been the movement into the labour force of a large proportion of women who had previously worked in the home. This has relieved frustrations which many, albeit not all, women had previously felt at being housebound. The urge on the part of women to self-fulfilment through employment outside the home has also been facilitated by wider availability and use of contraception, which can secure either the earlier termination of childbearing or postponement of the initiation of this process. Initially, it was used by women primarily for the former purpose, more at first on health grounds than with a view to resuming employment but latterly it has been employed mainly with a view to initiating, maintaining, and prolonging a career, through the postponement of both marriage and childbearing.

Delays in the family initiation process have, however, failed to resolve, indeed may even have intensified, the tensions inherent in women's dual capacity as bearers and early nurturers of children and also as people with a capacity to play an equal role with men in the labour force. This problem may currently be particularly acute in Ireland where, to a greater extent than in some other countries, the increase in the number of young women in the labour force has taken the form of full-time employment and where, in the 1980s at any rate, husbands of employed women spent only four more hours a week in housework than husbands of women engaged full time in the home.[5]

It should, perhaps, be added that, because of the lesser provision of childcare in Ireland, lone mothers here are less likely to be employed than in other EU countries.[6]

The resolution of all these tensions has not been helped by the fact that the pattern of work outside the home that had been evolved by men over centuries has not proved suitable, and has not been adapted to, the needs of those women endeavouring to fulfil this demanding dual role. The failure to accommodate our system of work to the fuller participation of women in the workforce, and more generally the failure of men to adjust their roles in the home to the new gender equality situation, are certainly elements that have aggravated the marriage breakdown factor.

Fourth, there is a clear correlation between the educational level attained by women and the postponement of marriage and childbirth. The rapid rise in Irish educational attainment in recent decades has thus been a significant factor in the shift towards later marriages and first births.

A fifth factor in the changes that have been taking place in relation to the family has been the rapid decline in religious practice, for there is evidence that in Ireland marriage breakdown is more common amongst people with no religious affiliation.[7] In many other industrialized countries this process began several centuries ago and was well advanced by the time social changes affecting the family began to emerge. In Ireland, however, these two processes have effectively coincided. We have squeezed into a single quarter of a century developments that in countries like Britain and France were spread sequentially over two centuries. This specifically Irish phenomenon has not, I think, been widely enough recognized.

In this country there has, in fact, been something of a backlash – recently intensified by the Church's handling of the clerical child abuse scandal – against the conservatism of the institutional Catholic Church. In the past the Church had acted as some kind of dam behind which, during the third quarter of the twentieth century, pressure for change built up on a scale that could not forever be denied. When that dam burst in the final quarter of the century, this led eventually to something equivalent to a storm flood.

What is now clear is that the primary source of societal constraints in relation to sexual behaviour in Irish society had previously been a purely religious ethic, the rational basis of which was fatally underplayed by the Catholic Church in particular. For with the evaporation, for one reason or another, of the religious authority behind a constraint which, to a much larger degree than most people realized at the time, had come to be felt to be an externally imposed set of values, many young people, and some older ones also, found nothing solid left to hang on to.

Successive generations were left largely in ignorance of the fact that most of the Christian Churches' moral teaching actually corresponded to a rational ethic, founded on the needs of society. The gap left in Ireland by the absence of a distinct, but closely linked, civic ethic, which could have provided a continuing firm basis for such societal institutions as marriage, has since proved very damaging indeed.

Moreover, however paradoxical it may seem, the delay in the introduction of civil divorce may also have contributed to the undermining of marriage. For, in the absence of divorce, marriage breakdowns during the 1970s and the 1980s led increasingly to the formation of informal unions on a scale that soon led to a ready acceptance of such arrangements as normal elements in society. It was, in fact, concern at the way in which marriage was thus being marginalized, in a manner damaging to social stability, that led me as Taoiseach to initiate the divorce referendum of 1986.

Unfortunately, neither side in that divorce debate proved willing even to address this key issue. The institutional Church chose to campaign on the basis of simplistic and unverified sociological assertions, bolstered up by a dubious 'floodgate theory', which was sometimes combined with theological statements of a kind that were irrelevant to the issue of civil divorce. And these Church spokesmen were backed by lay advocates who deployed emotive arguments about property, designed to frighten those who owned assets of various kinds, especially land.

Meanwhile, on the other side, most of the advocates of divorce were largely content to make a specious claim that something called a civic right existed to repudiate marriage contracts that had been entered into on the basis of indissolubility, backing up this claim with hard cases of the kind that make bad law.

There was simply no willingness to debate seriously the issue of whether we had or had not reached the stage at which the absence of any kind of divorce was creating a society in which the proliferation of unrecognized unions was undermining marriage to a greater extent than the availability of divorce was likely to do. Whilst I recognize, of course, that the merit of that argument was, and remains, necessarily a matter of judgement, I have to say that the way events developed since 1986 has strengthened my belief that in the interest of social stability divorce should have been introduced a good deal earlier, probably in the 1970s.

To the five factors just mentioned, a sixth should be added. Just as in the past social pressures and example helped to maintain the older pattern of marriage and childbearing, as well as rejection of premarital sex, such pressures and example now operate in the opposite direction. Those who have adopted a lifestyle that includes premarital sexual activity and postponement or abandonment of marriage are often motivated to justify this stance by creating social pressures favouring this new way of life. Young people, who are strongly influenced by peer pressures, may find it difficult to resist such a prevalent climate of opinion within their own generation.

The range and scale of the pressures that now operate against marriage, and which also favour late marital childbearing, is such that it is not easy to see what effective measures can be taken to counter them. Moreover, the climate of social opinion is predominantly hostile to 'judgmental' interventions that favour one lifestyle as against another. Indeed, sociologists point to the often perverse effects of past judgmentalist approaches, for example, the impact of judgmentalist attitudes towards non-marital births upon the tolerance of, and growing resort to, abortion by Irish young people in and after the 1970s.

However, these considerations have somewhat less force in today's permissive climate and, whilst the case for caution in respect of interventions designed to influence social mores is a strong one, it would be wrong to rule out consideration being given to steps that might improve the working of our society. Only very dogmatic liberals would absolutely oppose any such intervention.

The problem is to devise actions that would help to reduce promiscuity, strengthen the stability of marriage, and reduce the pressures that are currently pushing ever-later the initiation of families but which would not at the same time prove counterproductive or have negative side effects.

One measure that would not be contested socially, and which would certainly alleviate pressures favouring late initiation of families, would be the introduction of paid parental leave in Ireland. In the EU only Ireland, Britain and Luxembourg lack this provision. Such a move might encourage many working wives to bring forward their first pregnancy to a much earlier date, to the advantage of both mother and babies. There would, no doubt, be strong pressure from business sources against such a move, all the more so because of the labour shortage that developed in the late 1990s. Nevertheless, I believe that the longer-term good of our society requires such a move.

The provision or subsidization by the State of childcare facilities, at least to the less well off, if accompanied by parallel measures to assist non-labour force parents caring for their children at home, would also help, as would much more generous Child Allowance provisions. Despite recent marked improvements, our Child Allowance provisions still remain less generous than in many EU countries. It would also certainly be desirable that positive disincentives to marriage in our income transfer system – income tax and social welfare – be eliminated.

Examples of the extent to which our present system discourages lone parents from marrying, are given in chapter 1 of the *Report of the Working Group examining the Treatment of Married, Cohabiting, and One-Parent Families under the Tax and Social Welfare*

Codes (September 1999). In some cases income losses of up to 35% can arise through marriage or, of course, through an admission of cohabitation. That Working Group offered five options designed to remedy, individually or in combination, these negative features of our existing transfer system, which have yet to be addressed.

A more difficult area is the provision of direct incentives for marriage. Opposition to this would come from those who would see this as involving a judgmentalism that would reflect negatively on people who for one reason or another are in unrecognized unions. To this objection there are several possible responses.

First of all, the widespread social acceptance of such unions today, and the fact that they are no longer effectively forced upon some couples by the absence of divorce, have weakened the anti-judgmental argument. Moreover, there is, I believe, a real difference between, on the one hand, positively discriminating against unrecognized unions – something that is still a feature of our Constitution and of some of our legislation – and, on the other hand, encouraging marriage, which is an institution that the State, on behalf of society, has a legitimate interest in supporting.

A bigger difficulty is that artificial incentives may achieve not only the purpose they are designed to achieve but may also have unintended negative effects. For example, it can be argued that incentives for marriage might over-persuade some couples who are ill suited to entering upon a permanent relationship, and thus eventually increase the marriage breakdown problem.

Nevertheless, given the scale of both postponement and abandonment of marriage in Ireland today, the idea of some kind of incentives for marriage should not be dismissed out of hand.

More generally, the case for much more intensified relationship education is a strong one in the wider social interest. Many of our family problems today are not due to inherent parental character defects but to lack of early preparation for this aspect of life – something that many parents clearly have difficulty about personally offering to their children. Leaving these matters to the much later stage of pre-marriage courses is irresponsible. In many cases, attitudes and habits have already been formed long before that point is reached.

The Churches, as well as the State, have a role to play here, given that the vast majority of children still attend confessional schools. This responsibility has not always been exercised sensibly or effectively.

On the one hand, when, as often happens during the later stages of childhood, religious authority is rejected, an earlier failure to establish in the minds of the children in question the fact that traditional teaching on issues related to marriage was founded on a rational appreciation of human needs, opens the way to irresponsible behaviour. Reason is not a dangerous rival to religion as some churchmen seem to believe. In areas like this it can instead provide a reinforcement of religious teaching.

Next, to the extent that the credibility of the Catholic Church's basic stance on marriage is undermined by some late accretions to that Church's teaching – such as the invalidity of non-Catholic marriages of Catholics, as well as the Pauline and Petrine privileges, and the bigamous remarriage of some undivorced partners of annulled marriages (the latter of which seems to have been a peculiarly Irish phenomenon) – these urgently need to be reviewed.

But, the biggest obstacle in the way of the Catholic Church being able to recover credibility in these matters remains the rejection by Pope Paul VI of the majority view of the Church's Commission on Contraception. That contraception can be – is indeed certain to be – abused by many is no more a reason for banning it than drunkenness is a reason for declaring the consumption of alcohol to be a mortal sin. And the alternative approach of attempting to make a fundamental moral distinction between 'natural' and 'artificial' contraception is not merely unconvincing but is the kind of thing that gives theology a bad name.

It is probably the case that until this blunder has been retrieved – if that be possible – the capacity of the Catholic Church to offer persuasive leadership in matters sexual will remain negligible.

More generally, it seems to me that in addressing societal issues we have suffered from the fact that intellectual life in Ireland, as in Britain, has been predominantly literary, rather than philosophical/political. At a time of rapid social change it is, I think, a serious deficiency that we seem to lack the wider intellectual interest in social and philosophical issues that has been such a characteristic of some other societies, such as that of France. This has led to a most disturbing absence of informed debate about the many recent developments that affect marriage in our society in a most fundamental way.

First of all, public awareness of demographic changes in our society lags far behind the reality: we are living in a society that is now quite different from the one to which we were accustomed in the quite recent past, and most people are only dimly aware of, or, to the extent that they are so aware, greatly underestimate the scale and significance of the changes that have taken place in social behaviour.

Second, such discussion as has taken place on these issues has tended to be simplistically polarized between often rather inarticulate conservative voices on the one hand and highly vocal liberal, and sometimes extreme feminist, writers and speakers on the other. This type of polarization, beloved of the media, and especially of television, kills serious debate.

Third, there does not seem to be any forum within which such a serious debate can be effectively organized. There is, of course, much discussion of social policy amongst professional sociologists, who through their research and publications are making a major contribution to our knowledge of aspects of these problems. But the wider community, including many opinion-formers, and others who ought to be opinion-formers, are not involved in this internal professional process, and are often unaware of many of the issues at stake.

It is, perhaps, time that we faced up to these deficiencies in our intellectual life.

8 The productivity of Irish education

There is an aspect of Irish education that seems to me to merit more attention than it has ever received, namely its high productivity in terms of the combined quantity and quality of its output, in relation to the resources that are devoted to it. I devote most of this chapter to this issue.

In 1998, the latest year for which at the time of writing international comparisons with Irish education were available from the OECD, the Irish educational system absorbed a considerably higher proportion of public spending than elsewhere in the EU: 13.5% as against an EU average figure of 10%. But, because in 1998 only 35.4% of Irish GNP was devoted to public spending as against 46.5% in the rest of the EU, (by 2001 the Irish public spending GNP ratio was slightly lower than in 1998), this higher proportion of our public spending devoted to education yielded a share of GNP close to that elsewhere in the EU – estimated at 5.3%, as against 5.7% in the rest of the EU. (Because of the ways in which they are derived the relationships between these sets of figures are approximate rather than perfect, but they are close enough for comparative purposes.)

Now, when we look at the average amount spent per student in that year, we find that when measured in terms of the purchasing power of money in different countries, Irish spending per higher education student was almost 10% above the EU average but spending per student at the primary and secondary levels was about one-third lower in 1998 than in the rest of the EU. At purchasing power parities measured in dollar terms, spending per primary student in 1998 was $2,745 as against approximately $4,000 in the rest of the EU. At second level the comparative figures were $3,934 for Ireland and c.$6,000 for the rest of the EU.

In the four years since that year spending per primary student rose in Ireland by 16%, i.e. pro rata with the cost of living, and in the case of the secondary sector by 22%, slightly more than the cost of living.

However, in those four years both GNP in current money terms and total public spending rose by far more than this, by 50% in fact. The fact is that public spending on education as a share of GNP has been in decline since 1994 and as a share of public expenditure it also fell between 1998 and 2000.

Why has spending per head at primary and second level been so much lower in Ireland?

First of all, in 1998 Ireland's per capita GNP was lower than in the rest of the EU, in purchasing power parity terms: at that time we were still poorer than our partners, a gap that has since been effectively closed.

Second, and much more important, the share of the Irish population accounted for by children of school-going age in 1998 was one-third higher than in the rest of the EU. In 1998, 24% of our population was in the 5–19 age group, as against an average of 18% in the rest of the EU. (By 2002 the Irish figure had fallen to about 22.25%.)

Because of the fall in the birth rate between 1980 and 1995, and the consequential sharp fall already under way in the numbers of new second-level students, we can expect a considerable reduction in the current pressure on resources in this educational sector during the next decade. The drop in numbers during the decade ahead is estimated by OECD at 24%, as against a forecast decline of 5% in the rest of the EU. But, for reasons given below, in the following decade starting around 2010 there will be a reversal of this drop, on quite a substantial scale.

However, at the primary level, where in the rest of the EU numbers are expected to fall by 12% in the next decade, the drop in our case over this period is forecast by OECD to be quite small. Moreover, this OECD estimate of a small drop may in fact now be out of date because I do not think it takes account of the rise of over one-fifth in the birth rate that has taken place since 1994 – although, of course, part of this has been accounted for by babies born to immigrants.

However, even if this rise in births is not sustained during the period ahead, the numbers of primary students in Ireland is more likely to have risen than to have fallen by 2010, in very marked contrast to the situation in the rest of the EU.

There is also a third factor affecting adversely the volume of teaching resources that can be provided with a given amount of finance. This is the fact that in Ireland in 1994 86% of educational spending was being used to pay teachers compared with an EU figure of 65%. (The Irish figure has since fallen to 76% of current educational expenditure.) OECD figures also show that in 1998 primary and secondary teachers' pay in Ireland was already somewhat higher than in most of the EU. In fact, if the exceptional case of Germany is excluded, Irish teachers' pay at all levels emerges as having been between 4% and 28% higher than in the rest of the EU in 1998.

Since that year pay has risen here by 22.5%. I have no information on teachers' pay increases elsewhere in the EU, but I greatly doubt that pay has risen by more than this figure in the rest of the Community.

Table 9: Teachers' Pay 1998 ($000s @ PPP)

		Ireland	*EU Average*	*EU Average Excl. Germany*
Primary				
	Bottom	22.0	22.0	21.0
	15 Years	35.5	29.5	27.5
	Top	40.0	35.5	34.5
Lower Secondary				
	Bottom	23.0	24.5	22.0
	15 Years	36.0	31.5	29.5
	Top	40.5	40.5	39.0

Given that teachers' pay has since 1998 risen by about 22.5% (about 7% more than the cost of living), and looks like rising further sharply from this level as a result of benchmarking, this factor, in combination with the abnormally high share of Irish educational spending that is already accounted for by teachers' pay, must raise further the Irish share of GNP that would be required to provide any given volume of teacher resources. It is, perhaps, worth remarking that these higher average pay rates of teachers probably reflect a higher entrance standard to the profession than in some other countries. Whilst I have no entrance standard data relating to teachers elsewhere, I doubt whether at primary level the standard in many other countries is equivalent to the 430 points level that applies to Irish primary teachers, or that at secondary level elsewhere the entrance standard is equivalent to a second class Honours degree, as has been the case in Ireland. (Incidentally the current entrance standard for secondary teachers is near the top of 2.2 range, and in view of the fact that current research is suggesting that honours standards here have been somewhat higher than in Britain, this is perhaps the equivalent of a 2.1 degree in the neighbouring island.)

When all these factors are taken into account, it must be clear that we have not hitherto been able to provide our students with material resources on the same scale as our EU partners enjoy and we are unlikely to be able to match them in this respect in the years immediately ahead. Our unique demography has posed, and for some time to come will continue to pose, a serious problem for the public authorities responsible for Irish education policy, although qualitatively we may compensate for these quantitative deficiencies.

An obvious casualty of Irish resource constraints in education is the student/teacher ratio at both primary and second levels. In 1999 the Irish primary student/teacher ratio was 21.1 as against 17.6 in the rest of the EU. (By 2000/01 the Irish figure had increased marginally to 20.3.) At second level the figures in 1999 were respectively 15.4 and 13.8, a smaller differential of about 10%, and by 2000/01 the Irish figure had fallen to 14.0, due to an increase of 6% in the number of teachers combined with a drop in numbers of students.

As recently as 1991 the Irish primary student/teacher ratio had been 35% below that of the rest of the EU and the second-level ratio had been 16% lower, so there have been considerable improvements in this respect during the past decade.

At 935 hours per year, Irish intended student hours at second level in 1999 were close to the EU average, although there may be a slightly lower rate of actual delivery of hours. The OECD figures show that ancillary spending (i.e. other than on teachers' salaries) in 1999 was lower in Ireland than anywhere in the EU outside Italy and Greece. A glance at Northern Ireland's school facilities shows how far behind we are in this respect. This is the area in which we have skimped most.

Recent figures show that in Ireland prose literacy is at the average EU level, and maths achievement is reported by OECD to be 3.5% better than the EU average. It is also notable that US industrialists have consistently cited the quality of the educational system in terms of the output of well-educated, adaptable and motivated workers as a major reason for having located in Ireland.

Moreover, the very high proportion of Irish school students who apply for, and the number who are subsequently successful, in higher education also testifies to their quality. So far as the age of departure from second-level education is concerned, with 74% still in education at age 18 in 1999 (63% full time, and 11% part time), Ireland was then at the mid point in the list of figures for educational participation of 18-year-olds in EU countries. However, because the very low UK figure of 53% (almost one-third lower than ours), has a disproportionate effect upon the EU average, Ireland emerges slightly ahead of that weighted average.

Table 10: Percentage of 18-year-olds still in education, 1999

Sweden	95	Ireland	74
Belgium	85	Italy	69
Finland	85	Austria	67
Germany	85	Portugal	66
France	80	Spain	66
Netherlands	80	UK	53
Denmark	76	EU Average	70

It is thus clear that primary and second-level education is under-resourced, to the tune of something like one-third. But the evidence also suggests that the average standard reached by Irish students is at or slightly above the EU average, and that the proportion who complete education to age 18 is slightly higher than the EU average. Thus in terms of what might be called 'educational productivity' – output in qualitative and quantitative terms related to inputs of resources – Ireland seems to have been performing about 50% better than the rest of the EU.

This clearly poses a question: what could account for this high educational productivity? I have been posing this question since I first made calculations of this kind in connection with speeches I had to make as Taoiseach almost twenty years ago, and I have been puzzled by the fact that no one, so far as I am aware, seems yet to have attempted to answer it. Clearly there are non-quantitative factors at work here, which must involve either the teachers, or the students, or both.

First of all I think that the high level of purchasing power of teachers' pay in Ireland relative to our average GNP per head, and thus relative to that of other workers in Ireland, has reflected the higher status and reputation of teachers here, by comparison with some other parts of the EU, for instance Britain.

It is, I believe, a diminution in this high relative status in the past few years, as other groups have secured significant improvements in pay not matched by the teaching profession, that has given rise to the recent unrest in the profession, especially as this delay in adjustment coincided with an exceptional rise in house prices which put reasonable housing, especially in Dublin, outside the financial range of those entering the profession.

This recent temporary drop in teacher morale arising from the delays in addressing this problem should not be allowed to obscure the fact that until this issue arose the morale of teachers in Ireland was good, arising from their high status and from the fact that, as a proportion of GNP per head, i.e. in relation to the rest of the Community, they were well paid. The fact that by comparison with other countries the position and status of Irish teachers has been favourable, and that their morale has traditionally been high, may, I suggest, have been an important influence on the fact that in Ireland, despite the marked absence of resources on a scale approaching that which other Western European educational systems have enjoyed, the output of the education system has been quantitatively and qualitatively equal to that of the much more generously financed educational systems of most EU countries.

The key test of the achievement of Irish teachers has in my view been the achievement of a high standard by pupils in the face of unfavourable student/teacher ratios, which, as recently as a decade ago, were one-third worse in primary and one-sixth worse in second level than in the rest of the EU.

Of course it does not follow that a better performance by Irish teachers' offers the whole of the explanation for the 50% higher level of educational productivity in Ireland. Indeed it would be surprising if the whole of this difference could be explained by this single factor. The students could also provide part of the explanation.

There is at least anecdotal evidence in favour of the thesis that most Irish school students are on average better motivated than students elsewhere. In this connection it is, I believe, relevant that although Ireland has been largely urbanized during the past half century, the proportion of people living in areas of urbanized disadvantage is lower here than in most other EU countries. The great majority of Irish people still live in rural areas, in small towns, or in those suburbs of cities that are not marred by social disadvantage. Moreover, many urban-dwellers have a rural background. Thus in the case of Dublin a significant proportion of the population – about three out of eight – were born elsewhere in Ireland (over one-sixth), or have a parent or parents born elsewhere in Ireland (one-fifth of Irish people in Dublin in 1961 had been born outside Dublin).

Now, rural Ireland has always had a strong tradition of respect for education. The hedge schools are not a myth; statistics exist showing a very significant minority of Irish children being educated in such schools well before the introduction of the national primary education system in the 1830s, a development which, at the instance of an Irish educational reformer, Sir Thomas Wyse, began some twenty years earlier than in Britain.

The extraordinary response to the introduction of free private as well as public second-level education in the late 1960s also demonstrated the continuing high educational motivation of Irish parents.

The source of this may lie in the fact that until the late 1950s only half of each age cohort survived in Ireland to age 35, and the vast majority of those who emigrated came from rural areas and had secured primary education only, with little prospect, therefore, of anything other than manual employment in the countries to which they emigrated.

Amongst what was still in the 1960s a largely rural population – in 1961 only 40% were living in cities, boroughs, urban districts or environs of such centres – parents were deeply concerned to improve the prospects of their children, in order to maximize their chances of employment in Ireland and to improve their prospects as emigrants. Parents thus responded with enthusiasm to the opportunity provided by the availability of free private as well as public second-level education from the late 1960s onwards.

That this rural-based concern for education remains an important factor today may be seen from the fact that the proportion of 19–21-year-olds attending universities is 45% higher in the case of the less well off west and south of Ireland than in the case of Dublin and the eastern counties.

A further indication of the high average level of student motivation is the fact that some 80% of school leavers apply each year for higher education. (In 1997 the number of applicants for higher education was almost 64,000, which was equal to 95% of that year's school leavers, but these included school leavers of earlier years as well as students from outside the state.)

The 1999 Clancy survey of the reasons why some students decline higher education offers shows that 10% of applicants were ineligible and a further 13% did not secure an offer, but the fact that these students had nevertheless applied for a third-level place shows that it is not only the better students who aspire to continue their studies. The fact that some 17% of school leavers take Post Leaving Certificate (PLC) courses also demonstrates a very positive attitude of school leavers to education.

High educational motivation of parents outside the relatively limited areas of urban disadvantage appears to have communicated itself to their children, whose motivation seems to compare very favourably with that of students in other more urbanized EU countries, notably Britain.

Thus, high student as well as teacher motivation may be a contributory factor to high educational productivity in Ireland.

So much for the productivity of Irish education. But whilst the proportion of Irish 18-year-olds who complete second-level education matches, may be slightly higher than the EU average, and whilst the standard of successful school leavers in Ireland may be at a level broadly comparable with that of such students elsewhere in the EU, does the system cater adequately for the less able, and those from disadvantaged backgrounds? That is less certain.

In the effort to produce a well-educated group of school leavers, half of whom will be capable of benefiting from higher education either in Institutes of Technology or universities, the present system may not be catering adequately for a minority of students with learning difficulties or from disadvantaged backgrounds that have made it difficult for them to develop their talents.

Whilst the provision of remedial teachers in recent times has gone some distance towards helping to resolve the first of these problems, there seems to have been resistance within the system to concentrating additional teacher resources on areas of disadvantage. This may need to be tackled more energetically.

9 State and Church

Because the informal relationship between State and Church in Ireland has been so intimate in the past, we cannot readily appreciate how strange the absence of any formal links between the two must appear to many Europeans who have come from a very different historical situation. For, to an extent that we in Ireland do not appreciate, many European states still carry some traces of the post-Reformation principle, '*Cujus regio, ejus religio*' – the religion of the ruler determines the religion of the state.

We are, of course, aware of the operation of this principle in neighbouring Britain, where the monarch is the 'Supreme Governor' of the Church of England and where the appointment of bishops of that church is a Crown prerogative, exercised by the Prime Minister of the day, whatever his religion, or lack of it.

In a number of Scandinavian countries the Lutheran Churches are state churches, the clergymen being civil servants, paid by the state. In Germany there are religious taxes to support the churches, from which citizens can exempt themselves, but at the cost of losing the right to the sacraments, e.g. holy communion, marriage and burial in a confessional churchyard. And there is a German concordat with the Holy See which regulates relations between Rome and Germany – including, anomalously, Alsace-Lorraine in France.[1] Moreover, in Greece the Orthodox Church is a State church, and Italy, like Germany, has a concordat, originally signed by Pope Pius XI with Mussolini in 1929, which regulates Church–State relations there. Moreover, whilst post-Franco Spain terminated its concordat with Rome, I believe it was replaced by four formal Agreements.[2]

Ireland is thus something of an odd-man-out in its absence of formal relations between Church and State. The unusual character of our situation was brought home to me quite forcibly in 1983 when the Government I led was advised by the Attorney General that the wording of a proposed amendment to the Constitution with respect to abortion that had been devised by Charles Haughey just before the November 1982 general election – which at the time I had accepted without adequate consideration – was defective because of dangerous ambiguities in the wording.

Concerned that the Roman Catholic hierarchy should not misunderstand the rationale of what had thus become a necessary revision of this wording, and in the absence of any formal channel of communication between the State and the Catholic Church, in the course of driving to an appointment in the west I called on a bishop whom I knew to ask him to convey to his colleagues what had happened and to initiate a meeting between the Government and the Catholic hierarchy on the issue. This courteous informal approach was flatly rejected by the hierarchy in favour of an indirect contact through an intermediary, which proved entirely abortive. I have to say that I formed the opinion at the time that this refusal stemmed from a view on the part of the hierarchy that it would be easier for them to reject any change in the wording regardless of the merits of the case if they did not have to face across the table the cogent reasons that had led to our decision.

Another case where I faced the curious absence of any formal channel of communication with the Catholic hierarchy arose a year or two later when I was informed through diplomatic channels that the Holy See was about to open full diplomatic relations with the United Kingdom, on a basis that would not prejudice the ecclesiastical role of the Dublin Nuncio with respect to Northern Ireland. (This was an arrangement that the Irish State had always been concerned to maintain, due to unhappy memories of the way in which contacts between the British Government and the Holy See in the pre-independence period had worked to the disadvantage of the Irish people.)

In the absence of any formal State–Church channel of communication, I took the initiative on this matter by ringing Cardinal Ó Fiaich directly. He told me at once that he had been aware of this development for some months previously. But although he shared the Government's concern that the Church in Northern Ireland should not be brought within the ambit of the about-to-be-appointed Nuncio in London, it had clearly never occurred to him to inform the Government of this impending development.

It also now seems clear that until very recently the institutional Catholic Church in Ireland felt little or no obligation to report to the civil authorities crimes against children by ministers of the Church, apparently because it felt itself bound only by its own canon law in these matters. A civil law/canon law clash also exists in relation to marriages. Whilst provision exists in Ireland for purely civil marriage ceremonies, the vast majority of weddings in Ireland are religious ceremonies which are then subsequently registered by the clergyman with the civil authorities.[3] This joint marriage system would create no particular problems were it not for the fact that State and Church in Ireland have always had different procedures for declaring marriages to be null and void. Until the foundation of the State there had existed a rarely-used provision for divorce by an Act of the Westminster Parliament, and, with the disestablishment of the Church of Ireland in 1869, the very restrictive Anglican nullity procedure of the Church of Ireland was incorporated into Irish civil law. But quite separate from these civil law procedures have been the Roman Catholic Church's own private arrangements for voiding the sacramental element of joint Church/State marriages.

The Catholic Church's nullity procedures have been increasingly liberalized over the years, to a much greater extent than those of the Irish State, and in quite a number of these cases the Church decree of nullity permits one or both parties to remarry in a church. (In addition to this the Catholic Church also claims the right to, and frequently does, dissolve marriages of non-Christians where one party wishes to marry a Roman Catholic, although I am not aware of any case where this has actually happened in Ireland.)

In Irish law the remarriage in church of a person whose marriage has been annulled by the Catholic Church but not by the civil courts is, of course, bigamous, and those involved are liable to prosecution under the criminal law. However, in practice, the law of the State, and the constitutional provision for the protection of marriage, have frequently been flouted through religious marriages in Catholic churches of couples one of whom was previously married but who has secured a church, but not a state annulment of that marriage. Such bigamous ceremonies are then not registered by the priest with the civil authorities in order to reduce the chance of prosecution for bigamy. No prosecutions have in fact been undertaken in such cases. The informal reason given for this is the alleged difficulty of securing witnesses to such events.

It would appear that Ireland may be unique in having had this particular form of conflict between Church and State law. In other countries, such as Britain where there are such conjoint marriages, this problem was avoided by the Catholic Church actually proposing to a Catholic whose marriage was annulled by the Church that he or she apply for a civil divorce prior to a second marriage – a course of action which the Irish Catholic Church felt itself precluded from proposing in 1986, as it was then opposing the introduction of civil divorce in Ireland, but which, I believe, it may since have adopted.

This issue was raised by Alan Dukes, then Minister for Justice, and I when we met representatives of the Catholic hierarchy in 1986 to discuss the proposed divorce referendum. What occurred at that meeting is a matter of some controversy, the details of which are set out in my autobiography.[4]

Discussion took place at the meeting about how this conflict of jurisdictions might be resolved without actually separating the religious and civil ceremonies, a procedure which I said I was reluctant to propose in view of what I believe to be the attachment of Irish Catholics to the present joint marriage arrangement. The representatives of the hierarchy (who, I should say, did not rule out a separation of civil from sacramental marriages, a move to which it transpired they had given some thought), suggested, however, that in these annulment cases 'a purely religious event was taking place which made no claim and gave no appearance of a civil ceremony' and they went on to propose ways of 'removing any ambiguity'.

This might be done, they suggested, by making a formal declaration disclaiming any civil significance for the marriage, or by holding such a ceremony in the absence of a priest. The government record of the meeting then records a proposal 'that the civil law be changed to provide that where a sacramental marriage could not be a legal civil marriage, because under the civil law one of the parties was still married, the sacramental marriage would not be a civil marriage'. Whilst the wording of this minute is somewhat obscure, and Cardinal Ó Fiaich later denied that such a suggestion was made, both Alan Dukes and I were clear that we were being asked, instead of amending the Constitution, to disregard it by abandoning its requirement to 'guard with special care the institution of Marriage' in order to get the Church off a hook of its own making. We reacted most vigorously against this proposal, to such an extent that the dialogue effectively broke down at that point.

It will be clear from these examples that while there are, of course, clear advantages to the Irish State deriving from the absence of a formal concordat or agreements with the Holy See, our kind of separation of State and Church brings with it its own problems, some of which arise from conflicts of civil and canon law. As Chancellor of the National University, I am reminded of this conflict of laws on a number of occasions each year when I confer an honorary LLD by uttering a traditional Latin phrase that ends with the words: '*doctoratus in utroque jure, tam civile quam canonico*' – doctor in both civil and canon law!

However, the issue of Church–State relations in Ireland runs much deeper than these fairly technical problems might suggest. For the society that our State inherited in 1922 was one in which earlier interactions of the Irish Catholic Church and the British State had left us with a very complex relationship between these two institutions.

It has to be recalled that during earlier centuries the 8% or so of the population who were members of the Church of Ireland held a virtual monopoly of power and wealth in the island. (By 1775 only 5% of the land of Ireland was still retained by the three-quarters of its inhabitants who were Roman Catholics.) From the wealth that that Church and its adherents had accumulated, extensive provision had been made for the social and educational needs of their section of the Irish people.

In the 1830s, however, a non-denominational national primary education system was established through the efforts of a newly-elected Irish Catholic Unionist MP, Sir Thomas Wyse, the right to Catholic membership of parliament having been won in 1829. But within two decades this had effectively been transformed into a denominational system.

For their part, from about 1820 onwards, Catholics, emerging from several centuries of penal laws, had set about building their own churches, and constructing and financing the subsequent running of their own secondary schools, hospitals, orphanages and so on, with, in most cases, very little help from the State. This represented a quite extraordinary achievement by a population who for much of the nineteenth century were living in abject poverty, on a scale matched within Europe only by the lands then comprised within the Turkish Empire. It required both a huge financial effort by an impoverished population and the dedication of a large number of priests, nuns and brothers who gave their services to their flock, in most cases with little or no reward.

The confessional character of the educational and social provisions available to the new Irish State at its foundation had thus been determined much earlier by that state's inheritance from an unhappy and divided past. And these divisions were all the more deep because on the Catholic side they were psychologically reinforced by folk memories of attempts to extend the membership of Protestant churches by such methods as the operation in the eighteenth century of property laws that favoured Catholics who changed their religion, and in the nineteenth century by such methods as the provision of food to starving Catholic families with the same end in view.

Those who today rail against the failure of the Irish State to provide educational and social services on a non-confessional basis tend to overlook completely what our new state inherited from its history. They also ignore the very limited resources that were available to a state the per capita resources of which for many decades remained barely half of those of neighbouring Britain – a state that was moreover faced with the need to rebuild an infrastructure ravished by a most destructive Civil War, and to pay for, and further develop, some welfare services that previous to independence had been financed by transfers from much wealthier Britain.

Later the Irish State was increasingly drawn into supplementing the resources the Churches were applying to educational services, whilst at the same time – partly because of a concern to minimize these subsidies – being unwilling to take responsibility for the conditions that prevailed in some of these institutions, most notably those catering for various forms of disadvantage and where young people were involved.

For its part the Catholic Church authorities jealously guarded their control of the institutions they had created or, in the case of the primary schools, had effectively taken over from the civil authorities in the mid nineteenth century. Moreover the Catholic hierarchy was also concerned to retain a virtual monopoly of secondary as well as primary education of Catholics, and for many decades this inhibited the provision of adequate secondary schooling.

When in 1930 the State sought to supplement Catholic secondary schools which charged fees – admittedly very modest fees in most instances – by establishing free local authority schools, the Church authorities sought a presence in these new educational institutions and also successfully insisted that these new schools concentrate on vocational training, and refrain from providing academic education that might compete with the confessional schools. It was only with great difficulty and after many decades that these local authority schools began to provide a free alternative to the academic education being offered by the confessional secondary schools.

The impact of the Church's attempted monopolization of secondary education for Catholic children was particularly marked in the case of boys' schools in the northern part of the state. North of a line between Dublin and Galway diocesan colleges dominated boys' education, religious orders being actively discouraged from founding boys' schools in most of the dioceses in that part of the state. Thus in this half of the state there were 50% more Catholic schools for girls than for boys, and the number of girls attending Catholic secondary schools was three-eighths higher than the number of boys. Moreover, in other areas such as Cork the only schools allowed to compete with the diocesan colleges were those run by lay brothers. The purpose of all these restrictions was, apparently, to secure for the dioceses concerned, as distinct from religious orders, a monopoly of vocations to the priesthood.

It was only in the mid 1960s that this discrimination against boys' education was exposed by the report *Investment in Education*, as a result of which it was finally tackled by State intervention. Community schools and colleges were founded in areas where educational opportunities for boys had been absent or lacking.

The almost exclusively confessional character of Irish primary and second-level education has recently come under some strain as groups of parents in some urban – and even some rural – areas have sought to escape from this traditional educational system. New types of school have gradually emerged: multi-denominational schools, inter-denominational schools, and *Gaelscoileanna*, each with its own different management arrangements. Furthermore, an increasing number of pupils are attending confessional schools of denominations other than their own.

Hitherto these new developments have been on a small enough scale to avoid disruption of the existing system, but at some point real problems are bound to arise. In a country in which by the end of the 1990s the number of children in primary schools was 20% below its peak and the number of second-level schools had fallen by 10%, it is clearly not going to be possible to keep on proliferating different types of school to meet competing parental demands.

The Constitution (Article 42) guarantees to respect the inalienable right and duty of parents to provide, according to their means, for the religious, and moral, intellectual, physical and social education of their children, in their homes or in private schools, or in schools recognized or established by the State. But it also commits the State to provide for free primary education, and when the public good requires it to provide other educational facilities or institutions, with due regard, however, to the rights of parents especially in the matter of religious and moral formation. Our confessional primary school system has been built up on the basis of State assistance for the construction and running of well over 3,000 schools which are vested in trustees, in almost all cases appointed by churchmen. Most of these, of course, are Roman Catholic schools, a minority being vested in trustees appointed by other Churches where the number of students of a particular denomination in a locality have been judged to warrant such a school.

The minority faiths seem to have accepted the views of the State on what number of students warrants the establishment and running of a school for children of their denomination, but as the number of parents opting out of confessional education grows, it may be more difficult to get agreement on the circumstances in which new non-confessional schools are needed.

On the one hand the guarantee of parents rights to primary education of their choice is firmly embedded in the Constitution, but on the other hand the State cannot be expected to provide for an indefinite multiplication of different types of school throughout the country. At some stage we are likely to come up against problems posed by the absence of a national system involving one local primary school, in each area, with separate provision for the religious needs of pupils of different faiths or none. But I find it hard to see just how in an increasingly pluralist society we can easily get from where we now find ourselves to a coherent system providing for a wider range of needs than we have so far had to cater for, and I am not clear that any thought has yet been given to this issue.

Another problem with our confessional primary schools is the fact that teachers in Catholic primary schools are required to teach the children the religion of that school. As the proportion of teachers who are believers and who are practising members of the Catholic Church declines, this must pose an increasing problem. Hitherto this issue seems to have been simply ignored, although in such cases it cannot be satisfactory from the point of view of Catholic parents, the great majority of whom still want their children to be taught the Catholic faith. Far from the Catholic Church addressing this problem, teachers have been remarking upon what they see as a growing lack of interest by some local clergy in the primary schools. It seems strange that the Church authorities should be content to allow such a situation to develop and to remain insistent that teachers continue to undertake a task which a growing number of them are not, and feel themselves not to be, equipped to perform. At some stage the Catholic Church authorities must surely assume their responsibilities in this matter.

The inherited dependence of the State upon social provisions created by and staffed and run by the Catholic Church has in the past been strongly reinforced by the extraordinary deference shown by both the politicians and the Civil Servants of the new State towards this Church and its leadership. Some, indeed, of these politicians and Civil Servants have had their own special links with the Catholic Church through membership of organizations such as the Knights of Columbanus, and in the past this may well have further inhibited the willingness of the State to take its full responsibility with regard to Church-run social institutions. In government in the 1980s I made sure, by making non-membership of such organizations a condition of Cabinet participation, that ministers, at least, would be free of such possible conflicts of interest.

It should, however, be added that, whilst during the last decade we have learnt much about appalling abuses in certain of these institutions whose staff had allowed themselves to be corrupted by the power they exercised over those under their care, in the vast majority of cases the record of care by religious of both sexes was exemplary, and it was through the generosity of the services they provided that huge resources were made available to cover many of the running costs of the institutions in which they worked, and also in many cases to supplement State provision for the expansion of the system in order to meet the growing needs of our society.

The weakness of this structure – a weakness which at the time was understood by very few – lay in the inherent tendency of all institutions, religious as much as lay, to hide their own defects and to cover up wrongdoing in order to 'avoid scandal'. Just like State structures and private organizations, Churches are poor at self-regulation, and in Ireland the inherited overdependence of the State upon religious institutions to provide a whole range of social services clearly inhibited it from exercising any serious supervision over what was being done under its authority by religious institutions. In the only case where any inspection or review was undertaken – the Carrington Commission seventy years ago – the report of this review was quietly shelved to avoid embarrassment all round.

Great hardship, and in some cases brutality and sexual exploitation, was thus inflicted on what we now know to have been a significant minority of those in institutional care – the scale of which no doubt grew as those responsible for these evils increasingly came to feel they were invulnerable. Nothing can excuse what was done to thousands of people, very many of them children and young people whose subsequent lives were in many cases distorted and embittered by a deep sense of hurt. Because it had to be borne internally and never expressed, this hurt was incapable of relief until, decades later, a different and more humane kind of Irish society discovered a capacity to open itself up to the truth about a terrible part of its past.

But whilst these revelations offer a better hope for the future, they do not provide a guarantee against any future recurrence of abuses of authority unless we build into every part of our society both mechanisms of inspection and opportunities for ventilating grievances, neither of which come easily to bureaucratic and institutional structures, which have a deep instinct to protect themselves against scrutiny. This is not an area where we can ever afford to relax vigilance, especially in a society like ours which is more unequal than many others in Europe.

So far as the institutional Church is concerned, whilst no doubt some lessons have been learnt from recent exposure of evils within its structure, there is still remarkably little evidence that its leaders have grasped what its members now expect of it. The Catholic bishops have clearly been shaken by recent events, but the laity have not received an impression that they share fully the sense of indignation and horror at recent revelations.

It may or may not be the case that in certain instances enforced celibacy is a factor in paedophilia – that remains an open question. But what has deeply disturbed many lay people, and above all those who are parents, has been the lack of evidence that those of our celibate clergy who have become bishops understand emotionally as well as intellectually that abuse of children and young people by those in authority over them is many orders of magnitude more horrifying than most of the other sexual sins about which churchmen in Ireland have traditionally been so exercised.

To put it mildly, the persistent cover-up of many cases of this kind by bishops here and elsewhere, and the way these revelations have subsequently been handled by them, has not conveyed the impression that celibate bishops' emotions are in tune with those of parents. And this aspect of celibacy has placed a totally new kind of barrier between laity and episcopacy.

I turn now to a less sensitive issue, one that we have debated quite comfortably, if not always calmly, for many decades past: the Church and politics.

It is important, I believe, to distinguish at this point between two different kinds of Church influence on politics. At least up to the 1950s many politicians, including ministers, clearly thought they owed some kind of duty of obedience to the Catholic hierarchy in the carrying out of these duties. That was evident at the time of the Mother and Child controversy in 1951, when even Noel Browne expressed himself in such terms to the Archbishop of Dublin, John Charles McQuaid.

It is evident from voting patterns in the Dáil in relation to contraception in the 1970s, and in relation to abortion and divorce issues as late as the mid 1980s, that this remained true of a minority of members of the Dáil until quite recently. Thus, on the issue of the wording of the 1983 abortion referendum, one-quarter of Labour deputies and one out of nine Fine Gael deputies voted against their parties because of Church pressures. But for a quarter of a century past, this does not seem to have been true at government level, and today such deference to Church authority may no longer be an issue with more than a small handful of deputies.

Even before recent scandals greatly weakened the authority of the Catholic hierarchy, its influence on politics had clearly shifted from a direct influence on politicians to an indirect influence through the electorate.

It is not clear that at any stage the institutional Catholic Church had much influence on political matters outside the sensitive area of sexual issues. Certainly as far back as eighty years ago the Civil War showed that bishops' fulminations on political issues had little effect. The way for this had, of course, been prepared much earlier when the Holy See had most unwisely taken up a negative position on the Land War, and the Parnell affair had also had its effect on attitudes.

The fact is that on issues of economic and social policy the institutional Catholic Church in Ireland has never played a significant role, although in recent times the hierarchy has had some wise things to say on social issues, and the Conference of Religious Orders in Ireland has recently been an important voice on behalf of the poor and disadvantaged. The views of the latter body have, however, been dismissed summarily by certain politicians such as Charles Haughey and Charlie McCreevy, the latter of whom has been very contemptuous about what he describes as the 'poverty industry'.

On foreign policy issues churchmen, including some in the hierarchy, have been on the left, and they undoubtedly influenced Irish foreign policy in relation to Central America in the 1980s. As Taoiseach I had to walk a narrow path at that time in expressing public concern about US policy in the region, a concern aroused largely by churchmen (and one that I have to say I personally shared), whilst not losing the support of the Reagan Administration in relation to the impending Anglo-Irish Agreement.

My speech at the dinner in Dublin Castle for President Reagan in 1985 must have been a model of diplomacy, for it evoked a telegram of congratulations from Bishop Eamon Casey (who had radical views on Third World issues and especially on Central America), whilst arousing only fairly mild concern amongst the US delegation – although that was partly because I was able to ensure that they did not get a copy of my remarks before they left the country!

One area in respect of which the Catholic Church in Ireland has always seemed me to have failed in its duty of moral leadership has been in relation to tax evasion. I cannot recall ever having heard a word of condemnation from the pulpit of this kind of criminal behaviour – tax evasion being, of course, the only way in which someone can steal from everyone else in the community including the poorest, for it must be clear that the revenue shortfall from unpaid taxes necessarily imposes a need for higher taxes upon everyone else.

One of the most fundamental changes in human attitudes throughout the developed world during the past century has been the collapse of authority, and of deference to authority. Until the end of the First World War the industrialized world, and Europe in particular, where all states except France and Switzerland were monarchies, was strongly marked by such deference to authority. The Roman Catholic Church, which remains monarchical in form, had for long relied more than most upon authority to support its stance on many issues. True, despite the mid nineteenth-century authoritarian and anti-democratic stance of Pope Pius IX, the Catholic Church eventually succeeded in escaping – by the skin of its teeth – from the trap into which its support for the pre-French Revolution *ancien régime* had earlier led it. And much later, in the 1960s, a real effort was made to turn an anachronistic Church of Authority into something approaching a Church of Prophecy, which had been its role in the post-apostolic period but from which in the fourth century the Christian Church had been distracted by Constantine's decision to recognize it as a State religion.

Unhappily, the theological revolution initiated by the Second Vatican Council was subsequently blocked by counter-revolutionary forces in Rome and elsewhere. By falling back again upon authority at the very time when authority was finally losing its grip on society, and also by misjudging its approach to the contraception issue and failing to move closer to the prophetic role towards the recovery of which Vatican II had been feeling its way, the Catholic Church has, for the moment at least, lost its way, failing to maximize its potential role for good in the modern world.

The impact of all this in Ireland has been dramatic. Because the Church's authority had survived so long here, acting as what eventually turned out to be a fragile dam against social change, there has in recent times been in Ireland a dramatic and most drastic foreshortening of the transition to modernity that other peoples had been experiencing at a much gentler pace from the nineteenth century onwards. If the Church in Ireland had been better manned at its higher levels it might, perhaps, have ridden this flood more successfully. But from the late 1960s onwards – a full decade before the emergence of John Paul II as pope – a traditionally conservative Irish hierarchy saw its role further eroded by an appointments system which gave priority to conformity to teaching on contraception over any other consideration.

Save in a handful of cases where the system seems to have slipped up, the absolutism of this anti-contraception stance effectively ruled out the appointment as bishops of people of intellectual distinction and leadership capacity. So, just at a time when the extraordinary pace of change in Ireland demanded Church leadership of exceptional quality, the intellectual level of appointments to bishoprics declined. This is all the more disappointing because these last couple of decades have seen a remarkable growth of serious interest in theology amongst the laity, especially among laywomen. Instead of this being drawn upon so as to revive the Irish Church, it has effectively been ignored and treated as a threat rather than as an opportunity, thus increasing rather than reducing frustration and tensions within the Irish Catholic Church.

So far I have been writing almost exclusively about the Roman Catholic Church in Ireland. The Presbyterian Communion in this island is primarily a Northern Ireland Church – only 4% of its members live in this state. By contrast the Church of Ireland has one-quarter of its members in this state, and the events of the past few decades in Northern Ireland have created a good deal of tension for its membership in the two parts of this island.

What these tensions have reflected has been a profound shift in the loyalties of Protestants in this state during the past half century, away from their earlier Unionism.

When the State was founded, the 275,000 Protestants in it were almost all Unionists, who, to put it mildly, regretted the secession of twenty-six Irish counties from the United Kingdom. Despite the efforts of the first Irish Government to protect them and their property from republican violence that was in some measure sectarian, and despite the fact that this 7% minority was accorded strong representation in the first Irish Senate – half that body's initial membership was Protestant – the new state was felt by most of them to be cold place.

The Protestant population of the twenty-six counties had been in decline for many decades before the foundation of the state. Between 1861, when census data on religious affiliations began to be collected in Irish censuses, and 1911, the Protestant population of what is now the Republic had fallen by almost 45%, or 1.2% a year, whereas in that fifty-year period the Roman Catholic population had fallen by only 30%. Both sections of the population suffered greatly from emigration during that time, but the faster decline of the Protestant population may have reflected a lower Protestant birth rate.

However, between 1911 and the first Irish State Census of 1926 – a period that included such traumatic events as the First World War, the 1916 Rising, the Anglo-Irish conflict, and the subsequent Civil War – the Protestant population of this area fell by 32%, that is to say, by an average of 2.4% a year, which was twice the rate of decline of the preceding half century. By contrast, between 1911 and 1926 the Roman Catholic population declined only marginally, by a mere 2%.

If one assumes that between 1911 and 1921 the rate of decline of the Protestant population had continued to run at about the same rate as during the preceding half century – although of course it would probably have been higher because of heavy wartime casualties – then in the immediate aftermath of independence, between 1921 and 1926, the Protestant population would have fallen by just over 50,000, or one-quarter, whereas in fact the decline in this period was over 106,000 – an extra drop of over 55,000.

Now, in 1911 the total number of members of the British Army, Navy and Police in Ireland had been 36,000, of whom three-fifths, over 20,000, were Protestant. Making allowance for the departure also of their dependants, as well as perhaps of some of the Protestant minority serving in the disbanded Royal Irish Constabulary (RIC), this factor could scarcely have accounted for more than about 30,000–35,000 of this 75,000 decline. So there may have been an extra outflow of some 20,000 other Irish Protestants during these five years, perhaps about one-sixth of the members of this minority, many of them leaving areas outside Dublin.

Close examination of the changes in the numbers of Protestants and Catholics in each age cohort during the following two decades (the period 1926–46), shows that, despite the more favourable socio-economic position of the Protestant population – a factor to which I return below – by the latter year the proportion of Protestants born between 1916 and 1936 who survived in Ireland into their twenties was lower than in the case of Roman Catholics.

During those twenty years emigration reduced the young Protestant population of the new State by a further 36%, whereas in the case of the Roman Catholic population the attrition rate during this period was only 22.5%. And only a small part of this differential could have been accounted for by a higher rate of Second World War casualties amongst young Protestants.

It is thus clear that during the period up to the end of the Second World War there was a higher rate of Protestant emigration from the new Irish State. But it is equally clear that thereafter this pattern was reversed. For throughout the period since the end of the Second World War the rate of emigration of the young Protestant population has been consistently lower than for Roman Catholics. Indeed, during the post-war period, in all age cohorts of the population, the Protestant minority declined more slowly than was the case with Roman Catholics.

This is certainly true of all those born up to 1966: for later births the process of youthful emigration was not yet complete in 1991, the year of the last Census in this State that recorded religious data. We have to await the outcome of the 2002 Census in the Republic to update emigration data of Protestants and Catholics, and because of significant immigration during the latter part of this period, it may not be easy to trace accurately the pattern of this more recent movement.

Looking back over the past eighty years it is clear that up to the end of the Second World War many Protestants in the Republic remained uncomfortable with their lot, with the result that, despite the greater job opportunities available here to a community which was greatly overrepresented in the business community and the professions, many young Protestants of that period preferred to make their lives elsewhere. However, in the post-war period that sense of discomfort, for some even alienation, rapidly disappeared, with the result that the more favourable job opportunities available to this well-to-do and well-educated community came fully into play.

Thus, the fact that the Protestant community in the Republic continued to decline up to the 1980s this was no longer attributable to differential emigration, as had earlier been the case, but was due rather to the way in which until the 1970s marriages between Protestants and Roman Catholics operated to reduce considerably the number of children brought up as Protestants. Although throughout this post-war period all adult Protestant age groups have maintained their numbers better than did the equivalent age groups of the adult Roman Catholic majority, it was because of this factor that the number of children brought up as Protestants continued to decline until the 1970s. The number of Protestant children under ten years of age fell from just under 30,000 in 1926 to barely 20,000 in 1946, and by 1961 had fallen further to 17,500.

This was the primarily a consequence of a 25% mixed-marriage rate by Protestants in a society in which until the 1970s Roman Catholics who entered such marriages were almost always extremely observant of their Church's stance on the upbringing of children. But in recent times, because of changing attitudes amongst the Roman Catholic majority in the Republic, the proportion of children of mixed marriages brought up as Catholics has been moving down to something between two-thirds and one-half, with the result that the erosion of the Protestant population of the Republic through the operation of this factor has greatly diminished.

It is particularly notable that throughout the whole history of the independent Irish State, the Protestant population of the Republic has fully maintained its favourable socio-economic position. Between 1926 and 1991 growing prosperity had increased the total number of people at work in the three highest socio-economic groups (commerce, insurance and finance; management and administration; the professions), raising from 17% to 22% the proportion of the workforce to be found in these categories.

In 1926 the proportion of the Protestant population in these three key socio-economic groups was over twice the figure for Roman Catholics: 32.5% as against 16%. But by 1991 the proportion of working Protestants in these three higher groups had risen by seven percentage points, to 39.5% of the Protestant population. This reflected upward Protestant social mobility during the history of the state, for much of this increase was at the expense of a drop in the proportion of Protestants engaged in clerical occupations, which in this period fell from 14.5% to 8%.

This upward mobility had the effect of fully maintaining the earlier socio-economic advantage enjoyed by Protestants in Ireland, for, by contrast, during this sixty-five-year period the increase in the proportion of the Roman Catholic population in these three socio-economic groups rose by only five percentage points – from 16% to 21%. Consequently in 1991 the share of the Protestant working population in these best-paid occupations still remained, as in 1926, twice the Catholic ratio.

It is also notable that in 1991 the Protestant minority – who then constituted 4.75% of the Republic's population – retained ownership of almost 10% of all farms of over fifty acres. And in a wide range of other occupations Protestants in 1991 were also three to four times overrepresented – to the tune of 13% to 17% of the available jobs.

This was the case with doctors and paramedics, writers and journalists, actors and musicians, professors and lecturers, government administrators, industrial designers, and those engaged in consultancy and research.

In addition, Protestants were also overrepresented between twice and three times (9% to 13%) amongst farm managers; ships' officers; architects and technologists; as well as in insurance broking, insurance, and business and professional services; and in films and broadcasting.

So it is not surprising that a Protestant community so well placed in the society of the Irish State and no longer uncomfortable with that State, should have experienced a lower level of emigration during the past half century than the Roman Catholic majority.

It is, I think, also interesting that not alone have the advantages thus enjoyed by the Protestant minority in the Republic never been challenged: so far as I am aware they have never even been publicly adverted to here. Whatever may have been the case eighty years ago, this situation has for long been accepted by the Roman Catholic majority as a matter of course. This reaction has no doubt been facilitated by the small size of the Protestant minority.

There are, of course, no statistics that would tell us how many of the Protestant community today remain Unionists, in the proper meaning of the word, that is, wanting Ireland to give up its independence and return to the United Kingdom. But whenever I have asked Protestants in Dublin or further south about this I find that they have great difficulty in identifying any actual Unionists amongst their numbers. Of course, further north, some Protestants in Monaghan, Cavan, or Donegal, may well identify with their hard-pressed coreligionist Unionist neighbours just across the Border, although whether they would actually wish to find themselves again inside the United Kingdom may be another matter.

But whether in Border areas or further south, in our state most members of the Protestant community retain a warm regard for Britain and many things British, which distinguishes them from the diminishing, but still significant proportion of the majority Catholic population which remains Anglophobic. Nevertheless, this Protestant population identifies primarily with the Irish State, for the most part feeling themselves Irish, rather than British and Irish as would have been the case with most Southern Irish Protestants eighty years ago. And Southern Protestants are clearly most uncomfortable with the stance of many of their strongly unionist coreligionists in Northern Ireland.

At the same time in Northern Ireland, many Protestants have also been moved by the events of the past thirty years to drop their former sense of a double Irish and British identity in favour of defining themselves as British only – although that does not mean that they feel comfortable with the British Government's role in Northern Ireland, or, indeed, with the attitude to their community of many people in Britain.

Thus the past fifty years has seen a movement apart by the Protestant communities in the two parts of this island, which in recent times has created visible tensions within the Church of Ireland. It may be said that this has been foreshadowed ever since the Home Rule crisis of 1886, and more particularly since Ulster Protestants began to pursue a partitionist stance a century or so ago. What was not foreseen then, or even half a century ago, was the extent to which Protestants living in this state would come to identify with it, ceasing to be, as most of their grandparents were, unionists in the full sense of that word.

10 Ireland and Europe

Historically Irish leaders looked to England's enemies in Europe for aid in their struggle to protect themselves from English power, or later to recover their country's lost independence. In the late sixteenth century they turned to Spain, Portugal and the Holy See, and in the late seventeenth century and the eighteenth to France. In the nineteenth century the Irish diaspora in the United States became the focus of attention for Irish revolutionaries, but some of them took refuge in France. In 1916 it was to Germany that the Military Committee of the Irish Volunteers turned, although as Pearse and Plunkett told my father in the GPO, and as Bulmer Hobson also told Ernest Blythe at the time, they had no illusion about the outcome should Germany win the War: a German monarch would replace their declared republic. But, in pursuit of Germany's interests with regard to Britain, Germany would, they believed, be happy to see Ireland becoming an Irish-speaking state, running its own affairs on the model of countries like Rumania and Bulgaria, where German monarchs had been installed in the nineteenth century.

Germany lost the War, and Ireland had to secure its independence without external aid. Indeed, by 1920 the President of the underground Dáil Government, Eamon de Valera, had come to realize that part of the price that would have to be paid to secure British assent to the emergence of an independent Irish State would be a guarantee that an Irish Government would never allow its territory to be used by any power hostile to Britain – possibly on the model of the relationship between Cuba and the United States after the Spanish–American war of 1898, which was, perhaps, a somewhat unfortunate analogy!

De Valera's public offer of such a guarantee during his sojourn in the United States may have been a factor encouraging the British Government to open its mind to a negotiated settlement during the first half of 1921, although the more immediate effect of its publication in the *Westminster Gazette*, before he had been able to explain its purpose to his Irish-American audiences, was to split Irish-America down the middle.

When the Anglo-Irish Treaty that brought the Irish War of Independence to an end came to be negotiated at the end of the following year, recognition of Britain's legitimate interest in securing itself against any possible future threat from this source facilitated Irish acceptance of the military clauses of the Treaty, and these clauses did not feature much in the subsequent political split that led to the Civil War.

The realistic approach of Irish political leaders to the radically altered relationship with Britain that would follow from Irish independence made it easier for Ireland to pursue, without undue tension in Anglo-Irish relations, its immediate political goal of converting its initial somewhat ambiguous status as a self-governing dominion of the Commonwealth into the sovereign independence that was formally recognized by Britain in the Statute of Westminster of 1931.

Whilst Britain was clearly unenthusiastic about, and in some measure resistant to, Irish initiatives on this issue during the course of the Imperial Conferences of 1926 and 1930 – as it had been to earlier Irish diplomatic moves to register the Anglo-Irish Agreement of 1921 at the League of Nations in Geneva, and to establish an Irish diplomatic mission in Washington – the unequivocal commitment of successive Irish Governments to ensuring that Britain would never be subjected to a threat from another power coming from its Irish flank, proved hugely important to the stabilization of the relationship between former colony and former colonial power.

When, in the late 1930s war loomed between Germany and Britain and France, Ireland, like all other European states and like the United States, chose to remain neutral unless and until attacked. (In the Irish case there was an unstated special reason for neutrality: concern lest participation in the war on the side of Britain and France might spark off a renewal of the Civil War of sixteen years earlier, in which some of the more Anglophobe elements in de Valera's Fianna Fáil party might be tempted to join with the IRA in alliance with Germany. It should be recalled that the IRA had 'declared war' on Britain earlier in 1939 and had set off bombs there.)

But Ireland, mindful of its commitment to prevent Britain's Irish flank becoming a threat to its security, initiated secret discussions with Britain in 1938 to help establish an Irish military intelligence system directed against possible German infiltration, and after Munich British consent was sought for the employment of a French officer to help train the Irish Army, a proposal that was turned down by the British because of their deep mistrust of the French even on the very eve of the Second World War!

When the war broke out de Valera warned the German Minister that Ireland 'would have to give a certain consideration to Britain', but, as the British were aware from decoding messages from the German legation in Dublin, Germany never learnt of the scale of that 'consideration'. Amongst the fourteen forms of secret Irish assistance listed in a report to the British Cabinet in February 1945 one was an arrangement under which in the event of a German invasion the Irish Army would be put under the command of the general in charge of commanding British forces in Northern Ireland, operating from a headquarters in Malahide, north of Dublin.

Although by 1931 the sovereign independence of Ireland and other dominions of the Commonwealth had been established by the Statute of Westminster, Ireland lacked the power to alter its almost total economic dependence upon Britain, which remained the only market open to Irish agricultural and most industrial products. And, as was mentioned in chapter 2, Britain as Ireland's sole market for most goods had, since the end of the nineteenth century, been consistently the slowest-growing market in Europe as well as the least remunerative for farm products. The latter situation was the outcome of Britain's policy of permitting free entry for foodstuffs from around the world with a view to keeping down wages and thus the prices of its manufactures.

Thus Britain, Ireland's only market, was also in important respects its worst possible market. And, largely for this reason, Ireland's growth potential was unrealized throughout the post-war period. When combined with a much-too-protective attitude towards the small and inefficient manufacturing sector, which offered no incentive to efficiency or to exports, this helped to ensure that the Irish economy, still led by conservative governments manned by ageing former revolutionaries, stagnated during that most dynamic of decades elsewhere in the world, the 1950s.

If Irish economists had been asked fifty years ago to imagine an ideal solution to this set of problems, their wish-list would have comprised unrestricted access for both Irish agricultural and industrial products to the more dynamic Western European continental market, and the assimilation of British farm product and food prices to the level prevailing in Europe, together with substantial grants to aid infrastructure investment.

Astonishingly, this is precisely what became a real possibility with the establishment of the European Economic Community in 1957 – if only Britain would abandon its traditional reticence about closer involvement with the Continent, and if Ireland could successfully prepare its inefficient, high-cost manufacturing sector for the rigours of free trade. Sean Lemass, the architect of the Irish industrial system, immediately saw the immense possibilities that the creation of the EEC had opened for Ireland and, as soon as he took over as Taoiseach from Eamon de Valera in 1959, he accepted this challenge.

To introduce a personal note here, I had resigned from Aer Lingus a year earlier. Fearing that the weakness of Irish industry would inhibit us from applying for membership of the EEC, I hoped to find some way of tackling the challenge thus thrown down. With a view to getting involved in the process of preparing industry for free trade I set about a research project in TCD involving an examination of the materials inputs into Irish industry, which brought me into direct contact with 250 firms, and required me to visit fifty of them. A year later I joined the Political Economy Department of UCD.

In 1960 I found that my ploy had worked for, in that year, encouraged by the new Taoiseach, Sean Lemass, to start preparations for the freeing of trade in the context of the EEC, the Federation of Irish Industries engaged another UCD economist, Gerard Quinn, and myself to undertake a pilot study of the survival prospects of one of the most highly-protected industries, the woollen and worsted sector.

In our report on that industry in April 1961 we suggested that the Federation and the Civil Service should jointly undertake similar studies across the whole range of Irish industries. This led to the establishment, simultaneously with the Irish application for EEC membership, of the Committee on Industrial Organisation, in whose work the trade unions also participated. And I became part-time Economic Consultant to the Federation, working on this Committee.

The Irish application to the EEC was, of course, turned down by General de Gaulle with that of Britain in January 1963 – although we now know that the French President had briefly dallied with the idea of admitting Ireland without Britain, partly, perhaps, because of his consciousness of his Irish roots – a MacCartan ancestor had left Co. Down for France at the time of the Treaty of Limerick in 1691 – but also perhaps because this would have been a way of teasing the British!

The consequent delay of twelve years gave Ireland more time to prepare for the negative effects upon indigenous Irish industry of free trade within the Community, a process that was speeded up by Sean Lemass's decision in 1965 to free Irish trade with Britain over a ten-year period, whilst awaiting British and Irish admission to the Community.

By the time Ireland and Britain, with Denmark, joined the EC in 1973, the Community's Common Agricultural Policy had already been fully implemented, with prices fixed at the high end of the price range of member states in order to accommodate high-cost German farmers. A Social Fund had also been established to finance training, especially in less developed areas of the Community. And a Regional Fund to contribute to investment in such areas was in preparation.

The delay in accession by these three states had, however, provided an opportunity for the original six members, who had a limited amount of waters within 200 miles of their coasts, to bring into effect a Community regime for sea-fishing that gave them access to British, Danish and Irish fish stocks. The disadvantages of this fishery regime for Ireland were, however, mitigated by a deal that I secured as Foreign Minister in 1976 which enabled Ireland to double its fish catches and increase their value by 40% within a few years and thereafter to expand their activity further whilst other member states were having to limit their catches because of over-fishing.

The benefits accruing to Ireland from EC membership were immense – far greater in relation to the size of the country than was the case with any other member state. This was true in relation to the impact on agriculture and the net flow of Structural Funds, but most of all in relation to the expansion of exports. Under all three headings Ireland benefited disproportionately, partly because of skilful negotiation, but also because of the goodwill of the European Commission and the generosity of its partners during the first two decades of membership.

Ireland made the most of the opportunities provided by the Common Agricultural Policy: the prices received for its farm products doubled within five years as depressed Irish prices moved up to the EC level. Not content with these accession increases, however, Ireland supported proposals for higher Community farm prices, although it was arguable – and as Minister for Foreign Affairs I argued unsuccessfully at the time – that Ireland's longer-term interest in increasing its market share might have been better served by opposing increases that were helping to keep less efficient German farmers in production.

When, in the mid 1980s the scale of the EC's milk surplus led to a decision to impose a system of milk quotas, due to the support of the German Chancellor, Helmut Kohl, and the active advocacy of President Mitterrand – both very friendly to Ireland – Ireland's exceptional dependence on this farm sector was recognized by according to it a bonus of a one-eighth additional quota.

Meanwhile, Ireland was securing a disproportionate share of the newly-established Social Fund for its expanding training programmes, receiving up to 13% of the Fund at one stage, although its population was only 1% of that of the EC. And when the Regional Fund was finally established in 1974 I negotiated for Ireland 6.5%, rather than the proposed 3.5% of the resources available – a negotiation that ensured that Ireland was the only member country to preserve its original allocation when the resources finally allocated to that Fund were virtually halved following the first oil crisis.

Ireland also secured the consent of the European Commission to replace its export tax exemption – banned by the European Commission as discriminating in favour of home production – with a tax of only 10% on all industrial profits. Given the very high level of corporate taxes in other EC states, this proved immensely valuable in attracting to Ireland industrial investments from outside the EC, notably from the United States. By the 1990s this low tax rate was helping Ireland to attract one-quarter of the *number* of all new US industrial investments in Western Europe, although not necessarily one-quarter of the *volume* of such activity.

These were remarkable achievements for a new member state, and they created a very favourable public climate in Ireland towards the Community. However, successive governments, including those in which I participated, were content to allow the popularity of EC membership to rest exclusively on these economic benefits that Ireland was receiving, without seeking to deepen Irish attachment to the Community by reference to its positive roles in creating a zone of peace in Western Europe and in leading the global development aid process.

There has never been adequate appreciation in Ireland of Europe's remarkable achievements in these and other respects during the decades after the Second World War. By 1945 Europe's infrastructure had been largely destroyed. The economies of most of its states were in grave difficulties and its peoples were threatened with hunger in 1947. Overnight the continent that had for so long held world leadership had lost this role with the emergence on to the world stage of two superpowers: the United States and the Soviet Union.

No one could then have foreseen the way this battered and demoralized continent would succeed in the decades that followed in reversing the tide of its history by initiating four major intellectual revolutions that ultimately transformed its role in global affairs.

The first of these was the decision in 1950 effectively to transfer the sovereignty of its states in relation to human rights to the supranational jurisdiction of a Human Rights Court at Strasbourg. Nothing in Europe's history had foreshadowed such a radical development, which ran against the tide of its history since the Renaissance, a history that had been marked by the aggressive assertion of unbridled state sovereignty.

A year later six states which had been at war with each other just half a dozen years earlier came together to create a supranational authority that would control two of their industries which historically had been the basis of their military power: coal and steel. And, six years later, these six countries laid the foundations of a united and peaceful Europe by agreeing to integrate their economies within a supranational political system. In this way they created a European zone of peace that in time was to spread to the whole of Western, Central, and North-Eastern Europe. Here again the tide of European history was reversed.

Meanwhile, during the twenty years after the end of the war Europe's colonial empires were dissolved, sometimes painfully and even, in the case of France, at a risk of domestic instability that threatened its democracy. But the transformation of Europe's relationship with the developing world went well beyond decolonization. Not merely did Europe abandon colonial exploitation – which had often involved the transfer of resources from poorer overseas countries to their European colonial masters – but Europe led the process of actually reversing these transfers by developing aid programmes to assist former colonies. Whatever imperfections these programmes may have – and some of them have included elements of neo-colonialism – the acceptance in principle of the concept that rich countries should help poor ones represented once again a reversal of the tide of history. Other developed countries have, of course, also played a part in this process, but on a much smaller scale: the development aid programmes of the two superpowers have involved much smaller proportions of their GDP, and have been dominated by a military element. The leadership in this revolutionary process came from, and remains with, Europe.

The fourth of these Europe-driven revolutions of the second half of the twentieth century has been the ecological revolution, the recognition of the need to restrain the growth of global pollution and the running-down of natural resources. However inadequate the steps hitherto taken towards this end, whatever has been achieved, or is likely to be achieved in the foreseeable future, is the product of European leadership: the United States, Russia and Japan have all lagged far behind.

But the unique role of Europe in these four crucial areas has never been fully appreciated in Ireland, where, paradoxically, those, often on the left, who are most concerned about the issues of human rights, peace, development aid and ecological issues are the most critical of Europe and of the process of European integration.

Meanwhile, as the budgetary transfers from the EU to Ireland in the form of Structural Funds – mainly the former Social and Regional Funds – have latterly diminished in parallel with the growth of Ireland's per capita GNP, and as the Irish electorate has come to take for granted the hugely beneficial access to Continental markets achieved through membership of the Community, earlier strong public support for European integration has begun to wane.

Irish Taoisigh from 1960 to 1981 – notably Sean Lemass, Jack Lynch and Charles Haughey – successively proclaimed Ireland's willingness to abandon neutrality and to engage in due course in a process of European defence, albeit with a proviso by Charles Haughey in March 1981 that this would need to be preceded by the raising of Irish GNP per head to 80% of the EC level and by the launch of a single currency. But from 1981 onwards this issue was made a domestic political football by Fianna Fáil in attempts to split Fine Gael and Labour on the neutrality issue.

This overnight opportunistic reversal of the earlier positive Fianna Fáil approach to European defence reached its climax in 1997 when Ray Burke in Opposition scapegoated the Partnership for Peace as a NATO adjunct and persuaded the Fianna Fáil Opposition Leader,

Bertie Ahern (who up to that time had had little experience of foreign affairs), to promise that Fianna Fáil in government would not join the Partnership without a prior referendum.

The subsequent failure of the Ahern-led Fianna Fáil/PD Government to abide by this commitment greatly strengthened left-wing anti-EU forces in Ireland. Indeed the whole process of resiling from earlier Irish Government commitments on European defence offered encouragement to Europhobe elements and led to a weakening of active support for the European Union in Irish public opinion. In turn this contributed to the failure of more than 16% of the electorate to vote in favour of ratification of the Nice Treaty in June 2000.

Whilst active opposition to the EU has always been confined to a relatively small, but committed, minority, comprising some of the Green Party, Sinn Féin, socialists, and some former development aid workers, as well as some right-wing Catholics who associate Europe with abortion, there also emerged more recently a small nationalist Eurosceptic element in Fianna Fáil. Moreover, the Progressive Democrats explicitly look to the United States rather than to Europe for their politico-economic inspiration, to Boston rather than Berlin, and while they supported the Nice Treaty some of their utterances on the subject had a negative effect on public opinion.

These shifts in the domestic climate in relation to the European Community – now the European Union – have, unhappily, been paralleled by a significant negative shift in attitudes towards Ireland on the part of some EU governments. This deterioration in Ireland's relations with some of its EU partners seems to have started around 1990, when the stridency of Irish Government demands for Structural Funds at the Edinburgh European Council, and the exaggeration and triumphalism about what was secured at that meeting, began to grate on some other European leaders.

As the Irish economy expanded rapidly during the 1990s, resentment against Ireland grew in countries like Germany, France and the Netherlands, where it was simplistically – and erroneously – assumed that the prime factor in this exceptional growth was the resources being transferred to Ireland from these countries through the Community budget. In fact, whilst the Structural Funds did help Ireland to catch up on its infrastructural deficit, and thus to reduce some capacity limitations on growth, their actual direct contribution to growth was quite small.

Much more important to the achievement of rapid economic growth have been domestic policies such as the rapid expansion of education, and the low rate of corporate taxation. This latter policy became a sore point with France and Germany during the course of the 1990s as the numbers of new US industrial investments in Europe locating in Ireland came to exceed substantially the numbers locating in the much larger German and French economies. By the end of the decade there were increasingly strident demands from the governments of these and some other member countries for harmonization of corporate taxation rates in the EU with a view to eliminating what was seen as an 'unfair' Irish advantage in attracting greenfield US investments.

The Irish Government's understandable resistance to this pressure at the time of the negotiation of the Nice Treaty, followed by a somewhat triumphalist reaction to its success in holding the line on this issue, did little to soften the negative reactions of some other member states.

Meanwhile, although the admission of Finland, Sweden and Austria reduced Ireland's isolation on the 'neutrality' issue, Ireland's failure to join the Partnership for Peace at the time of its establishment in the late 1990s isolated it for a period upon a related issue, in a way that also proved damaging to its reputation in Europe.

Of course, as Ireland during the 1990s moved rapidly from being by far the poorest country in Northern Europe to a level of GNP per head equal to the EU average – higher than that of France by 2001, for example – it was inevitable that some of the sympathy that it had evoked from several larger states in the early years of its membership would evaporate. Changes in the composition of Europe's leadership during this period – the disappearance from the scene of President Mitterrand and Chancellor Kohl, both of whom had been very sympathetic to Ireland's problems and needs, accelerated this process.

This inevitable shift in the climate of opinion towards Ireland might have been less marked if Irish Governments in the late 1990s had shown more sensitivity towards and had evinced a more evident positive interest in the future development of the European Union. In particular, Ireland could have avoided exacerbating its increasing problems with its partners if in June 2000 the Government of the day had bestirred itself to campaign actively for ratification of the Nice Treaty by way of referendum, instead of passively allowing, through inertia, a mere 18% of the electorate to defeat ratification.

Government overdefensiveness in the course of the Nice Treaty negotiations had contributed to some negative reactions to the new Treaty, as did excessive emphasis by the Opposition parties on the fact that the outcome of the Nice discussions secured a partial restoration of the voting strength of larger countries, which had been eroded through successive enlargements involving the accession of seven small states but only two new large ones. The fact the Nice Treaty had made much smaller institutional changes affecting the balance between large and small countries than had been thought likely was never communicated to the electorate.

Moreover, several interventions by the European Commission in favour of locally unpopular environmental protection measures, and against excessive state aid to the national airline Aer Lingus, as well as the Commission's valid criticism of the excessively expansionist 2000 budget, all produced unjustified negative reactions from some ministers, and this found populist echoes with the media and with some sections of public opinion.

Particularly disturbing has been the fact that these events were allowed to obscure the reality that the legislative role of the Commission – its exclusive power to initiate legislation – provides invaluable protection for small countries against efforts by larger ones to dominate the Community. Misplaced demands by Irish Eurosceptics and others for greater 'democratic' control of this 'unelected body' has played into the hands of larger countries which would like to see the Commission's role downgraded. Preservation of the Commission's monopoly of legislative initiative has always been Ireland's most important single vital interest in the Community, and efforts by some Irish politicians of the left to weaken this role have been singularly misplaced.

In the Convention launched in Brussels in March 2002 Ireland has an opportunity to identify and pursue longer-term objectives designed to improve the working of the Community and to ensure a balanced development towards a European Union of States.

One of the matters that requires urgent attention is the inadequate linkage between the Community's activities and democratic opinion within member states. Many national parliaments, including notably the Oireachtas, have hitherto failed to scrutinize Commission proposals and to feed their views to the Government in advance of deliberations on these matters by the Committee of Permanent Representatives and ultimately by the Council of Ministers.

Successive Irish Governments – my own included – have been happy enough to allow this form of democratic deficit to persist, fearing that a greater involvement of the Oireachtas in the Community decision-making process might reduce the margin of manoeuvre of governments in subsequent negotiations and lead to Government/Oireachtas clashes on such matters.

This has been a shortsighted view, and persistence with it could intensify the alienation of the Irish electorate from the European process. As in the Danish case, preservation of the Irish Government's negotiating position at critical moments can be ensured by holding pre-Council parliamentary committee meetings in private to discuss sensitive bargaining issues in respect of which it would be unwise for the Irish Government to show its full hand in advance of the Council debate.

A related issue is the question of how best to secure a stronger public sense of democratic involvement in the Community process. In the past I have been inclined to the view that this might be achieved by the election of the President of the Commission by the prevailing majority within the European Parliament, although I have also been attracted by the idea of a direct election of the President by the people of the member states.

The first of these processes would replicate the democratic procedures to which we are accustomed within our own states: it would involve shifts backwards and forwards in the political complexion of the Commission in response to such movement as may occur in the membership of the Parliament arising from periodic elections to that body. But by introducing a more ideological element into the institutional structure, this might, perhaps, create new, and unnecessary, tensions between the Commission and those member states which at any given time had a government with a different ideological stance.

The second procedure – direct election of the President by the people – would engage the electorates of member states in the European process, from which at present they feel themselves remote. But as the candidates most likely to emerge from a popular election might be more widely-known figures from larger states, this might tend in time to alienate the peoples of smaller states, and perhaps also to increase tensions between larger states.

An alternative process that has been suggested, and that has been supported by the Irish Government representative to the European

Convention, would involve members of national parliaments becoming an electoral college, presumably on a basis that would give to each parliament's votes an appropriate weighting, proportionate, for example, to the number of seats allocated to that state in the European Parliament or to its weighting in the Council of Ministers. Such an arrangement would clearly enhance the roles of national parliaments within the Community. However, especially given the weakening public respect for parliamentary institutions both in Ireland and elsewhere, it might not generate an increased sense of popular engagement with the institutions of the EU on the part of the public.

The debate now taking place within the Convention on these issues may help to clarify the relative merits of these alternative approaches to the choice of future Presidents of the Commission. From an Irish viewpoint – and from that of other small countries – what is important is that, by whatever means, the role of the Commission as the initiator of Community legislation be strengthened in order to meet the danger of this role being taken over de facto by a European Council dominated by the larger states.

That the Community has hitherto been a benign structure for smaller states is due primarily to the entrenchment of this power of legislative initiative within the European Commission. Had either of the other two European political institutions – the Council and the Parliament – been given such a role by the Rome Treaty, the larger states would have been enabled eventually to dominate the Community through the influence they could then have brought to bear upon the initial shape of legislation, for whoever prepares the first draft of any document inevitably has a disproportionate influence upon what emerges at the end of the process.

Although, of course, the members of the European Commission are appointed by national governments, and although they cannot totally divorce themselves from their national backgrounds, the fact is that their oath of office, in combination with the conventions that have been established over many decades, has ensured that in the preparation of legislation its members acting collectively have almost always been guided in this process by a sense of the European common good, and by a concern to ensure that such legislation does not bear harshly on the legitimate interests of any member state, however small. I cannot in fact recall any case where since we became members of the Community Ireland's interests have been seriously prejudiced by proposals brought forward by the Commission, and I can recall many cases where our interests have in fact been safeguarded by that body.

Not surprisingly, larger states have from time to time found that this approach by the Commission to its duties has frustrated their desire to pursue particular policies. Moreover, even where no particular national interest of a large state is at stake, there has sometimes emerged a sense of frustration amongst the governments of larger states at the failure of some Commissions to act with sufficient drive and energy – for, to be blunt about it, over the years there have been weak Commissions as well as strong ones.

At certain times it has been possible to detect a wish on the part of larger states to secure for themselves a de facto power of initiative which the Treaty of Rome legally denied them, and the present may well be one of these times. In the past such moves have emanated from France or Germany, but now that Britain has a Prime Minister who personally aspires to a leading role in Europe, it is from this source that a further effort of this kind could originate.

In 1975, at a time when the Commission had temporarily lost its impetus as the initiating organ of the Community, it was France's new President, Valéry Giscard d'Estaing, who sought to turn what had previously been occasional meetings of Heads of Government into a series of multi-annual European Councils through which the larger states might direct the future development of the Community. As we may now be facing another attempt of this kind, and as I was personally involved in the events that followed this French initiative of twenty-seven years ago, and fought with some success to prevent such Heads of Government meetings replacing the role of the Commission, it may be worth recounting here the main features of those events, as seen from the inside.

It all began at the end of Georges Pompidou's presidency of France when the first of what subsequently became a regular series of six-monthly informal meetings of Foreign Ministers took place at Gymnich near Bonn. At this meeting Jim Callaghan, who had just replaced Alec Douglas-Home as British Foreign Secretary, enquired what was meant by a phrase 'European Union', used in the communique after an earlier Heads of Government meeting in Paris, apparently on the proposal of President Pompidou.[1] The phrase, he said, presumably did not mean a union like that between Britain and Ireland, which, he said had not exactly been a success, nor like that between England and Scotland. I intervened to suggest that it might perhaps mean changes in the structure of the Community that would modify the unanimity procedure in the Council of Ministers, increase democratic control by Parliament, and bring the political and economic aspects of our activities closer together – all objectives of Irish policy at that time.

In the discussion that followed, the Foreign Ministers of the Netherlands, Germany, Luxembourg, Italy and France all stated that in fact no one knew what this phrase meant! The French Foreign Minister then proposed that the matter be delegated to representatives of Heads of Government meeting *without* the Commission, but a number of us forthwith shot down that dangerous proposal.

President Pompidou died shortly afterwards and Valéry Giscard d'Estaing was elected in his place. By appointing an ambassador rather than a political figure as his Foreign Minister, he made it clear that he intended to run France's foreign policy himself. It soon became evident that he was not prepared to drop General de Gaulle's insistence on the retention of the veto in Council decision-making: that had to await an initiative of François Mitterrand's a decade later.

On 14 September 1974 Giscard d'Estaing invited the Community's Heads of Government to a dinner at the Élysée, after which his Foreign Minister sought to persuade his colleagues on the Council of Ministers that our Prime Ministers had agreed at the dinner to a series of proposals. These included the initiation of a series of regular joint meetings of the Council of Ministers and of ministers dealing with Political Cooperation (the formal name given to foreign policy coordination) which would be attended by Heads of Government.[2] These meetings would be serviced by a 'light' secretariat, replacing the Council Secretariat, and foreign policy issues would be confined to European matters. (Apparently the larger countries were to handle the rest of the world!)

Intergovernmental discussions were to take place on a whole range of specified issues, a number of which were in fact already Community competences. And there were to be direct elections to the European Parliament – something we could, of course, support – but the Parliament was to be given a certain right of initiative, which would clearly undermine the Commission's exclusive role in legislation. All this was to replace the 1972 Paris Summit idea of a European Union which, the French Foreign Minister said had been 'idiotic', an odd phrase to use about a proposal by a former French President.

Little of all this had filtered through to us Foreign Ministers from the dinner at the Élysée, let alone that it had all been agreed by our Prime Ministers. That bluff was firmly called by all those present – except, significantly, the German and British Ministers: Callaghan was enthusiastic about these ideas whilst the German Minister said he was 'happy' with them.

There is no need to describe here how the consequent battle was fought – successfully – during the three months that followed: I enjoyed the process.[3] All that needs to be said here is that the European Council that emerged from the December 1974 Paris Summit did *not* take the form of a decision-making Council of Ministers of the Community; there were to be *no* intergovernmental meetings on matters that were Community competences; the Parliament was *not* to be given a right of legislative initiative that would undermine the Commission's; meetings of the European Council were to be serviced by the Council Secretariat and *not* by a separate secretariat; and Political Co-operation was *not* to be confined to European matters, leaving the rest of the world to the big countries.

All that was agreed was that there would be direct elections to the European Parliament (which, on an Irish proposal, were, in fact, held a year earlier than the French had suggested), and that there would be informal European Council meetings of Heads of Government two or three times a year. As the Heads of Government of the larger countries seemed to feel that it would be beneath their dignity to act on proposals by the Commission, the European Council was not to act as a formal Council of Ministers; it would simply give 'orientations', rather than make decisions.

This brief account demonstrates two things: first that the larger states will go to considerable lengths to substitute a 'Directoire' of three larger states for the existing carefully-balanced Community structure, but, second, that they cannot force such a change on the smaller states if these take a firm stand on the treaties.

We must be as vigilant today as we were in 1975 in opposing any fresh attempt to increase the role of the European Council at the expense of the Commission. However, because of Ireland's current unpopularity with its partners, we may not be as well placed as we were in 1975 to lead a move to block such an attempt, but should certainly encourage other smaller countries to fight this issue and should support their efforts.

We should all be clear that our single most important national interest lies in the preservation of the independent role of the European Commission. Some critics of the Nice Treaty who do not understand the workings of the Community mistakenly want to bring the Commission under what they describe as 'democratic control', but in practice this could all too easily mean control by the larger countries.

It is, perhaps, worth adding that at the final stages of an Intergovernmental Conference, convened to consider possible amendments to the treaties underlying the Community and the wider European Union, the decisions on outstanding issues are taken by the Heads of Government meeting without officials present, and sometimes even without their Foreign Ministers. Whatever merit there may be in Heads of Government meeting in this way so as to exchange views freely on outstanding issues involving the European Union, as a method of drafting outstanding clauses of a treaty, this process is chaotic and ultimately very dangerous. Such meetings tend to end up taking crucial decisions on the future of Europe in the early hours of the morning, without any adequate objective record being made of what may have been agreed.

After the Amsterdam Treaty it took a month to get agreement on what the Heads of Government thought they had agreed. And I recall that after the meeting at which the Nice Treaty was finally negotiated by the Heads of Government, four days elapsed before it could be established whether it had or had not been decided to hold all future European Council meetings in Brussels.

In future the final terms of a new Treaty should not be agreed without the presence of competent officials to record what has been decided, and the Heads of Government should not conclude the meeting until these officials have been able to verify the final text.

11 Ireland, Britain and Northern Ireland

The relationship between Ireland and Britain is hugely complex, with many subtle nuances. The two countries have been so closely engaged with each other over such a long period, often negatively, but also in some important respects, positively, that the relationship cannot be described in simple, easily comprehensible, terms.

It is inevitable that there should have been negative aspects to the relationship between the new Irish State and the State from which it had seceded. Conquest leaves behind a residue of mutual antipathy: not merely of resentment on the part of the conquered but of hurt also on the part of the withdrawing conquerors at their rejection by the conquered – a sentiment sometimes mixed with at least subconscious guilt. And when there is a religious difference between conquered and conqueror, that can greatly intensify these negative reciprocal reactions.

Of course, different kinds of conquests can leave different legacies, depending *inter alia* upon the degree of differentiation of the dominant and subordinated cultures, and on the completeness of the process of conquest, evidenced by the extent to which the native culture and language of the conquered is eliminated or survives.

In the historical period Ireland experienced sequentially three rather different conquests. The first, by Norman lords from Wales in the twelfth century (with the consent of, and soon brought under the control of, the Crown), was geographically incomplete. Moreover, the descendants of these Norman lords to some degree assimilated the native Gaelic culture.

But in the second stage, during the sixteenth and seventeenth centuries, the English government brought the whole of Ireland under its direct control. And with the departure of what remained of native Irish leadership at the end of this period, almost all land ownership was transferred to English landlords, who, together with English commercial interests, formed a small colonial governing elite. By 1775 the operation of penal laws against the Roman Catholic Irish had led to only 5% of the land remaining in Irish ownership. The indigenous Irish had become tenants at will of English landlords.

However, in one part of the island, the north-east, there was a third and different kind of colonization which involved the actual installation of English and Scottish settlers on the land, the Irish in this region being confined to poorer land often in surrounding hills or boggy tracts. This latter process was very similar to that which took place simultaneously in North America. But in the Irish case the lesser technological and genetic differentiation between conquerors and conquered prevented the elimination of the indigenous population by warfare and disease – the process which so strikingly marked the contemporary settlement of North America by much the same kind of immigrants as those who settled in parts of Ulster.

By the end of the seventeenth century the Irish population throughout the island had been left absolutely leaderless, control of both administration and commerce being in the hands of the relatively small minority of colonists. From about 1700 onwards that indigenous population began gradually to adopt English as their language, both around the various coastal ports and along the main routes from Dublin to the west and south, and also in the hinterland of the Ulster settlement area. By 1800 up to one-half of the total population was English-speaking, and as the nineteenth century progressed the Irish language became increasingly confined to areas between these main axes and outside the hinterlands of the ports, areas which eventually shrank to the small Gaeltachts that we know today.[1]

In the late eighteenth and nineteenth centuries some of the indigenous population had begun to gain entry to trade and to certain of the professions, providing the nucleus from which a new leadership of that population began to emerge. Whilst some of this emerging native leadership were prepared to accept and work with the colonists, others chose from time to time to challenge their power and that of Britain – as England and Scotland had by then become. From the late eighteenth century onwards the disabilities under which the indigenous Irish Catholic population laboured were gradually removed and an increasing proportion of the adult population acquired the right to vote for the Westminster Parliament, and from 1829 onwards to be elected to that institution.

Finally, towards the end of the nineteenth century several British Governments sought to remedy the evils of the landlord and tenant system that had originated in the seventeenth century. This was accomplished by financing the purchase of the land from the landlords so as to install the tenants as owners, subject to small long-term repayments of the borrowed money to the British Government.

But although the land reform issue was settled in this way towards the end of the nineteenth and early in the twentieth century, for much of the period from 1885 onwards British politics was bedevilled by the Home Rule controversy. The extent to which the British democratic system was put at risk by this issue may be seen from the fact that at one stage it actually led the Conservative Opposition to threaten civil war. It is only relatively recently[2] that we have been made aware that on 26 January 1914 the Opposition Conservative leader, Bonar Law, told King George V that 'there are now only two courses open to the Government – either they must submit their [Home Rule] Bill to the judgment of the people [by holding a third general election] or prepare for the consequences of civil war'.

This extraordinary threat led the King to tell the Prime Minister, Asquith, that a course open to him would be to follow the example of William IV in doing something that had come to be accepted during the reigns of Victoria and Edward VII to be no longer constitutionally open to the monarch in Britain's evolving democracy: namely, to dismiss his ministers despite their parliamentary majority and send for the leaders of the minority Opposition party to form a government. As such a government would not have had a parliamentary majority, it would immediately have sought a dissolution of Parliament, which the King would have granted.

What persuaded John Redmond to accept at that point an amendment to the Home Rule Bill – one that eventually took the form of a clause permitting Ulster to opt out of an Irish Home Rule Parliament for six years – was the fact that, even if the Liberal Party had been returned to power at an ensuing election with the backing of the Irish Parliamentary Party – which was far from certain – under the provisions of the hard-won Parliament Act 1911 a further three years would then have had to elapse before a revived Home Rule Bill could have been enacted by Parliament.

As a result, by the time the Anglo-Irish Agreement of 1921 was negotiated, partition was already a fait accompli, and this issue consequently played little part in the debate about that Agreement, or in the subsequent split that led to the Civil War. Nevertheless it has to be said that this part of the 1921 Agreement had not been well negotiated.

On 16 November 1921, in the context of a proposal that Northern Ireland be permitted to opt out of the new Irish State, the British Government had proposed that 'A Commission shall be appointed to determine in accordance with the wishes of the inhabitants the boundaries between Northern Ireland and the rest of Ireland.' But the wording of the relevant clause of the Agreement as finally drafted and signed was qualified by an additional over-riding phrase that severely limited the changes that would eventually be proposed by this Boundary Commission four years later: 'The Commission shall determine in accordance with the wishes of the inhabitants, *so far as may be compatible with economic and geographic conditions,* [italics mine] the boundaries . . . ' I have never seen any explanation of how this over-riding clause came to be inserted in the draft Agreement, or of how the Irish negotiators failed to appreciate its significance at the time.

The Irish negotiators were in any event naive to have believed that the major transfer of territory that they mistakenly expected to be proposed by this Boundary Commission would have made Northern Ireland non-viable. As the southern and western areas of Northern Ireland which they hoped would be transferred to the Irish State were the poorer parts of the region, the reduced area that would then have remained under the jurisdiction of the Northern Ireland Government would have been financially *more* rather than *less* viable. And I cannot see any basis for the belief that the residual area would not have been large enough to be politically viable.

The abandonment by the Irish Government in late 1925 of the Boundary Commission's recommendations, because its very limited proposals for Border adjustments in favour of the Irish Free State were most unexpectedly accompanied by offsetting proposals for the transfer of some parts of Monaghan and Donegal to Northern Ireland, had a hugely negative effect on the morale of that embattled government. So negative, indeed, was this effect that, having agreed to suppress the report, the members of that government seem effectively to have switched off Northern Ireland thereafter. An exception was Kevin O'Higgins, who at the time of his murder by three IRA men was actively pursuing an idea – which today seems strange to most people – of uniting Ireland under an Irish/British dual monarchy, akin to that of Austria–Hungary between 1867 and 1918.

For his part, de Valera in power cannot be said to have ever addressed the Northern Ireland issue seriously. It is true that during the negotiation of the 1938 Anglo-Irish Agreement he raised both the partition issue – which he pursued longer than some of his colleagues and advisers thought sensible – and that of discrimination against the nationalist minority in Northern Ireland. But his inevitable failure to make any progress with partition seems to have led him to abandon the discrimination issue, on which the British knew that they were very vulnerable. Ultimately in that negotiation he left Northern Ireland to its fate, contenting himself with the return of the British-controlled naval bases in Cork and Donegal together with a trade agreement that ended the economic war.

The low priority de Valera accorded to Northern Ireland was explicitly confirmed by him a year later, when in a speech to the Senate[3] he said that, speaking for himself, he 'would not to-morrow for the sake of a united Ireland give up the policy of trying to make this a really Irish Ireland – not by any means'.

In that speech he had no hesitation in making it clear that for him the revival of the Irish language and the maximizing of Irish sovereignty both took precedence over the ending of the political division of Ireland. Of course, the priority he gave to these other aims ran directly counter to the achievement of Irish unity by consent, for – as he must surely have realized, at least subconsciously – the more 'Irish' he made this state, the greater the obstacle to the achievement of the goal of reunification.

(Once, before I entered politics, I had an opportunity in 1963 to challenge de Valera's Fianna Fáil party directly on this issue. I was asked to address a party seminar in Dún Laoghaire on the Irish language issue – flanked, of course, by two safe advocates of Gaelicization. When I argued strongly that the Gaelicization policy was driving a wedge between North and South, this stance raised such a measure of support from members of various working groups that the chairmen of two of them refused to report their heretical views back to the plenary session. Because I gave priority to reunification over Gaelicization, one of them described me, rather curiously I thought, as an 'Orangeman'! In my final address to the seminar, looking straight at several Fianna Fáil ministers in the front row, I said that I was happy to have converted what seemed to have been one-third of the Fianna Fáil audience to a genuine concern about partition. I was never asked back!)

The lower priority that de Valera gave to Irish political unity over other issues may also have been a factor in his rejection of proposals made by Malcolm MacDonald in June/July 1940, on Neville Chamberlain's initiative with Winston Churchill's agreement. These involved a declaration of a united Ireland in principle and the establishment of a joint North–South body to work out the constitutional and other practical details of such a Union, in return for the immediate setting up of a joint Defence Council and Irish entry into the war on the Allied side. Memories of how John Redmond had been let down by a British Government over Northern Ireland a quarter of a century earlier may, of course, have raised doubts in de Valera's mind about the sincerity of this offer and he seems also to have been at least momentarily persuaded by Joe Walshe, Secretary of the Department of Foreign Affairs, that at that stage Germany had already won the war.[4]

The lack of realism, and indeed lack of seriousness, on the part of Irish political leaders of both political complexions about Northern Ireland was to be further demonstrated later in that decade both by de Valera's opportunistic anti-partition world tour in 1948 and by John A. Costello's 1949 clarion call to 'hit Britain in its pride, pocket and prestige'. That call was in retaliation for the British decision to include in the Ireland Bill recognizing Ireland as a republic a provision that the consent of the Northern Parliament would be required for Irish unity.

In the decades that followed, Irish politicians and governments, whilst simultaneously failing to address effectively the very real issue of the treatment of the Northern minority, pursued internationally a futile and counterproductive 'sore thumb' policy against partition, demanding that Britain hand over 'our lost Six Counties', regardless of the wishes of a majority of the population of that area. Understandably, the failure of Southern politicians to address seriously the grievances of Northern nationalists, and their preference for speech-making at home and abroad about partition, made Northern nationalists cynical about politics in the Irish state. The truth is that the record of the Irish State in respect of Northern Ireland during the first half century of its existence left it with little moral authority to challenge

Britain's gross failure throughout this period to secure the good governance of Northern Ireland.

The institution of a local Home Rule Parliament in Belfast in 1920, followed by signature of the 1921 Anglo-Irish Agreement establishing the Irish State seems to have convinced the British establishment that they had finally solved the Irish question. The fact that from the outset questions about Northern Ireland were not allowed to be put in the Westminster Parliament represented a quite extraordinary abdication of authority by the British state – an abdication that eventually reaped its own prolonged whirlwind. Thereafter, there was huge opposition in London to the re-opening of any element of the settlement – such as would have happened if a British intervention in Northern Ireland to eliminate some form of discrimination against the minority or in relation to a security issue, were to have precipitated the resignation of a Northern Ireland Unionist Government.

This British determination not to allow any aspect of the Irish settlement to be re-opened turned a threatened resignation of the Northern Ireland Cabinet into an enormously powerful Unionist weapon. Because of this weapon all British Governments from 1922 until 1972 proved unwilling to tackle misgovernment in Northern Ireland, and the knowledge that this potential threat carried such a powerful charge enabled Unionist Governments for fifty years to pre-empt any pressure for reform that might have emanated from London.

In this situation the Home Office, which dealt with Northern Ireland throughout the whole of this period, was a convinced and determined supporter of Unionist Governments, and that unfortunate tradition later came to affect the way in which, after direct rule had been reinstituted, that department's administrative offspring, the Northern Ireland Office, addressed many of its tasks up to and including the botched legislative implementation of the Patten Report on policing.

What was remarkable about Anglo-Irish relations during most of the post-war period was the very limited character of the contacts between the two governments. Thus between 1948 and 1965 each of our countries had five different governments, but there were few meetings between ministers of the two states throughout this period, and very few significant contacts between the leaders of these governments.

Nevertheless it was during this fallow period in Anglo-Irish relations that a rethinking of the irredentist Irish approach to Northern Ireland began. From 1948 onwards I had been writing articles critical of this stance, but, as I recall it, the first major challenge to traditional irredentist anti-partitionism was made in 1959 by Donal Barrington – subsequently a Judge of the European Court and of our Supreme Court – in a pamphlet of his published by Tuairim.[5]

In the autumn of 1969 both within Fine Gael and Labour there were successful moves, led by Conor Cruise O'Brien in Labour and by myself in Fine Gael, to abandon the irredentist stance to which both parties had been committed at least since the controversy over the Ireland Act in 1948. Whilst Jack Lynch, like Sean Lemass before him, personally shared our approach, he did not feel able to commit his party to it, and after 1975 Fianna Fáil, on the initiative of Michael O'Kennedy, reverted to its traditional line of calling for British withdrawal from Northern Ireland. It was not until the Downing Street Declaration of December 1993 that Fianna Fáil formally repudiated its traditional irredentism.

However, between 1969 and 1972 events in Northern Ireland and some of the reactions to these events in this state – in particular the Arms Crisis of 1970 – had alerted responsible politicians in all Irish political parties to the dangers that this irredentism posed to our society. In the debate in the Dáil on Thursday, 3 February 1972, following the Derry massacre and the previous day's burning of the British Embassy in Merrion Square, an inflammatory speech by Neil Blaney early in the debate evoked an instinctive and spontaneous reaction by all subsequent party speakers that was clearly designed to calm emotions in a situation that momentarily seemed to have developed a potential to destabilize our democratic system.

At least from that moment onwards Irish government policy became directed primarily towards seeking peace and stability in Northern Ireland, both for its own sake and also in order to protect our state against the possible overflow effects of Northern Ireland violence. The new mood that this reflected was reinforced by the British Government's decision two months later to suspend Stormont and introduce direct rule in Northern Ireland.

That British decision reflected the fact that from 1965/6 onwards the British Government had been receiving 'explicit warnings of a recrudescence of violence in Northern Ireland' and by February 1969 it had already 'subjected the crisis to a rigorous analysis, which included the preparation of a draft Bill for the introduction of direct rule in Northern Ireland', although 'that could never be publicly admitted because the strategy of minimizing British engagement meant trying to govern through Stormont'. By contrast in Ireland, 'the Trappist silence on the subject of Northern Ireland in the minutes of the new Cabinet that took office after the election of June 1969 reflects the dangers of discussing the matter when the differences between ministers were so acute. No references are recorded in the minutes of the first eleven meetings (between 3 July and 7 August), and after the spate of emergency Cabinets devoted to Northern Ireland in mid-August a veil of silence again descends.'[6]

The British plans for direct rule were held in abeyance until March 1972, when in the aftermath of the Derry massacre Stormont was abolished and Willie Whitelaw was appointed Secretary of State for Northern Ireland. By the end of that year preparations were under way for what a year later became the Sunnningdale Agreement.

As just mentioned, elements of Fianna Fáil in Opposition reverted in 1975 to calling for a British withdrawal from the North and in the first six months of 1980 the new Haughey Government briefly succumbed to pressure from Neil Blaney to modify the anti-IRA policy in the United States that had been pursued by all governments for many years past. However, thereafter Irish policy in respect of Northern Ireland became directed consistently towards the restoration of peace and stability there.

For all Irish Governments recognized that in some respects the IRA campaign of violence represented more of a threat to the Irish State than to Britain. The Dublin riots of 1972 and 1981 offered warning signs of what could happen if the violence in Northern Ireland were to overflow to the Republic, with its unarmed police force and its small army, which was severely overstretched because of local political pressure to spread its manpower over a large number of barracks around the country in order to maintain employment in these areas.

From 1972 onwards the main thrust of Irish policy became a sustained effort to persuade the British Government to modify its security policy in Northern Ireland, which effectively operated as a recruitment system for the IRA and which for much of the period was eroding support for the SDLP amongst the nationalist population. This concern became a major preoccupation of my second government, which took office at the end of 1982.

The problem that I faced as Taoiseach in early 1983, as I reviewed our Northern Ireland policy with key ministers and advisers was that the British Prime Minister with whom I had to deal belonged to a wartime generation with its memories of Irish neutrality, and nothing I knew of her career – nor anything in my contacts with her since 1975, as Foreign Minister, Opposition Leader, and, in 1981 as Taoiseach – suggested that she could easily transcend that background.

It is worth dwelling briefly on this factor: the impact of Irish wartime neutrality upon British public and political attitudes towards Ireland during most of the second half of the twentieth century. For in Ireland the effects of these British memories has been greatly underestimated.

In the post-war period the earlier British combination of a sense of guilt over past behaviour in Ireland and a sense of relief at having, as they thought, at last 'solved' the Irish problem, had been replaced by bitterness at Irish neutrality during the Second World War. Given the extremity to which Britain was reduced in the years after the fall of France, and the very narrow margin by which it survived the Battle of the Atlantic, it was understandable that Irish neutrality should have been resented by the people of Britain during that war. It was hardly to be expected that they would recognize that in remaining outside the war until and unless attacked, Ireland was no different from any other European country, or indeed the United States.

Moreover, neither during nor after the war were people in Britain aware that their own Chiefs of Staff opposed the occupation of the ports in the south of Ireland because of the drain that the protection of these ports would have imposed on limited British military resources, and also because, once France had fallen, the southern ports were no longer of strategic use to them. Thenceforth convoys had to use the northern route, which was protected by naval vessels based in the ports of Northern Ireland and Scotland, and by aircraft from bases in Scotland and Northern Ireland. With the secret permission of the Irish Government the latter flew to and from the North Atlantic across the territory of the Irish State. Because details of this and many other forms of secret Irish assistance given by de Valera to Britain during the war did not emerge until decades later, a quite false impression of the nature of Irish wartime neutrality has persisted ever since, in Ireland as well as in Britain.

In addition to this, neither in Britain, nor indeed in later times in Ireland, was there any understanding of the fact that the virtual unanimity of Irish politicians in favour of wartime neutrality reflected a deep-seated fear that entry into the war on the Allied side might have precipitated a recurrence of the Civil War that had ended only sixteen years earlier, this time, however, with German support for an IRA whose ranks might have been greatly strengthened by elements breaking away from Fianna Fáil. And that would have made matters worse rather than better for Britain.

Because of all this, I believe that many of the generation in Britain who remembered the war – which included Prime Ministers up to and including Margaret Thatcher – had their view of Ireland significantly distorted by their recollection of Irish neutrality. It was not until the emergence in the 1990s of a new political generation in Britain, led by people like John Major and Tony Blair, who had no personal memories of that conflict, that British attitudes to Ireland could be normalized.

When in January 1983 I contemplated an initiative designed to alter radically Britain's approach to security in Northern Ireland, I was conscious also of the fact that Margaret Thatcher was notably lacking in empathy with anything outside her own frame of reference, which seemed to be more or less confined to Southern England.

I also realized that whatever goodwill I had painstakingly built up between 1975 and 1981 was likely to have been seriously eroded by Charles Haughey's intemperate handling of the Falklands affair in May 1982. Because of its potentially negative impact on Irish relations with the British Government, I had strongly opposed Charles Haughey's abandonment of sanctions on Argentina after the *Belgrano* sinking, but I doubted whether my stance would have impinged on Margaret Thatcher sufficiently to have undone the damage that this gesture had inflicted on the Anglo-Irish relationship.

There was, in truth, little reason to believe that the British Prime Minister would respond positively to any proposal by me to modify British security tactics in Northern Ireland with a view to reversing the dangerous growth of support for Sinn Féin there. The problem was that from 1970 onwards British policy on Northern Ireland had been dominated by a belief that what they faced there was a *security* problem that could be overcome by intensifying security measures – an approach that persistently aggravated what was, of course, primarily a *political* problem of nationalist alienation. It was that approach that I had to challenge with, many of my colleagues believed, little chance of success.

This is not the place to rehearse the course of those negotiations, which are set out in some detail in my autobiography.[7] Suffice it to say that in 1985, with the assistance of an able Irish team of ministers and Civil Servants, and helped by British Civil Servants like Sir Robert Armstrong and Sir David Goodall, and by the Foreign Secretary, Geoffrey Howe, Margaret Thatcher was finally reluctantly persuaded, at least intellectually, of the need to adopt a quite different approach. But she was never emotionally convinced by our arguments, and no sooner was the Agreement signed than she reverted to her obsession with security, and, of course, in the late 1990s expressed regret at ever having signed this Agreement.

But for the force of the Unionist reaction against the Agreement, the fact that the British side did not implement some of the changes in security policy that had been agreed between us might have had the effect of undermining much of its impact. That overreaction convinced many nationalists that the Agreement must represent a major step forward, as indeed it did, in ways the details of which were, however, only imperfectly understood by nationalists at the time. This positive nationalist reaction to the Agreement soon led to a switch of one-third of the Sinn Féin vote back to the SDLP, and, in time, to a radical rethinking by the IRA/Sinn Féin of its 'Armalite and ballot-box' strategy.

These and later negotiations between the two states highlighted for me the fact that a British Government can call on vastly greater human resources than Ireland can, and I was very impressed by its capacity to negotiate skilfully and constructively, under the guidance of a small hand-picked Cabinet Committee.

But I was equally unimpressed by the frequent lack of coherence of Britain's general Northern Ireland policy. On the one hand British Secretaries of State for Northern Ireland often seemed to me to succumb to intense pressure from their own Northern Ireland Office staff to avoid any action that might upset the Unionists or the security forces. That was a dangerous recipe for inaction, from which only some of the ablest Northern Ireland Secretaries, after an initial submergence in this negative atmosphere, managed to escape.

Moreover, these Secretaries of State were also under pressure from another direction. Many of them came up against preoccupations of other British Government departments, pursuing their own distinct agendas, which often seemed to cut across the ultimate policy interest of the British Government in securing peace and stability in Northern Ireland.

This problem became very evident in the early months of 1988, just after the retirement as Cabinet Secretary of Sir Robert Armstrong (now Lord Armstrong of Ilminster), who had given close and constructive attention to Irish affairs. In the months that followed his retirement, the absence of any overall coordinating mechanism permitted the Defence Secretary to reinstate in the Army a soldier who had not long before been convicted of a murder in Northern Ireland. At about the same time, the Attorney General, Sir Patrick Mayhew, decided that the 'public interest' required the abandonment of the Stalker prosecutions – 'public interest' being apparently interpreted as involving the protection of the security services rather than the pursuit of Britain's interest in weakening support for the IRA in accordance with British policy on the lines set out in the recently-signed Anglo-Irish Agreement.

The Home Secretary also chose that moment to make the Prevention of Terrorism Act permanent. And the Prime Minister pursued her own private agenda by authorizing the Gibraltar shootings.

What chance had the Secretary of State for Northern Ireland against that chaotic administrative background?

I was told at the time that this series of debacles had led to the belated establishment in the late spring of that year of an Inter-Departmental Committee to try to achieve some measure of coordination of policy with respect to Northern Ireland, and matters did seem to improve thereafter.

Nevertheless, throughout the whole period, right up until the Labour Government was elected in 1997, Britain's Northern Ireland policy appeared to me to have been dominated, or at any rate distorted in a most damaging way, by the unwillingness of the Ministry of Defence to control some of the activities of the British Army in Northern Ireland. Conservative Governments did not wish to interfere with the freedom of action of the Army, and Labour Governments appeared afraid of possible reactions if they did so. I recall a former British Cabinet Minister telling me two decades ago that the failure to pre-empt the Ulster Workers' Strike in 1974 by prompt action before it could gain widespread support had been due to British Government memories of earlier fears about overstraining the Army's loyalty at the time of the Rhodesian UDI crisis in the 1960s.

Amongst many episodes that raised questions in my mind about civilian control of the British Army in Northern Ireland I particularly recall how furious I was in the mid 1970s at the discovery that the British Army in Northern Ireland had known for eighteen months that explosives being used by the IRA there were being stolen from a particular explosives factory in our state, but had not told us about this, apparently because they preferred to use this leakage as a propaganda weapon against us than to save lives in Northern Ireland by stopping it.

In 1981 there was an exceptionally unfortunate instance of policy incoherence on the British side when an approach by London to the IRA sabotaged an arrangement being worked out between the Justice and Peace Commission of the Roman Catholic Church and the British Minister of State in Northern Ireland that would have ended the hunger strike on terms acceptable both to the hunger strikers and to the British administration there.

I believe that the intermittent incoherence of British policy in Northern Ireland, reflecting a failure to coordinate the activities of different ministries in that complex government structure, contrasted unfavourably with the tight control of this policy area that was exercised by most Irish Governments, usually through a Northern Ireland Committee of our Cabinet.

Of course, it is much easier for a small power to act coherently than for a large power, in whose affairs both a big army and several security services inevitably play a bigger role. So I make this point not particularly by way of criticism of British governance but rather in order to challenge the widespread Irish belief – spawned by what is now, happily, a diminishing inferiority complex – that the British are enormously clever operators, with whom the poor simple Irish cannot hope to cope. In my experience much of what some Irish people have often attributed to Machiavellian British manoeuvres has been due rather to the incoherence of a governmental system in which at times one part knows nothing of what other parts are doing.

More generally, I think that it is also fair to comment that the British seem to have had more difficulty about adjusting to a post-imperial world than the Irish have had in carrying through a rethinking of nationalism that was necessitated both by our entrance to the EC and also by our almost simultaneous recognition of the dangers that our irredentism posed to peace in Northern Ireland.

Here once again the smaller size of our country and of its governmental system worked in our favour, for, whilst it is clear that the rethinking of Irish nationalism that has occurred here in recent decades has been incomplete – the Nice referendum of June 2000 demonstrated this – this ability to rethink aspects of our nationalism has certainly had a major impact on Anglo-Irish relations.

In looking back over the past eighty years of a divided Ireland, I cannot help reflecting on the paradox that it was in fact the Irish State that has created most of the new divisions between North and South that arose during that time, as its leaders sought effectively to create in their territory a Roman Catholic post-Gaelic society. In truth, since 1922 much less has been changed in Northern Ireland than in what is now the Republic: the drifting apart of the two parts of the island has primarily been as a result of initiatives taken in the Republic rather than in the North.

And, whilst the inhabitants of independent Ireland quickly developed a loyalty to the State that soon involved a fundamentally partitionist outlook on Northern Ireland, the Unionists of Northern Ireland never lost their sense of being a threatened minority in the island of Ireland. To this extent they retained an all-Ireland mentality that the inhabitants of the new Irish State soon lost. The fact that at this deeper psychological level both of these communities thus came to think of themselves in the opposite way to that in which they claimed to see themselves has not made the Irish problem any easier to resolve.

Under the new dispensation created by the Belfast Agreement efforts are now being made to put together again some of the elements of Northern and Southern politics that had moved apart over that period. And in contrast to the situation that existed thirty years ago at the time of the Sunningdale Agreement, those Civil Servants from the Republic who are engaged in these all-Ireland activities are now very positive about this exercise, for which back in 1973 their predecessors showed less enthusiasm.

Nevertheless Northern fears of impending Irish political unity are much more vivid than Southern ambitions for such an outcome would seem to justify. Indeed if the people of the Republic believed that reunification was likely to take place in the near future, many of them would probably be more worried about this prospect than enthused.

How likely is reunification to become a live issue within a foreseeable future? How realistic are the expectations of Sinn Féin and its supporters that within a decade or two a majority will emerge in Northern Ireland favouring Irish political unity?

At the time of writing, the 2001 Census data in respect of the religious affiliations of the Northern Ireland population is awaited. In 1991 fractionally over 50% of those under 15 are estimated to have had a Catholic background, but there is uncertainty as to whether this proportion has remained constant or has fallen slightly since then. Allowing for deaths, which have a greater impact upon the Protestant population which is more elderly, and for the moment ignoring the question of differential migration of people of Catholic background, the Catholic population may by now have risen from about 41% in 1991 to just under 43%.

But, whereas the Catholic proportion of the population under 18 has remained constant or may have fallen slightly since 1991, the larger number of deaths amongst the predominantly Protestant older population, together with the movement into the over-18 category of those who in 1991 were aged 8–17 (about half of whom are of Catholic background), may have raised the proportion of Catholic voters somewhat more sharply, by three percentage points, I would judge, from around 37.5% to about 40.5%, again ignoring differential migration effects.

However, in this connection it is, perhaps, worth remarking that – after making allowance for the fact that some Catholics vote for the Alliance party – the proportion of votes actually cast for nationalist candidates suggests that a somewhat higher proportion of those actually voting in Northern Ireland come from a Catholic background, perhaps 42%–43%. In other words turn-out from the nationalist community appears to be higher than amongst those of Protestant background.

There may also be a differential migration effect that would over time increase the Catholic proportion of the electorate. It is true that population estimates for Northern Ireland over the past decade do not suggest that there has been a significant net flow of people in either direction, although the 2001 Census may show a different picture. But there is in fact evidence of a significant net outflow of young Protestants in the 1990s, in particular through the higher education system – an outflow that over a period of time could have a negative influence on the ratio of Protestants to Catholics amongst both the population and the electorate in Northern Ireland. (Incidentally this larger education outflow of Protestants helps to explain the fact that in both the Northern Ireland universities Catholic students have for some time past been in a majority, a fact that has reinforced the tendency for Protestant students to go elsewhere in the UK.)

In the late 1990s there was evidence that whereas only 22% of Catholics in Northern Ireland entering higher education went to universities in Britain, 46% of Protestant entrants did so. It is estimated that at best one-quarter of these students returned to Northern Ireland on graduation (although some may return at a later stage), and it is speculated that the return rate for Protestant graduates may be lower than for Catholics.

As 40% of school leavers were estimated to be entering higher education in the late 1990s, these figures would suggest a differential emigration rate for Protestant and Catholic graduates of about 1,000 a year. That may not seem much, but, if it continued indefinitely, this higher education net outflow means that the net loss from each cohort of young people would be about 14% in the case of Protestants, as against 6% in the case of Catholics, which would be equivalent to an 8% differential in the birth rate. The persistence of such a differential outflow of young Protestants could bring forward by some years the distant moment when the Catholic electorate might conceivably outnumber the Protestant voters.

There is, however, another factor to be taken into account in any attempt to calculate whether and when there might be a majority in Northern Ireland that would vote in favour of a united Ireland. Opinion surveys there up to 1998 consistently showed that one-third of Catholics preferred to remain in the United Kingdom rather than to unite with the Republic, partly, no doubt, for fear of losing the very large transfers from Britain that sustain Northern Ireland's living standards at a level very much higher than its level of output would justify.

Since 1998 this proportion of Catholics preferring to remain in the United Kingdom has fallen back to 15%–20%. Nevertheless, when this is taken in conjunction with the fact that currently not much more than about 40% of voters are from Catholic backgrounds, this suggests that if at this point a Border Poll were held, as David Trimble has proposed, the vote for remaining in the United Kingdom might be close to 65%. If that is the case then, despite Sinn Féin's optimism on the issue, Irish reunification would be a fairly distant prospect.

Even if the Catholic fertility and birth rates were to remain above those for Protestants – and this is far from certain, for the Catholic proportion of births seems to have started to fall after 1986 – it would seem that, all other things being equal, many decades would have to elapse before the number of voters coming from a Catholic background would equal the number of Protestant voters – although, of course, if the turn-out of Catholic voters were to remain higher than that of the Protestant electorate, this period might be somewhat foreshortened.

On the assumption that the present settlement survives the pressures to which even four years later it remains subject, it is worth considering where in fact the interests of Northern Ireland lie in the twenty-first century, with this part of the United Kingdom and the Irish State both being part of a European political and economic union. The development of the European Community towards such a union carries implications for the interests of Northern Ireland which have not yet, I think, been adequately addressed. Fundamental decisions affecting the life and economy of Northern Ireland are now being taken in two different centres outside the North, namely London and Brussels.

London remains of major importance because of the scale of the transfers effected through the United Kingdom budget to Northern Ireland as also, in a somewhat lesser degree, to other parts of the UK such as Northern England, Wales, and perhaps Scotland. Whilst a significant part of the British transfers to Northern Ireland still reflect direct or indirect consequences of the security situation, there is an important residue, possibly in excess of £4bn. a year, that might be described as genuine peace-time transfers from Great Britain. This residue represents a significant proportion of Northern Ireland's GDP, and the people of Northern Ireland have a clear interest in retaining it.

However, Northern Ireland is now also the beneficiary of resource transfers from the European Community. These transfers at present are significantly smaller than those from Great Britain, but the real disproportion is less than the apparent one. The mechanism by which the British Treasury negotiates for and controls the distribution of EC transfers has meant that the amount coming from the EC budget directly to Northern Ireland has been a good deal less than it might be.

An example is to be found in the Structural Funds provision for the region. The Republic's share of the Structural Funds over the last five years of the twentieth century was £3bn., which would suggest a figure of £1.5bn. as the amount that Northern Ireland might have received if it had had a direct relationship with the Community institutions. The fact that the actual EU transfers to Northern Ireland were only about one-third of this amount, i.e. £500m., reflected, I believe, the influence of the British Treasury.

This does not, of course, mean that Northern Ireland will necessarily have been deprived of £1bn. during this period, but rather that the Treasury preferred for its own reasons to substitute its financial flows for Community transfers. If account is taken of this factor it will be seen that the potential transfers from the Community to Northern Ireland may now be not hugely less than the level that 'peace-time' transfers from Great Britain would represent in the absence of this factor.

Moreover, quite apart from the resource transfer issue many other decisions affecting Northern Ireland, particularly in areas like agriculture, are now taken in Brussels rather than in London and, broadly speaking, it seems likely that the importance of decision-making in Brussels for the material interests of Northern Ireland will ultimately be close enough to that of London.

At the same time the interests of Great Britain and Northern Ireland in matters to be decided by the Community do not necessarily coincide, and in certain areas such as agriculture and regional policy may, in fact, as is the case of the Irish State, even be inversely related. What suits Britain's interests may be precisely what does *not* suit the interests of Northern Ireland. In these circumstances the fact that Northern Ireland's interests in the EU are represented exclusively through London, and that there is no prospect of any direct input to the Council of Ministers or the Commission from Northern Ireland, could become a matter of considerable concern.

Northern Ireland is unusual, and may even be unique, in finding itself in this position. I cannot, offhand, think of any other region within the Community the interests of which are potentially so divergent from those of the rest of the member state of which it is part as is the case with Northern Ireland – although it is probable that a somewhat lesser divergence of interest may exist between Spain and Italy and some of the regions of those states.

Northern Ireland therefore has a strong and growing interest in direct representation within the institutions of the Community and may be uniquely disadvantaged if over time it fails to secure such a position. The concentration on the, still very important, link with Britain, to the exclusion of the establishment of a direct link with the European Community, could, I feel, work to its long-term disadvantage.

Just as the Irish State rethought at a fundamental level its stance in relation to Europe in the early 1970s, so also Northern Ireland may in time need to reconsider its position with respect to the European Community. I do not think that any simple solution can be found to the problem thus posed. Objectively, Northern Ireland has two parallel – and in magnitude not hugely different – interests to pursue in its economic relationships with Great Britain and with the European Community, a dichotomy which cannot readily be resolved within traditional political structures.

Given the unique character of the Northern Ireland problem this could argue for some reconsideration of those traditional structures. Some would say that Northern Ireland has in recent decades had the worst of all worlds with its uncomfortable domestic political arrangements, its security situation, its prickly relations with the governments of both Great Britain and of Ireland, and the weakness of its linkage with the European Community. What Northern Ireland might eventually wish to consider is whether it might not stake a claim to getting the best instead of the worst of both worlds by seeking – even demanding – that the governments of Great Britain and of Ireland and the Community all accept the logic of its unique situation by agreeing to permit it to operate in relation to the Community in a more flexible way.

For Northern Ireland's interests to be adequately served it would be desirable that it have direct access to the Community decision-making mechanism. Clearly this cannot be achieved within the present structure, which involves the handling of Northern Ireland's interests exclusively through the mechanism of the British State. Nor does independence for Northern Ireland provide an appropriate channel, for the risks and dangers of such independence are seen by the two communities within Northern Ireland and by the two States concerned to rule out such a solution.

However, there is a possible alternative channel, that is the securing of an equal share in the Irish State's involvement in the Community process. This would entail a change in political structures of the Irish State in order to give Northern Ireland such a role, as well as the acceptance by the British Government that Northern Ireland, whilst remaining in the United Kingdom for as long as its interests and the emotional commitment of the majority of its people so require, could, in matters where its interests so demand, channel its relationship with the Community through joint and equal participation in the Irish involvement in Community structures.

It can, of course, also be argued that Northern Ireland's interests in security could be met ultimately by joint and equal participation with the Irish State in the organization of security throughout the island, but that is a separate issue and, within both Northern Ireland and the Republic, a more sensitive one.

Ideas like these may be rejected on various grounds, as too complex, as conflicting with traditional concepts of the structure of states or, of course, because the need for changes of this kind is not seen as sufficiently compelling to warrant such innovations. I am not concerned to advocate here any particular structure but rather to illustrate the necessity in a rapidly changing world to be open to new arrangements corresponding to developing needs.

In the meantime, the Irish–British relationship has been transformed by the way in which the two Governments have had to work together constructively in order to bring to an end the violence that tore Northern Ireland apart during the past thirty years. The success of a series of Irish Governments in persuading their British counterparts to abandon their commitment to repressive security measures, which alienated the minority community, in favour of an approach designed to end that alienation, has opened the way for a constructive peace process. The tensions that had earlier affected relations between two governments then pursuing conflicting approaches to the Northern Ireland crisis have evaporated, and their common interest in bringing violence there to an end by an agreed approach has brought them closer together than anyone previously had thought possible. Indeed, no two European governments have today as close a political relationship as those of Ireland and Britain – which is scarcely the outcome the IRA expected when they initiated their campaign of violence three decades ago!

It has to be said that this outcome owes a good deal to the personal relationships that gradually developed between the Prime Ministers of the two States. My own relationship with Margaret Thatcher was better than what had existed between earlier Irish and British leaders, and produced a concrete result in the form of the 1985 Agreement, but it remained underneath the surface a fairly combative one, marked by underlying tension as well as by a measure of mutual respect. Because of the previous relationship between John Major and Albert Reynolds within the EC Economic and Finance Council and because, as pointed out earlier, John Major was the first British Prime Minister without hang-ups about Irish neutrality, these two leaders developed a new kind of relationship which made possible the launching of a peace process based upon their joint Downing Street Declaration of December 1993.

John Bruton, as leader of the Rainbow Coalition, and John Major brought the Framework Document to a successful conclusion, which provided a starting point for the negotiations leading to the Belfast Agreement of April 1998, and the conclusion of that Agreement under George Mitchell's auspices was made possible by the extraordinarily close cooperation that developed between two new government leaders, Bertie Ahern and Tony Blair. Keeping this Agreement alive and securing the implementation of its provisions in the face of huge difficulties has owed an enormous amount to the personal working relationship that developed between these two men.

This constructive evolution of the Anglo-Irish political relationship has been accompanied by a parallel improvement in relations between the two countries at the level of public opinion. Anglophobia amongst Irish people is not yet dead – many Irish people still share with the Scots a tendency to enjoy British sporting discomfiture, and the growth of support for Sinn Féin in the Republic, especially amongst young people, reflects in part at least a persistent element of Anglophobia. But this is less widespread and more superficial than in the past and, during the World Cup in the early summer of 2002, the evidence of a new warmth of feeling towards Ireland on the part of people in Britain has served to challenge the persistence of an element of anti-British feeling on the Irish side.

The evident improvement in the Anglo-Irish relationship at several levels, paralleled by an increasingly cordial relationship between the UUP and Irish ministers in the North–South context, augers well for the future of our archipelago.

Of course, the future of Northern Ireland is still uncertain and the political settlement there could yet be upset by the displacement of the SDLP by Sinn Féin and/or of the UUP by the DUP in the 2003 Assembly Elections. In that event, the new more positive relationship between the Irish and British Governments could come under some strain. But it seems unlikely that the capacity for constructive co-operation that the two Governments have displayed in recent years would, at this stage, be seriously disrupted even by such a breakdown of the settlement agreed in Belfast in April 1998.

The common interest of the Irish and British States in preserving the relationship forged by having faced together the challenges posed by Northern Ireland in the closing years of the twentieth century is a new and powerful stabilizing factor in the historical development of these two islands.

Notes

2: Economic comparisons

1 Garret FitzGerald, 'The Irish Economy: North and South', *Studies*, XLV, 180, Winter 1956, pp. 373–88.

2 Garret FitzGerald, *Towards a New Ireland* (Dublin: Charles Knight, 1972), ch. 4.

3: The Irish Constitution

1 J.M. Kelly, 'Fundamental Rights and the Constitution', in Brian Farrell (ed.), *De Valera's Constitution and Ours* (Dublin 1988).

2 James Casey, *Constitutional Law in Ireland*, 3rd ed. (Butterworth, Sweet & Maxwell, 2000), p. 315.

3 Kelly, 'Fundamental Rights and the Constitution', p. 169.

4 David Gwynn Morgan, 'Judicial Action – Too Much of a Good Thing?', in Tim Murphy and Patrick Twomey (eds), *Ireland's Evolving Constitution* (Oxford: Hart, 1998), pp. 107–11.

5 David Gwynn Morgan, *A Judgement Too Far: Judicial Activism and the Constitution* (Cork: Cork University Press, 2001).

6 Brian Walsh, address at McGill Summer School, 1987.

7 Declan Costello, 'The Natural Law and the Irish Constitution', *Studies*, 1956, pp. 405–6.

4: The Irish party system

1 Mary Daly *The Buffer State: The Historical Roots of the Department of the Environment* (Dublin: IPA, 1991), p. 59.

2 Ibid., p. 70.

7: Irish demography

1 Niamh Flanagan and Valerie Richardson, *Unmarried Mothers: A Social Profile*, Department of Social Work/Social Science Research Centre, UCD, and Social Work Research Unit, Holles Street Hospital, 1992, p. 30. [Also Green Paper on Abortion, September 1999, par. 6.071.]

2 Flanagan and Richardson, *Unmarried Mothers*, p. 30.

3 Valerie Richardson, *In and Out of Marriage* (Collection of essays), Family Studies Centre, UCD, 1992, pp. 77, 82.

4 Claire Camey, *In and Out of Marriage* (Collection of essays), Family Studies Centre, UCD, 1992, p. 48.

5 Margaret Fine-Davis, *First Joint Report of Second Joint Committee on Women's Rights*, pp. 70–71.

6 Valerie Richardson, *Irish Family Studies*, Family Studies Centre, UCD, 1995, pp. 133, 137.

7 Maire Nic Ghiolla Phadraig, *In and Out of Marriage* (Collection of essays), Family Studies Centre, UCD, 1992, p. 10.

9: State and Church

1 I discovered this some years ago when the appointment of an Irish-resident theologian friend to the University of Strasbourg appeared to be blocked under the German Concordat.

2 In 1976 a post-Franco Foreign Minister visiting Ireland expressed his astonishment at the absence of any Concordat between Ireland and Rome, and asked if he could send someone to examine what he saw as an anomaly. Whilst, because of a change of government in Spain shortly afterwards, this visit did not take place, on a visit to Madrid in 1980 I was told by a member of the Communist Party that Spain had in fact terminated its Concordat with Rome, but had replaced it with four formal Agreements. It is my recollection that my interlocutor told me that the Communist Party had voted against two of these on technical grounds, but had supported two others. And he expressed puzzlement about how Ireland could have managed without some such formal arrangements with the Holy See!

3 It should, perhaps, be explained that, after the Reformation, the Church of Ireland as the Established Church in Ireland had a statutory monopoly of marriages, but gradually religious marriages by other churches came to be informally recognized as 'common law marriages'. Finally in the nineteenth century a series of laws were enacted to give statutory recognition to marriages in different Churches, as well as to introduce civil marriages.

4 See my autobiography, *All in a Life* (Dublin: Gill & Macmillan, 1991), pp. 226–29 and Appendix 2.

10: Ireland and Europe

1 It should, perhaps, be explained that the term 'European Union' is, of course, now the name given since the Maastricht Treaty of 1990 to the combination of the European Community with two parallel intergovernmental pillars, dealing respectively with Foreign and Security Policy and Justice and Immigration issues.

2 Hitherto the French had insisted that these two sets of matters be dealt with at separate meetings. Some months earlier, because of this insistence, all the Foreign Ministers had had to fly from Copenhagen to Brussels in order to separate the two parts of our discussion on these issues!

3 See FitzGerald, *All in a Life*, pp. 133–36.

11: Ireland, Britain and Northern Ireland

1 For details of this process see *Estimates For Baronies of Minimum Level of Irish-Speaking amongst Successive Decennial Cohorts 1771–1781 to 1861–1871*, Garret FitzGerald, Royal Irish Academy, 1984.

2 See Nicholas Mansergh, *The Unresolved Question* (Yale: Yale Univeristy Press, 1991), pp. 63–66.

3 *Seanad Éireann*, 22 (7 February 1939), pp. 988–89.

4 A few days after that rejection Walshe wrote to de Valera to the effect that if at that point Ireland were to have entered the War on the Allied side it would provoke 'the deservedly complete loss of our independence'. His curious choice of adverb reflected his personal conviction that Germany was already victorious. Soon Walshe was to develop the idea of a grouping of four Catholic states – Salazar's Portugal, Franco's Spain, Pétain's France, and de Valera's Ireland – within Germany's triumphant New Order. National Archive, Department of Foreign Affairs File A2, Secretary to Taoiseach.

5 Tuairim was a combined think tank and debating club which from the late 1950s onwards sought to stimulate discussion of political, economic and social issues. Its role in the modernization of Ireland has hitherto been largely ignored but, I believe, deserves study.

6 Ronan Fanning, 'British and Irish Responses to Northern Ireland, 1968–69', *Irish Studies in International Affairs*, 12 (2001), p. 58.

7 FitzGerald, *All in a Life*, chapters 16 and 17.

Index

De Valera, Fianna Fáil and the *Irish Press*

The Truth in the News?

Mark O'Brien, NUI, Maynooth

'Mark O'Brien's story of the birth, life and death of the Irish Press is not merely the tale of how a great newspaper group fell . . . It is also part of the warp and woof of twentieth-century Irish history. I commend his book to anyone interested in that history.'

Tim Pat Coogan

' . . . the most important book published this year'

The Irish Times

This book examines the relationship between the Fianna Fáil party and the *Irish Press*, both founded by Eamon de Valera. The *Irish Press* gave voice to de Valera's vision for Ireland and Irishness, and provided him with a means to counter hostility in the media, orchestrated particularly by the *Irish Independent* and the *Irish Times*. The author gives a fascinating view of the war of words between the two papers, their fight for rural readership and the role of *Irish Press* in bringing Fianna Fáil to power.

288 pages 2001
0 7165 2733 2 cloth **€32.50/£25.00/$35.00**

John Hume and the SDLP

Impact and Survival in Northern Ireland

Gerard Murray, The University of Edinburgh

'The die has been cast, however, and this book points out the irony that it is up to the unionists – by working the Belfast deal – to save the SDLP.'

Belfast Telegraph

'Gerard Murray has written a much needed and extremely useful book on the SDLP . . . Murray has performed a much needed task in his study of the SDLP. In addition he has done so with an engaging narrative which sets out sufficient detail for the reader to draw their own interpretation of events.'

Irish Political Studies

'Murray has made readable what few journalists could be bothered to do, and has dug up areas worth further investigation.'

Scotland On Sunday

342 pages 1998
0 7165 2644 1 €35.00/£27.50/$39.50
New Directions in Irish History